Waterloo
CASUALTIES

Waterloo CASUALTIES

PAUL L. DAWSON

To Jean-Charles and Hélène
Thank you, my friends, for your work at Vincennes and continued friendships

Fonthill Media Language Policy

Fonthill Media publishes in the international English language market. One language edition is published worldwide. As there are minor differences in spelling and presentation, especially with regard to American English and British English, a policy is necessary to define which form of English to use. The Fonthill Policy is to use the form of English native to the author. Paul L. Dawson was born and educated in the United Kingdom; therefore, British English has been adopted in this publication.

Fonthill Media Limited
Fonthill Media LLC
www.fonthill.media
office@fonthillmedia.com

First published in the United Kingdom and the United States of America 2024

British Library Cataloguing in Publication Data:
A catalogue record for this book is available from the British Library

Copyright © Paul L. Dawson 2024

ISBN 978-1-78155-902-4

The right of Paul L. Dawson to be identified as the author of this work has been asserted by him in accordance with the Copyright, Designs and Patents Act 1988.

All rights reserved. No part of this publication may be reproduced, stored in a retrieval system or transmitted in any form or by any means, electronic, mechanical, photocopying, recording or otherwise, without prior permission in writing from Fonthill Media Limited

Typeset in 10.5pt on13pt Sabon
Printed and bound in England

CONTENTS

Acknowledgements   7
Introduction   9

1	1815	12
2	15 June	23
3	16 June	28
4	Fatal Perambulations	35
5	Durutte Attacks at Ligny	42
6	17 June	48
7	18 June	59
8	Marbot's Patrol	70
9	Battle is Joined	79
10	The Allied Response	89
11	Durutte's Offensive	97
12	Jacquinot's Counterattack	103
13	The Cuirassiers	112
14	Durutte's Second Attack	120
15	The Prussians' Next Move	138
16	Domon and Subervie	147
17	6th Corps is Sent to Stop the Prussians	155
18	Prussians and More Prussians	176
19	Plancenoit	188
20	D'Erlon's Last Offensive	199
21	Rout and Retreat	205
22	Conclusions	211

Endnotes   220
Bibliography   237

Acknowledgements

This book originated from a discussion with the late Neil Faulkner: as part of the celebrations marking the 200th anniversary of Waterloo, I penned an article for *Military History Monthly* on the action at Plancenoit. This coincided with writing about the battle in general terms, producing *Waterloo: The Truth at Last*. I had hoped to return to the defence of the French right wing and the action at Plancenoit, but in June 2016, I suffered a severe traumatic brain injury: this book had been at the planning stage, its lengthy delay being the result of a long period of rehabilitation. The COVID-19 pandemic and complications from long COVID added further delays to a text that was already years behind schedule.

The discovery of bones in an attic belonging to the victims of the fighting at Plancenoit has reignited interest in the action here: Robin Schäfer approached me to provide research for a TV documentary about the bones, released during the summer of 2023, and was the prompt I needed to reassess my own writing and add in new discoveries from the archives and auction houses.

Without support from Sally Fairweather, this book would not exist. She has accompanied me on my various research trips, patiently recorded the casualty data from the regimental muster lists, and unfailingly helped me day and night during my recovery—coping with my speech impediment, seizures as my brain healed, and impaired cognitive ability; Sally has done her best to make sense of my notes and essays, some of which are almost a decade old, and has melded them into a format that makes sense to the reader. The cognitive impairment from my injury means my memory of what I did yesterday is non-existent, which means repetition and poor articulation of argument has been a battle I hope Sally has won. I owe her a huge vote of thanks. This book is the result of our combined labours. I dare say it owes 60 per cent to her editing and writing, as, in all honesty, the cover deserves to have her name on the front to recognise her huge contributions to making this book exist.

My esteemed friend Jean-Charles Lair acted as my 'eyes and ears' in French archives while I was incapable of international travel due to rehabilitation, allowing the research for the book to continue. His contribution in research amounts to perhaps 25 per cent of the total sum of this book; my efforts in comparison to Sally and Jean-Charles are slight: their work stands foremost over my original writing and editing of this book. I must also thank long-term friend Hans Karl-Weiß for his comments and generous provision of Prussian material.

Furthermore, I must also acknowledge the tremendous and most generous assistance in the provision of research material by Ronald Pawly and Yves Martin. Ronald has been of great help in our many hours of discussion and debate on the campaign and sources available to researchers. Bravo gentlemen. Alasdair White has been of great assistance in our numerous discussions of the action on the French right wing. Ian Smith has provided a learned ear and sage council and advice in discussing the thesis presented.

I need to also thank Martin Lancaster for our discussions on the empire, the emperor, and Waterloo over our twenty years of friendship.

Erwin Muilwijk and John Franklin deserve a special word of praise; without their assistance in the provision of source material, this book could never have come to fruition. Stephen Beckett must also be thanked, as must Pierre Juhel.

Lieutenant Colonel Timmermans must be thanked for providing some illustrations. I heartily encourage visitors to his excellent website Napoleon-monuments.eu/.

Anthony Dawson must be thanked for his additional comments and creative writing skills.

Variation in spelling of place names over time is commonplace, and while consistency has been strived for, some soldiers have spelled (or misspelled) names in their writings which have been maintained to sustain the integrity of the source.

Paul L. Dawson BSc Hons MA MIFA FINS
5 May 2023

Introduction

Can anything new be said on Waterloo? Surely nothing lies in dusty archives to be found? Yes, actually. Waterloo was a battle of two halves: one well known, as the eyewitnesses spoke English and concerned the action on Hougoumont and La Haie Sainte. The other half of the action—arguably the most important half for the outcome of the battle—was witnessed by non-English speakers, primarily French, Dutch, and German. These written sources are far more limited than the copious accounts of Hougoumont, and therefore to understand the fighting, we have to rely on both the eyewitnesses as well as other sources, most notably the records the French made of the losses sustained in the campaign.

The discovery of the campaign diary of Drouet d'Erlon while searching in the *Archives Nationales de France* in Paris—Saint Denis really—for material relating to Irish émigrés, and also a new account of General Lefol in the Diplomatic Archives while on the same quest, was groundbreaking. As too was finding new eyewitness accounts of the battle in the French Army Archives at Vincennes; these are legal documents that give time, place, and mode of death and provide a further degree of collaboration to regimental records of the losses of officers and men killed during the campaign, adding vital, fact-based information that can be used to unlock the story of Waterloo, and crucially the French right wing, which this book sets out to do.

In creating our narrative, we have endeavoured to let the primary sources speak for themselves without having to fit what they say into a superficial construct, created by other authors. We must be aware, however, of the limitations and failings of these memoirs as a source of empirical data. The memoir, as Paul Fussell has established, occupies a place between fiction and autobiography.[1]

Neuroscientist John Coates conducted research into memory; his study undertaken between 2004 and 2012 found that what is recalled from memory is what the mind believes happened rather than what actually happened. This effect is often referred to as 'false memory'.[2]

False memory is created by the eyewitness in two ways. First, reading material since the event described took place has overwritten their own memories; they then write down and recall what they have read since the event rather than what they actually witnessed. Secondly, false memory can be created by the mind recording memories of what it thinks ought to have happened; this occurs even if the subject is not contaminated by other sources of data. The story of Waterloo is 'plagued' by false memory, as we shall see.

The historian's primary aim is decoding the language of the source used, to understand the ideological intentions of the author and locate it within the general cultural context to which the source material belongs.[3] The letters cited in this narrative were written down by combatants or by family members long after the events had taken place and are not necessarily an accurate reflection of events that happened. Each of the writers of the letters included in this work had a personal and unique view of Waterloo—what they experienced will be different from participant to participant. The letters left by the participants recorded what was important to them. However, the closeness of the written narrative to the events that took place will affect what is recorded.[4]

Whom the writer is writing to will also impact on what they say. If writing to parents, the writer will subconsciously edit out a lot of the detail. If writing to a brother, then the content may be more graphic. In both cases, the writer will concentrate on their regiment's achievements above others. A diary entry will be more candid and honest about what took place. When an author writes about events they cannot have seen or experienced, then we must question the whole content of the text. If the writer has constructed a narrative of events they did not take part in, clearly this is based on what they have been told or read, which may include all of what they have written.

The further the written narrative shifts away from a diary or the events, the closer the written narrative becomes to a figurative fiction. The recollection of crucial events will be re-evaluated and re-contextualised throughout the life of the author to the point of creating the written record—personal memoirs become influenced by the sociopolitical and socioeconomic environment, and the experiences of the author will have an impact on how they recall an event.[5] As time passes between the event and the recollection of it by participants who were there, the degree of cognitive processing distorts the memories even further and various biases creep in, the main one being that people come to believe that the version of events that they recall is actually correct because they recall it. This becomes self-reinforcing until they are unable to accept their original recall was incorrect. However, the biggest issue with memory recall after time is almost always that the person recalling the event has been influenced by other memories (their own and from other people), which have combined to create a new version of the event.

Part way between memoires and data come orders written in 1815 concerning troop movements and operation. Consulting the various archive boxes at the *Service Historique de la Défense* at Vincennes in Paris quickly reveals that a lot of accepted facts on the battle cannot be verified.

A high percentage of orders relating to the Waterloo campaign are actually from handwritten manuscripts compiled between 1863 and 1865 taken from the collection of the marquis du Casses or made by the sons of Marshals Ney and Grouchy. We do not know if the material is a word-for-word copy of the original. We have to trust that the copies are genuine.

Finally, we must also stress the role of the interpreter in the creation of the narrative. We all have preconceived ideas and personal biases about historical events based on political, economic, sociological, and ideological grounds; these will impact the way the historian interprets the source material. No historian is free from bias.

A perceptive British officer writing in 1835 notes that the accounts from eyewitnesses that mention events that they cannot see are not reliable:

> Indeed, I maintain it to be impossible, that they could give a correct account. The clouds of smoke from the artillery and musketry of both armies, rendered observation impracticable to them, while many an interesting 'war passage' took place in the melee, easily distinguishable by those near at hand, (who could just see what was passing around them,) which was lost to a looker-on at a greater distance. Therefore, you must not expect from me, who was then a subaltern officer, commanding a company, an account of the 'whole battle'.[6]

1
1815

Paris in the spring of 1815 was restless—continuing unemployment and financial hardships caused by rampant inflation, despite the longed-for peace, had not endeared the people to the king. In fact, peace had been a huge contributor to the economic woes that France faced that spring. With peace, thousands had been made unemployed with the closure of clothing and equipment factories that had been established to supply the army. In addition, the Napoleonic state had required a huge bureaucracy to function, and with the change of government, many hundreds of pen-pushers were without work, and men who had served the state, in many cases for over a decade, found their posts were being given to returning royalists. Economic hardships were not helped by the new government levying heavy taxation to endeavour to put money back into the government's coffers—France was virtually bankrupt. To save money, the army, now on a peace footing, had jettisoned thousands of men, who now flooded onto the labour market. The duke of Wellington, the British ambassador, reported on the mood in Paris to the British government. Thankfully for the new government, the large number of malcontents had no unified voice of opposition, nor could it agree on what it opposed. The opposition lacked a figurehead around whom they could rally.

The Congress of Vienna was busy endeavouring to redraw the map of Europe. The process was not going smoothly at all. France—backed by her allies, Austria and Great Britain—seemed on the brink of declaring war over the fate of Saxony, one of Napoleonic France's allies against the expansionist aims of Prussia. To face this crisis, the French army needed to be brought up to a war footing and brought up to strength. One of the last acts of the monarchy in the spring of 1815 (on 9 March) was to call up 12,000 half-pay officers and 30,000 half-pay men, of which it seems some 8,952 men returned to the army.[1] We need to note that an amicable agreement was made on 24 October 1815 to solve the Saxon problem; the former Napoleonic duchy of Warsaw was cut up among the allied powers—Russia received most of it, the district of Poznań was handed to Prussia, and Kraków became a free city. In addition, Prussia received 40 per cent of Saxony—later known as the province of Saxony—with the remainder returned to King Frederick Augustus I as the kingdom of Saxony. Prussia would later gobble up Bavaria, Westphalia, Württemberg, and what remained of Saxony in expansionist wars in the middle years of the decade.

The call-up of men to face the Saxony crisis returned many of these unemployed soldiers back to the army, diluting the opposition to the monarchy. Yet we accept that 'Why am I on half pay and not someone else like x y z' was perhaps the primary grievance former soldiers had with the monarch as opposed to being die-hard Bonapartists. Opposition to the monarch was not solely restricted to disgruntled soldiers—many were Republicans, die-hard Jacobins, Orleanists, and Liberalists, all having their own agenda on how France should be governed. For Napoleon to succeed in rallying France behind him, he had to appeal to the disparate opposition groups, which led fundamentally to his own downfall as he had no single power base. Unlike 1799, Napoleon had to win over key sections of society to support his new government in a coalition as opposed to the virtual dictatorship he had enjoyed since 1799. The new regime was divided in its loyalties, as was the country: France faced civil war both in the Vendée and northern departments. The events that followed the emperor's return reflected the fractured nature of France.

To rally the state to the new regime, at the *École militaire* in Paris on 1 June, the army swore an oath of allegiance to Napoleon and the people accepted the new constitution which had been voted for in a democratic referendum. An eyewitness was Colonel Noel of the Horse Artillery, who reflects the mood of the army:

> On 1 June, the ceremony took place on the Champ-de-Mars.
>
> Deputations from the military intermingled with the state bodies and authorities, occupied a huge circular amphitheatre built against the front of the military academy and rising to the level of the first floor. In front of this an altar erected, and beyond, arranged on both sides were the troops of the National Guard stretching to the banks of the Seine.
>
> The Emperor entered from the first floor of the military school, and took his place on a golden throne in the middle of the terraces. He wore a purple robe embroidered with gold and lined with ermine. He has on his head a black cap, surmounted with feathers held in place by a large diamond.
>
> Upon arrival, everyone stood up and he was acclaimed by all the spectators. His family was coldly received. They were not very popular and had cost France dearly.

At the coronation, I was part of the deputation of the first horse artillery, the Champ-de-Mai, I am part of the 4th regiment under my command, and I can see it at 1 June 1815 [there] are more cheers than 2 December 1804. They seem less formal and sincerer. Many sympathies were returned to Napoleon.

The Bourbons and their entourage had made themselves so unpopular that, although it had a thirst for peace, they still preferred the Emperor, even with the prospect of war. We knew he had tried everything to keep the peace, and that the allied sovereigns had refused to receive his envoys, he was humiliated and angry. We sincerely believed that he had become open to more liberal ideas. The drafting of the Additional Act, entrusted to Benjamin Constant, the leader of the Constitutionalists, the choice of Carnot as minister of the interior, restored freedom of the press, his moderation, the absence of persecution against his enemies, gave pledges for the future, he was well aware, moreover, that the opinion had worked.

Finally, fate put us struggling with the whole of Europe, and it was felt that the genius of Napoleon alone in the terrible circumstances where we were, gave us some chance of success. One could deplore his return, but France has again chosen him for sovereign, there was no alternative but to follow him.

The Emperor has sat on his throne, a Mass followed by a sung *Te Deum*, there is nothing like the imposing ceremonies of Catholic worship, accompanied by military pomp. There were 50,000 men under arms and 100 pieces of cannon.

The show was great and severe.

The faces of those present did not seem to be giving thanks to the heavens, but implored it for help. Everyone seemed to feel their help was were needed.

The oath to the Constitution was sworn on the Gospel and was followed by the distribution of eagles to the National Guard and deputations from the regiments. The whole ceremony was beautiful.[2]

Nominated as tribunes to the new government were several of Napoleon's marshals, who had sat in the Chamber of Peers during the previous Napoleonic administration, namely, Marshals Massena, Lefebvre, Seurrier, Moncey, and Kellerman; Marshal Ney was also appointed a tribune.[3,4] Napoleon was escorted by Marshals Soult, Grouchy, Oudinot, and Jourdan. Myth implies very few marshals rallied in 1815, when in fact ten were present at the Champ de Mai. Indeed, Soult, Ney, Jourdan, and Grouchy were mounted and rode alongside the emperor.[5] Mortier is noticeably missing as is Brune, and for some reason, Davout was not present either. Oudinot, we are told, rode as part of the emperor's cortege, but his biographer makes it clear he was not involved in these events and had not rallied to the emperor.[6,7]

As the army swore its oaths, it was all too apparent that war was inevitable. With the allies ranged in opposition to him, Napoleon's hand was forced into taking military action. To prevent an invasion of France, Napoleon made plans to attack the mobilised allied troops under Wellington and Blucher in the Netherlands. Despite being outnumbered, as in the 1814 campaign, Napoleon's *modus operandi* was to keep the two forces separate, over which he had a numerical advantage, and defeat each army in turn by rapid concentrations of the French army, just as he had so effectively done in 1814. While he would attack in the Netherlands with the *Armée du Nord*, the borders of France would be controlled by *Corps d'Observation*:

General Jean Rapp's 23,000-man *Armée du Rhine* was in position to stop the Austrians of Schwarzenberg once they started their advance.

General Lecourbe's 8,400-man *Armée du Jura* faced Bachmann's 37,000 Swiss.

Marshal Suchet's 23,500-man *Armée des Alpes* was ready to protect Lyons against the Austrian-Piedmonts army.

Marshal Brune's 5,500-man *Armée du Var* observed the Neapolitan army of Onasco.

In the rebellious department of the Vendée, General Lamarque was dispatched with 10,000 troops, including elements of the Young Guard. Furthermore, Napoleon sent two armies in the field against the Spanish-Portuguese threat: the *Armée des Pyrenees Orientales* (7,600) was commanded by General de Decaen at Toulouse and the *Armée des Pyrenees Occidentales* (6,800) was commanded by General de Clausel at Bordeaux. The minister of war, Marshal Davout, had 20,000 troops to protect Paris.

The Campaign Begins

Jean-Baptiste Drouet d'Erlon was the son of a master carpenter, and he joined the army in 1782. Ten years later, he joined the Army of the North. In 1793, Drouet was with the Army of the Moselle when he finally became an officer, being elected *capitaine* of his battalion. The next year, he joined the Army of the Sambre and Meuse and he became an aide-de-camp to General Lefebvre, beginning a long working relationship with the future marshal. Over the course of 1794, he received promotion to *chef de bataillon* and to *chef de brigade* in 1797. Later that year, he joined the

Army of the Rhine. He became Lefebvre's chief of staff in 1799 and was rewarded with promotion to the rank of *général de brigade* and would fight at Zurich under the orders of another future marshal, Eduoard Mortier.

Promotion to *général de division* came in August 1803. He led the 2nd Division of Bernadotte's 1st Corps at Austerlitz. He was back on Lefebvre's staff in 1806 and was at Danzig before being moved to the staff of Marshal Lannes to act as chief of staff, and was wounded at Friedland. Due to wounds, he withdrew from frontline service and took up command of the 11th Military Division at Bordeaux in 1808. In 1809, he became Count d'Erlon, and then in May, he joined Lefebvre again as a chief of staff. He served with Lefebvre in Bavaria and the Tyrol and then took command of the Bavarian VII Corps when Lefebvre left. In August 1810, he took command of the IX Corps in service in Spain, and then in September, he fought at Valladolid; the following year, he was named commander of V Corps in Andalucia. He served under Soult, and was present at the debacle at Vittoria and actions across the Pyrenees into spring 1814. A good chief of staff, he was quietly competent, but as a field commander, he lacked finesse and skill. Yet he found himself named commander of 1st Corps. His staff comprised aide-de-camps Colonel de Salaignac, Captains Cassolet and Crepieux, and Lieutenants Drouet d'Erlon and Novion.

Chief of staff was *Maréchal de Camp* Baron Delcambre, assisted by two adjutant-commandants, Viala and Babut. His aide-de-camp was Lieutenant Hix. Officers attached to the staff were Captain Millicent de Mousse and Lieutenants Rousseau and Cheron. The staff comprised Major Leroi; Battalion Commanders Lefebvre, Quersval, Poulet, Moller, Reyand, Cardon, Merlin, and Forbi; and Captains Colomb, Bourain, Cartret, Vendel, and d'Herbignie. Baron des Salle commanded the artillery; he has left us his eyewitness recollections of the campaign. Des Salle's aide-de-camp was Captain Marquis, and his chief of staff was Colonel Bernard, assisted by Major Mouchel, the former's aide-de-camp being Lieutenant Evrard, formerly of the Imperial Guard Foot Artillery.[8]

On 3 June, Napoleon informed Marshals Soult and Davout that Marshal Grouchy had been named commander-in-chief of the cavalry of the *Armée du Nord*. Grouchy joined the Imperial Headquarters at Laon on the 5th and began to work with Soult on establishing the movement orders for the forthcoming campaign. Grouchy has left preserved his own diary of his operations before the campaign and of the opening stages of the campaign; this is a vital source of information. As with the campaign diary of General Noguès, which unfortunately has the period from 13 June torn out, this needs to be published to be brought to a wider audience.

The Imperial Guard left Paris on 8 June 1815. Two days later, Marshal of the Palace Betrand issued the following order:

> The Emperor's intention is still to leave on Sunday the 11th at 9 o'clock in the evening and be at Soissons at 4 o'clock in the morning, to leave the place at 9 o'clock, to arrive at Laon at noon, and to leave there in the evening to arrive at Avesnes at 2 o'clock in the morning on the 13th.
>
> The Emperor's intention is that that Army Headquarters will be on the 12th at Avesnes; where the Imperial Guard will arrive on the 12th, that Avesnes will be evacuated by the 2nd Corps which will position itself behind Maubeuge; that you have General d'Erlon draw closer to Maubeuge behind the Sambre and close to the 2nd Corps. Finally, you will have the 6th Corps advance; so that it will be in front of Avesnes, to the rear of 2nd Corps, that of General Vandamme being to the right, and that the Corps will establish itself between Beaumont and Avesnes, and manoeuvre in such a way that the army will be located as follows on the 12th:
>
> The 2nd Corps in the centre.
> The 1st Corps to the left.
> The 3rd Corps to the right.
> The 6th to the rear.
> The Imperial Guard in Avesnes.
> The siege artillery, reserves and pontoon train in front of Avesnes.
> The Corps of the Armee du Moselle, will continue its march to arrive in the same location at the 3rd Corps.
> Marshal Grouchy and the four reserve cavalry corps will be in front of Avesnes.
>
> In these provisions the Emperor will see during the day of the 13th, Generals Reille, d'Erlon, Vandamme, and will be on the 14th at Maubeuge to head to Mons in the hope of attacking the English swiftly, or by marching to the right to follow the Prussians at Charleroi.
>
> The Army Corps must therefore be placed so that they can either arrive at Maubeuge and Mons or manoeuvre on the right.
>
> I have the honour of sending you this order of the day which indicates the position of the army on the 13th. This order must be kept secret. I am sending General Reille, d'Erlon, Lobau, Vandamme, and I pray Your Excellency to communicate it to Marshal Grouchy, to the *Ordonnateur en Chef*, and the commander in chief of the artillery.
>
> General Drouot sent orders to the Imperial Guard and Marshal Mortier. The Emperor's Household and equipage are receiving the order to head to Avesnes. Please give orders that no cannon be fire in Avesnes or Maubeuge, so that the enemy will not be made aware of any movement, The cannon may be fired in Laon.[9]

On 12 June, Napoleon left Paris and headed for Soissons, where the headquarters for the coming campaign were established. Arrayed along the Belgian border were two allied armies: Field Marshal Gebhard Leberecht von Blücher commanded a force of 116,000 Prussians and Saxons, centred at Namur; the second comprised 93,000 British, Dutch, and German troops based at Brussels. These men were commanded by the duke of Wellington. The emperor's plans called for a thrust to Mons: Reille and 2nd Corps were directly south of Mons and were to be centre of any thrust. The order also made provision for a second thrust to Charleroi (with Vandamme at the centre with 3rd Corps)—at this stage of operations, an advance along two parallel roads was being developed. This made sense—the army would march quicker on two roads than one, and not exhaust local supplies of fodder and food. The goal was for the attack to begin on the morning of 14 June.

At some stage, Napoleon abandoned the idea of two thrusts into Belgium and instead favoured an all-out attack at Charleroi. To this end, in a letter of 12 June, Soult ordered Gerard to arrive at the Sambre by 14 June, and Delort with the 14th Cavalry Division was to move to Beaumont.[10] This is where things began to 'unravel'. Communication is key. Soult's staff had been hamstrung by Davout in Paris, and he was short of horses, secretaries, and essential personnel. Without officers and men to transmit orders, event planning quickly broke down. At the same time, communication between the major general and the emperor's personal staff (Soult was not with the emperor at this stage) failed. Used to having Berthier always with him, Napoleon began sending orders in the name of General Bertrand to direct the movement of the army. On the same day as Soult issued his order, Napoleon sent an order changing Gerard's destination to Beaumont rather than Rocroi: his original destination for the advance on Mons. Napoleon had changed his plans, but for whatever reason judging on extant archive documents, the cavalry reserve under Grouchy was still being concentrated on the attack on Mons.[11]

What was going on? Soult was issuing orders from the Army HQ, yet Marshal of the Palace Bertrand was issuing orders directly from the emperor. Neither man seems to have been aware of the other's intentions. Napoleon had changed his mind about the plan of operations and not told his major general. Lack of and failure of communication was a major problem from day one of operations as it were.

Soult—at this stage with the headquarters—was not with the emperor. Due to the distance to transmit orders between Avesnes and Laon and the time delay on orders, it meant that Soult was issuing orders hours behind those of Bertrand, and thus conflicting orders were issued; two staffs working to separate ends to achieve the same result is not a good idea. Yet as early as 5 June, the emperor had planned a frontal assault on Mons, with a feint towards Charleroi; the Prussians knew this plan as soon as the emperor had decided upon it.[12] No one except Napoleon is to blame for this fiasco.

When we look at the paper archive generated during the campaign, we note that on 29 May, the emperor sketched out his outline plan of operation: to defeat the Prussians and then turn on Wellington via a rapid thrust on Brussels to separate the two allied armies. Many commentators on the military operations of 1815 cite the defection of de Bourmont with copies of the emperor's plans on 14–15 June as a vital tipping point in informing the allies of the operations of the French army. Yet since the end of May, the allies had known what the French army was going to do: attack Brussels via Mons or Charleroi, starting with the Prussians. What the allies did not know was when.

Spy networks feeding information to allied sources as well as divided loyalties among the French top table of officers gave the allies a vital insight into the planning process and Napoleon's mind. The allies knew where the French would be and made plans accordingly. The emperor needed a surprise, sudden attack. If he could strike while Wellington and the prince of Orange were still in Mons, the road to Brussels was open. Any delay in the attack by twenty-four to forty-eight hours gave the allies time to concentrate. The debacle over Mons or Charleroi caused the late arrival of Gerard and 4th Corps to their starting positions, as well as the cavalry, meaning that twenty-four hours were lost. The campaign was lost from that point. Any advantage the French had had was lost.

The importance of the change in focus of operations and the time it took to reorganise the army, which allowed the allies to concentrate their forces, has often been overlooked in studies of the campaign. Why the original plan of operations was changed we do not know. It was a clumsy mistake committed when the advantage lay squarely with the French. While the allied strategy was to maintain a united front, Napoleon as usual sought one great battle at a point where his enemy's forces were split, concentrating his own forces at that point and destroying them. He intended then to deal with Russian and Austrian armies approaching France from the east. To carry out this plan, he divided his forces into two attacking wings and a strategic reserve, which consisted as in former years of the Imperial Guard.

Having settled on a thrust on Charleroi, in the early hours of 15 June, the French army began to move across the frontier. Napoleon was confident of the expected outcome, so much so that the order of the day, issued the previous day, proclaimed:

Soldiers, today is the anniversary of Marengo and Friedland, places where the destiny of Europe was decided on two occasions. Accordingly, like after Austerlitz and Wagram, we believed the arguments and the oaths of the princes that we left on their thrones! Today, however, in their coalition against us they take offense [*sic*] at the independence and at the most sacred rights of France. They started their aggressions on in a precise manner: let us therefore march to meet them; they and we, are we not the same men?

Soldiers, at Jena, against those same Prussians, who are today so arrogant, you were one against three, and at Montmirail, one against six.

That those of you who were prisoners of the English tell you their stories of their Pontoons and of the horrible evils that they suffered.

The Saxons, the Belgians, the Hanoverians, the soldiers of the Rhine Confederation, groan at their obligations to help the cause of the princes who are enemies of the justice and the rights of all people. They know that this coalition is insatiable. After destroying twelve million Italians, one million Saxons, six million Belgians, she will devour the smaller States of Germany.

The fools! One moment of good fortune blinds them. The oppression and the humiliation of the French people are above their power! If they move into France, they will find their graves.

Soldiers! We have to make forced marches, give battles, take risks; but, with steadiness, victory will be ours: the rights, the honour and the welfare of our country will be retaken.

For each Frenchman who has the courage, the moment has come to win or to die![13]

The emperor's plans called for a concentric advance of three columns to Charleroi. Reille's 2nd Corps and d'Erlon's 1st Corps formed the left wing of the army and were to march from Solre-sur-Sambre, via Thuin, to Marchienne-au-Pont, a short distance outside of Charleroi. Pajol's cavalry in the centre, supported by Domon's cavalry, was to advance from Beaumont to Charleroi, with General Vandamme's 3rd Corps to follow under the protective screen of cavalry. At the rear were Lobau's 6th Corps and the Imperial Guard. The right wing comprised General Gérard's 4th Corps protected by one of Milhaud's cuirassier divisions.

Napoleon's plan was that if the army left its positions at 3 a.m., some 60,000 men would be at Charleroi by midday, but this carefully timetabled plan soon started to unravel. At 7 a.m., *Général de Division* de Bourmont deserted to the Prussians, which flung his division into chaos. He was the first but not the last officer who deserted the army. Vandamme did not get his marching orders as the courier carrying them, we are told, broke his leg, so he only moved off at 7 a.m.—already many hours late. Even worse, 3rd Cavalry Corps was out of position: it was still heading to its starting positions to attack Mons. Clearly, someone had bungled. Yet the staff had received no word from Kellermann for days. What was going on? Why was Kellermann operating on 'radio silence'? As discussed elsewhere, Kellermann's command was 'far from happy': the Carabiniers contained many officers and men who would rather have been with the exiled King Louis. Perhaps in trying to win the 'hearts and minds', Kellermann's focus on his operations had become impeded. We simply do not know.

On the morning of 15 June, General Kellermann and the 3rd Cavalry Corps were at Vervins, a town in north-east France, some 80 miles from Quatre Bras.[14] Kellerman's staff work was so abysmal that on the morning of 16 June, Soult's headquarters had no real idea where Kellermann was as he had sent no reports for almost forty-eight hours. At 5 a.m. on 16 June, Marshal Grouchy reported to Soult about his cavalry force:

> The 1st Cavalry Corps was placed at Lambusart on the road from Gilly to Fleurus;
> The 2nd Corps was at Lambusart in the rear of the valley;
> The 4th Corps was based around the village of St François;
> The location of the 3rd Corps was unknown, with a best guess between Charleroi and Gilly.[15]

Grouchy acidly remarked to his superior that he had no idea where Kellermann actually was and, moreover, had had no dispatches from him during the course of 15 June.[16] Poor staff work and a failure to cooperate and communicate was symptomatic of the improvised nature of the army. It is undeniable that Napoleon's top table of officers were hardly a dream team. D'Erlon at the head of 1st Corps was hardly a great soldier and had a track record of failure; Reille at the head of 2nd Corps was competent; Vandamme was the architect of the disasters at Kulm in 1813; Gerard commanding 4th Corps was capable; and Lobau at the head of 6th Corps was possibly the best field officer commanding a corps on the field of Waterloo.

Of Napoleon's immediate subordinates, Ney and Soult had taken posts out of political expediency. Soult was an excellent tactician and staff officer, but was perhaps not the ideal man to be major-general; he had no experience of working with the emperor in this capacity. He had years of experience commanding troops in Spain as his own man, but he had no recent understanding of how Napoleon worked, having last served directly under him at Austerlitz. Ney was a hothead with no staff. Making matters worse, from 16 June, Grouchy would not be replaced as head of the cavalry due to a lack of senior officers, and Mortier's position at the head of the Imperial Guard was still vacant. Of Grouchy, history has damned him as a traitor who caused the downfall of the empire, but as the author has argued in multiple previous books, and as this work will show, Grouchy was the easy target for blame. His aristocratic background made him an obvious scapegoat as a royalist sympathiser, who deliberately disobeyed orders. This is, of course, all slander.

Serving officers who would rather have been at home in their châteaux and commanders and staff still joining their divisions as the campaign started were issues that were detrimental to the combat performance of the army. General Allix never took his appointment in 1st Corps as he did not get to Paris in time to partake in the campaign, for example. Lack of competent senior officers and a lack of senior officers in vital command and control positions was a huge weakness. All command was vested on Napoleon: with missing key subordinates, Napoleon was in total command of the French forces at Waterloo. If he won, then the glory was all his; if he lost, then no one else was to blame except him. Charles Esdaile remarks that the *Armée du Nord* was nothing like the *Grande Armée* and was less likely to win battles or to be able to sustain defeat.[17]

2

15 June

Our story begins with d'Erlon's own journal entry for the campaign. This key text has, to the best of my knowledge, not been widely used to study the campaign or been accessible to readers in French or English. The text is the centrepiece of the story that follows. It is not our intention to give a blow-by-blow account of the campaign or the battle—that can be found in other books by the author; it is our intention to present the campaign as d'Erlon understood it firsthand, with commentary from other eyewitnesses and primary sources of data.

The first entry in d'Erlon's campaign diary concerns 15 June:

All of 1st Corps was ordered to head to Thuin where it would relieve the 2nd Corps. The 1st Division and the brigade of cavalry under the orders of General Gobrecht to remain at Thuin to guard the bridge over the river Sambre and to observe for any troops debouching from Nivelles and to transmit this news to Maubeuge. The equipment train was at [word missing]. The other troops of the 1st Corps headed to Marchienne au Pont, and once they had crossed the Sambre were to unite with the 2nd Corps. The 3rd Division passed Marchienne au Pont [and] gained the main road from Charleroi to Mons. A squadron of Hussars was employed in reconnaissance patrols in the direction of Fontaine l'Eveque. The 2nd and 4th Divisions were to position at Jumet, the cavalry to be established behind the village [remainder missing].[1]

Reille, with the leading elements of 2nd Corps, was at Jumet by 3 p.m., and from there began his movement to Gosselies. He ordered Piré's cavalry to sweep the countryside in front of the infantry and to pass to the left of the Monceaux wood, through which his infantry marched. This movement was, in theory, to be supported by 1st Corps. Around 10 a.m., Napoleon was at Jamignon.[2] Here, he ordered General Reille and 2nd Corps to pass the Sambre and to 'form several lines one or two miles in front as to be astride the main road to Brussels, passing in the direction of Fleurus':

> The Comte d'Erlon and 1st Corps will be formed at Marchienne, in line of battle on the road from Mons to Charleroi, where he will be within range of support if need it in Charleroi. If you are still in Marchienne when the orders arrive, make your movement by Marchienne, but always fulfil the above provisions.[3]

To d'Erlon, the following order was passed:

> The intent of his majesty is also that you pass the Sambre at Marchienne or Ham, to take the highway from Mons to Charleroi, where you will form, over several leagues, and take positions by moving closer to the Count Reille, linking your communications and sending parties in all directions, Mons, Nivelles, etc. This movement would also be appropriate, if the Count Reille was forced to make his passage by Marchienne. Give me your account of your operations and what happens to you. The Emperor will be in front of Charleroi.[4]

In the centre came 3rd Corps. General Lefol, who served under Vandamme in 3rd Corps, reports:

> [Lefol did] not encounter any obstacles and arrived on the plains of Charleroi ... the army corps formed up on this plain and was soon on the march to pass through Charleroi before taking position one and a half leagues beyond the city, just in front of the village. It was just before 1 o'clock in the afternoon. The Emperor who was positioned just outside Charleroi witnessed the entire army corps march past, I can't tell you how ecstatic the troops were. The march of the 11th division was gruelling. The army marched through Charleroi all united: infantry, cavalry, artillery, Guard and Line all marched past together. General Vandamme had a heated argument with the Major General and the Emperor about this. By this time we were in the presence of the enemy, who occupied the road to Fleurus and were well positioned.[5]

As Lefol reports, the central column met the Prussians at Gilly and attacked. After successive charges by the cavalry, the Prussians fell back at Sombreffe.

Reille arrived with 2nd Corps at about 5.30 p.m., in sight of Frasnes; the lancers of the Guard were received with cannon fire. General

Edouard de Colbert notes that the village was occupied by an infantry battalion and a battery of light artillery. Although the allied infantry troops perhaps numbered only 4,500 men with six guns, they were sufficient to defend Quatre Bras against the 1,700 lancers and chasseurs of Lefebvre-Desnouettes, supported by a single light infantry battalion. Ney contented himself with ordering a few rather feeble charges against the Nassau infantry, in position in front of Quatre Bras, and directing to the east of this point, on the side of Sart-Dames-Avelines, a reconnaissance that did not even approach within musket range of the allied troops' outposts.

In the afternoon of 15 June, d'Erlon wrote to Soult regarding his troop movements:

> Conforming to the general orders, one of my cavalry brigades has passed through Solre and Bienne-sous-Thuin, and a division of infantry at Thuin, Lobbes and Abbey d'Aulnas. My other troops continue to arrive at Marchiennes, following the 2nd Corps, and are yet to cross the Sambre. I will position a brigade on the road to Mons, and another brigade on the road at Marchienne, and the other division will head to Gosselies.[6]

About the operations of 1st Corps on the night of 15 June, d'Erlon reported his positions to Soult as follows:

> Conforming to Your Excellency's order of three o'clock, I moved to Gosselies. Upon arriving, I found the place occupied by the 2nd Corps, so I placed the 4th Division to the rear of this village, and the 2nd Division at Jumay [sic.] as well as a brigade of cavalry.
>
> The 3rd Division has remained at Marchienne-au-Pont, and the 1st at Thuin, with my other cavalry brigade at Solre and Bienne-sous-Thuin, so my troops are greatly dispersed; I request Your Excellency to let me know if I can recall those troops left in the rear.[7]

In response, Soult wrote:

> Comte d'Erlon, it is the emperor's intentions that you concentrate all of your corps on the left bank of the Sambre, and unite with 2nd Corps at Gosselies, in line with the orders that you will be given by the Prince of the Moskowa. Also, recall the troops you have left at Thuin, Solre and that area. You are always to send out numerous patrols to cover the road to Mons.[8]

This is the last we know of d'Erlon that day. Thuin was 20 miles away from where Bachelu and other elements of 1st Corps spent the night. D'Erlon had failed to keep in contact with Soult, failed to operate with Reille, and failed to keep his corps concentrated. The outcome of the following day was largely a consequence of d'Erlon's bungling during the course of the 15th. Ney reported his positions to Marshal Soult at 11 p.m. that night:

> Gosselies 15 June 1815. 23.00
>   To His Excellency marshal major-general
>   M. marshal, I have the honour to inform Your Excellency that in accordance to the emperor's orders, this afternoon I occupied Gosselies, from where the enemy was dislodged by the cavalry of General Piré and the infantry of General Bachelu. The enemy's resistance was most obstinate and a discharge of twenty-five to thirty rounds of artillery fire repulsed them in the direction of Heppignies via Fleurus. We have taken between 500 and 600 prisoners from the corps of General Zeithen.
>   Here are the dispositions of my troops:
>   General Lefèbvre-Desnoëttes with the lancers and chasseurs of the Guard at Frasné.
>   General Bachelu and the 5th Division at Mellet.
>   General Foy and the 9th Division at Gosselies.
>   The light cavalry of General Piré at Heppignies.
>   I do not know where to find General Reille.
>   General d'Erlon occupies the terrain around Jumet with the majority of the corps, but he has not sent to him his exact dispositions, I will send them one when they get to me. I attach a report by General Lefèbvre-Desnoëttes.[9]

Jacques Martin narrates:

Our corps did not cross that day, it followed that of Reille, responsible for the attack, and it's in the footsteps of the latter that I saw for the first time in eighteen months, the wounded and dead lying on the ground. This show, which announced the upcoming return so quickly to so many bloody scenes, seriously impressed me: my heart beat, I remember. Why do I say not, since it does not prevent me from completing my duty then?

However, the day was winding down and we were up from two in the morning and we had done, without food, a march of eight leagues, made more painful by a heat that became stifling. We were ordered to bivouac on the road to Brussels, a league ahead of Charleroi. That night was better than the last. It did not rain, the soldiers went to find wood and straw, and as is usual, seeking wood in the roofs, they found the wine stores. This is an unavoidable evil; to go to forage, we must enter houses: we are pleased when it happens without serious repercussions. Among those who were in charge of this duty was one of our soldiers who had fought in Spain. He went straight to the village priest and, as he knew the uses of these gentlemen, descended to the cellar and we brought a few bottles of excellent old wine, we drank to the health of the good priest.[10]

The French army bivouacked for the night in an area of 10 square miles. On the left, Lefebvre-Desnouette's cavalry was around Frasnes, with Reille's 2nd Corps between that point and Gosselies. Girard's division of that corps was at Wangenies, near Fleurus, while d'Erlon's 1st Corps was covering the ground from Marchienne to Gosselies. On the right, Marshal Grouchy had Pajol's and Exelman's cavalry divisions south of Fleurus, around Lambusart. The 3rd Corps under Vandamme was between Charleroi and Fleurus, while Gerard's corps camped on both sides of the Sambre river at Chatelet. In the centre, under Napoleon's direct orders, were the guard around Charleroi and Gilly, and to the rear, perhaps not yet across the river, were Lobau's 6th Corps and the cavalry corps of Milhaud and Kellermann. Grouchy had initiated a skilful cavalry pursuit that was stopped by Zieten's reserves.

3

16 June

Sombreffe became the concentration point for Blücher's army following the delaying actions fought on the previous day. The gently undulating battlefield was covered with growing crops, and was divided approximately in half by the Ligny stream. The steep-banked stream was 1–4 metres wide with banks overgrown with willows and bushes. There were four bridges along the stream. Near the wood of Bois du Loup was a marshy meadow. The highest point was the Bussy Mill, between Brye and Ligny, where Blücher's observation post was located. The second highest point was Point du Jour, where General Thielemann established his headquarters. The villages were well built, each having a number of stone buildings and church towers. Some villages also had ditches and hedges around their perimeters.

Napoleon was on horseback at 4 a.m. on 16 June and in good spirits, intending to reach Brussels as soon as possible. Of course, he did not know of Wellington's movements, but considered that in all probability the Anglo-Belgian army would take ground in front of Brussels and make a stand there. In this event, he would push them back to Antwerp, along their lines of communication, causing them to be separated still further from their Prussian allies. Before this plan could be put into operation, however, Napoleon had to be sure that Blücher would not be able to come to their assistance.

The Prussian corps of General Zieten had to be driven back past Gembloux, denying Blücher the use of the Namur–Wavre–Brussels road. Unfortunately, at about 8 a.m., Napoleon received a note from Marshal Grouchy informing him that the Prussians were preapring to make a stand. In response, Soult sent the following order to Marshal Ney:

Charleroi, 16 June

The emperor has sent orders to the Comte de Valmy, to unite his corps and to direct his movement to Gosselies, and to make it available to Marshal Ney.

It is the intention of the emperor that the cavalry of the Guard that went along the Brussels road is to move to the rear and to rejoin the main body of the Imperial Guard; to prevent them from making wrong moves they are to be placed a little behind the line. General Lefèbvre-Desnoëttes will send officers to take orders. You will inform me whether the corps had carried out this movement, and the positions this morning the 1st and 2nd Corps occupies along with the attached cavalry divisions, as well as making known to us what news you have and what troops are in front of you.[1]

Following this order, Napoleon via Soult wrote: 'Order the Comte de Valmy to unite his 3rd Cavalry Corps and to move to Gosselies and to be placed at the disposal of Marshal Ney'.[2] Later that morning, more orders were sent to Ney by the emperor:

Charleroi 16 June

Mr marshal, the emperor orders that you are to march with 1st and 2nd Army Corps as well as the 3rd Cavalry Corps, which is now at your disposal, and lead them to the intersection of so-called Trois-Bras of the Brussels roads, where you will take up position. You will undertake reconnaissance along the Brussels and Nivelles roads, along which the enemy probably withdrew. His Majesty desires, that despite any setbacks, you are to establish a division with cavalry at Genappes and he orders you to send another division to Marbais to cover the area between Sombreffe and Trois-Bras. You can place with this division the cavalry of the Imperial Guard commanded by General Lefèbvre-Desnoëttes as well as the 1st Regiment of Hussars which was seconded to you yesterday to stand at Gosselies.

The corps that is to be placed at Marbais may also be used to support Marshal Grouchy in his movements on Sombreffe, and also support the position of Trois-Bras, as it may become necessary. You are to instruct the general who will be at Marbais to scout in all directions, particularly to Gembloux and Wavre.

If, however the division of General Lefèbvre-Desnoëttes is not standing on the Brussels road, it is to be replaced at Marbais by the 3rd Cavalry Corps under the orders of Comte de Valmy, as well as the 1st Hussars.

I have the honour to notify you that the emperor will be moving onto Sombreffe, where Marshal Grouchy will debouch with the 3rd and 4th Corps of Infantry and the 1st, 2nd and 4th Corps of Cavalry. Marshal Grouchy will occupy Gembloux. Please send a report of your news and arrangements to the emperor, and execute the order I sent you.

His Majesty charges me to remind you to tell all generals commanding army corps to concentrate their men, and draw back in all isolated men, to maintain the most perfect order amongst the troops as well as to concentrate your artillery and ambulances which may be in the rear.[3]

The order clearly defined Ney's mission objectives: he was to occupy Quatre Bras, as well as Genappe, and move a division towards Sombreffe to support Grouchy at Ligny, who was well aware of the situation (that Ligny was the primary objective and Quatre Bras the secondary objective). At some stage that morning, the emperor clearly changed his mind, as a conflicting set of orders was sent to Ney. Based on Ney's actions that day, it is clear he did not fully understand his mission brief:

I am sending you my aide-de-camp, General de Flahaut, who brings you the present letter. The major-general [Imperial Headquarters] should have given you my orders, but you will receive mine earlier because my officers have better mounts and ride faster than his. You will receive the movement orders of the day, but I want to write them to you in detail, because it is of the greatest importance. I'm sending Marshal Grouchy, with the 3rd and 4th Infantry Corps towards Sombreffe. I'm taking my Guard to Fleurus where I will be also before noon. I will attack the enemy if I meet him, I will scout the way to Gembloux. There, after what will have happened, I will make up my mind, maybe at three o'clock in the afternoon, maybe this evening. My intention is that you should be ready to move towards Brussels, immediately after I have made up my mind.

I will support you with the Guard who will be at Fleurus, or at Sombreffe, and I want to arrive in Brussels tomorrow morning. You will have to move this evening after I have made my decision, early enough to be able to inform you, so that you can move three to four miles this evening, and be at Brussels tomorrow at seven o'clock. You should be able to dispose of your troops in the following way: one division at two miles in front of Quatre Bras given there will be no inconvenience in doing do so; six divisions around Quatre Bras and one division at Marbais, in order to be able to get it closer to Sombreffe if I should need it there. This division will not delay your movements. The corps of the Comte de Valmy, who has 3,000 elite cuirassiers, will be posted at the intersection of the roman road and the road to Brussels, in order that I can move it towards my position, whenever I should need it. As soon as I have made up my mind, you will send him [the Comte de Valmy] the order to join you.

I would like to have with me the division of the Guard that is commanded by General Lefèbvre-Desnoëttes and I will send you the two divisions of the Comte de Valmy, so as to call him back, when I need him, and to prevent General Lefèbvre-Desnoëttes from making wrong moves, because it could be that I will decide this evening to move to Brussels with the Guard. Nevertheless, cover the division of Lefèbvre-Desnoëttes with the two cavalry divisions of d'Erlon and Reille in order to spare the Guard, because should there be a clash with the British, I prefer that this should happen to the Line, rather than to the Guard.[4]

General Flahaut confirms this:

> I remained with him [General Lefèbvre-Desnoëttes] while awaiting the arrival of the troops under Marshal Ney and we saw, quite some distance in front of us, the English staff officers, who appeared to be examining our position. General Lefèbvre-Desnoëttes had some cannon shots fired at his cavalry, even though they were out of range. Finally, Marshal Ney appeared and the affair started, but there was no coherence in the dispositions. We took, as it is said, the bull by the horns, and launched the troops successively in the order they arrived.[5]

The order seemingly tells Ney that he has eight divisions at his disposal, plus Kellermann. He is told not to send a corps but a division to Marbais. An eyewitness to the events that day writes:

> The morning of the 16th, the Emperor sent word to Marshal Ney, ordering him to move to Quatre Bras; I took a good horse and reconnoitre a good position on the Brussels road, and to guard the roads from Nivelles and Namur and to occupy the right and left of the roads. This order was carried to the Marshal by General de Flahaut.[6]

Once the reconnaissance had been made, at 11 a.m., Ney issued orders to Reille and d'Erlon to begin the advance to Quatre Bras from Frasné:

> Conforming to the instructions of the emperor, the 2nd Corps will begin its movement and will occupy the following positions.
> The 5th Division will be in the rear of Genappes on the heights that dominate the town, the left flank lying against the main road. A battalion of two [illegible] will debouch in front along the Brussels road. The park and reserve will be deployed in the 2nd Line.
> The 9th Division will follow the movement of the 5th, and will take up a position in line on the heights, deployed to the right and left of the village of Banterlet.

> The 6th and 7th Divisions will debouch at Trois-Bras where I shall establish my headquarters. The first three divisions of the Comte d'Erlon will take up position at Frasné, the right-hand division will be established at Marbais with the 2nd Division of light cavalry of General Piré; the first is to cover your march and you are to send out reconnaissance patrols towards Brussels and on both flanks. My headquarters will be at Frasné.
> For Marshal Prince of the Moskowa
> Colonel aide-de-camp, Heymès
> The two divisions of the Comte de Valmy are to establish themselves at Frasné and Liberchies. General Lefèbvre-Desnoëttes and Colbert's division of the Guard are to remain at Frasné.[7]

Ney had arrived with no staff whatsoever; he had very little clear idea of what the situation was. Beyond reasonable doubt, at 11 a.m., Ney had no knowledge that Girard was at Wagnelée, nor did he know that Kellermann was 40 miles to the south—in fact, no one really knew where he was—and to make matters worse, 1st Corps was yet to arrive, being scattered between the Sambre and Gosselies as d'Erlon's performance to keep his corps concentrated on 15 June had been appallingly bad. Ney's caution in not attacking the allied forces at Quatre Bras perhaps owed a great deal to not knowing what forces were to his front and what troops he actually had to command.

The 1st Corps was spread out in a wide arc almost 30 miles deep from Quatre Bras. The closest element of the force to Quatre Bras was Durutte, and he was at Gosselies—7 miles south of Quatre Bras, around three hours away at most. Quiot was at Thuin, 26 miles away, or around seven hours at most by line of march, which would have taken him through Charleroi. Donzelot was at Jumet, some 9 miles to the south and perhaps three hours away. Marcognet was at Marchienne-au-Pont, 13 miles (four hours) away. Jacquinot's command was split with a brigade 26 miles to the south-west at Solre-sur-Sambre (a forced march of around six hours), and his other brigade at Bienne-sous-Thuin, some 21 miles from Quatre Bras.

D'Erlon's concentration order was sent at 3 a.m. and the courier had to cover 26 miles—perhaps an hour on horseback—so, in theory, Quiot would have had his orders by 5 a.m. and been on the march an hour later, perhaps as late as 7 a.m. With 26 miles to cover, he could have reached Quatre Bras in seven hours, assuming he did not get into a traffic jam crossing through Charleroi, where 6th Corps was. In spite of this, Quiot could have been at Quatre Bras around 4 p.m., which seems realistic based on Durutte's time of arrival. Jacquinot's men clearly hit the route march with speed to cover the distance and join with Durutte.

Ney's caution may be explained in a report from Adjutant Jeanin's intelligence report to the emperor transmitted that morning:

Sire,

In conforming to your orders that Your Majesty had given me, Adjutant-Commandant Jeanin has made contact with the corps commanded by M. Marshal Prince of the Moskowa. This officer informs me that the troops are in echelon in the environs of Gosselies and the village of Frasné. It is hard to tell with any precision if the enemy is there in force as the terrain is mostly forest. The colonel has spoken to numerous senior officers, some of whom have interrogated some deserters, to gain information about the enemy, which they say is about twenty thousand men. Due to the nature of the terrain, only a small number of sharpshooters are at present engaged.

I am yet to take position in front of Charleroi. In accordance to Your Majesty's orders I have replaced the battalion in the town for police duties and also to protect the large number of wounded.

Charleroi 16 June 1815

Lieutenant-general aide-de-camp to the emperor,

Commander-in-chief of 6th Corps

Comte Lobau

PS—Colonel Jeanin has reported that Colonel Tancarville, chief-of-staff to Comte de Valmy, and had been transmitted to him from Comte d'Erlon, that a large body of enemy troops has been seen marching from Mons towards Charleroi.[8]

Lobau's dispatch is interesting on a number of accounts. First, by the time that Jeanin had arrived, Ney had not yet begun a major action, but small clashes of vedettes were taking place. The heavily wooded terrain was not an ideal combat zone; aware that 20,000 allied troops were in the area, Ney was outnumbered, and he seems to have decided to do nothing other than send out cavalry patrols till his troops had all assembled. Yet in choosing this line of action, the tardiness of Ney was to have major implications in the outcome of the day as it allowed the small Dutch–Belgian garrison at Quatre Bras to be reinforced by Wellington.

The longer Ney waited for d'Erlon to arrive before beginning the attack, the stronger his opponent came. If he had attacked at first light, he would have quite easily taken the position—the Ney of 1805 would have attacked, while the Ney of 1815 was lethargic and wasted valuable time. At dawn, Ney was faced by a few thousand, of whom we believe that Jeanin was well aware that Wellington was coming to their aid. Ney, it seems, suffered from option paralysis: attack now or wait for the allies to present themselves in full, by which time his forces would have arrived. This delay in unifying the command cost a decisive action at either Quatre Bras or Ligny and ultimately the outcome of the campaign. That blame falls squarely on d'Erlon. He was far from a capable commander and hardly the man for the job. Yet, despite his poor performance in Spain, he got the top job in 1815.

At 2 p.m., Soult sent the following order to Marshal Ney:

> In front of Fleurus 16 June about 14.00 hours
> Marshal,
> The emperor charges me to let you know that the enemy has united a corps of troops between Sombreffe and Brye, and that at 14.30 hrs, Mr Marshal Grouchy will attack it with the 3rd and the 4th Corps; it is the intention of His Majesty that you will also attack what is in front of you, and that you, after having repulsed it vigorously, fall back on us in order to surround the corps I just mentioned to you. If this corps is pushed before, His Majesty will move in your direction in order to hasten your operations. Instruct at once the emperor of your arrangements and of what is happening on your front.
> Marshal of the empire, major-general,
> Duc de Dalmatie.[9]

This order presumably arrived between 3 and 3.30 p.m. but we cannot be sure. The order outlined that Ney was to conduct a *'manoeuvres sur les derrières'* against Blücher. However, the general concept of the situation was not explained to him in the wording of the written text, but we must assume the verbal portion of the order did so. However, rather than holding the allies at bay, the order made Ney commit himself even more into the action at Quatre Bras, as the order made it clear that the occupation of Quatre Bras was to be completed before he was to manoeuvre towards Ligny. Ney did not realise that the action at Quatre Bras was of secondary importance and that the decisive battle was raging at Ligny.

4
Fatal Perambulations

The emperor's plans now began to unravel due to a combination of bad luck and incompetence on the part of Ney and d'Erlon. Around 3.30 p.m., Soult ordered d'Erlon to Ligny:

In front of Fleurus
  Mister the Comte d'Erlon,
  The enemy lowers his head into the trap that I intended for him. Bring at once your four divisions of infantry, your division of cavalry, all your artillery, and two divisions of heavy cavalry which I place at your disposal, carry you, say I, with all these forces the height of Saint-Amand and descend on Ligny. In doing so *monsieur*, the Comte d'Erlon, you will save France and will cover yourself with glory.
  Napoleon[1]

Simultaneously, the emperor wrote to Ney:

In front of Fleurus, June 16, between 15.15 and 15.30.
  Mister the marshal,
  I wrote to you, one hour ago, that the emperor would make an attack on the enemy at half-past two in the position which it took between the villages of Saint-Amand and Brye; at this moment, the engagement is very marked. S. M. [His Majesty] gives me the responsibility to say to you that you must manoeuvre at once so as to envelop the right of the enemy and fall quickly on his rear; this army is lost if you act vigorously; the fate of France is in your hands. Thus, do not hesitate a moment to make the movement which the emperor orders you and directs you on the heights of Brye and Saint-Amand to contribute to a perhaps decisive victory. The enemy is taken in the act at the time when it seeks to unite with the English.

The marshal of empire, major-general,
Duc de Dalmatie.[2]

We are missing the verbal portion of all the orders written in the period, but we assume that the aide-de-camps passed the imperial will and intentions on to the receiving officers. An eyewitness notes the following about d'Erlon's move to Ligny:

> The Emperor ordered that a column of 8,000 men with cavalry and 28 pieces of artillery was to be detached from Quatre Bras to attack Bry and the rear of the enemy army ... to hold the Anglo-Dutch army in its position and to envelop the right and rear of the enemy.[3]

On receiving his orders, d'Erlon sent word to Ney, it seems, to confirm his orders. An eyewitness to the events, writing on 22 June 1815, was a young aide-de-camp, Alexandre de Chéron:

> General d'Erlon requested an officer of good courage to serve on his staff: I presented my self [sic.] and was charged with asking for orders from Marshal Ney, I left at the gallop.
> I went to search for the field of battle at Quatre Bras and found the staff of Marshal Ney. I found him in the midst of a melee with a single lancer. I recognised him on his grey horse, I asked him for orders for Count d'Erlon and far from taking this request seriously for his part, said that he did not need anyone sending and swore f... me and f... the Count d'Erlon to whom I reported a more honest response, informing him that the prince did not need him, which meant that we became benevolent spectators of battle for the rest of the day when on the contrary we could have been of great help to Marshal Ney, and would undoubtedly have decided to take this important point.[4]

Reading between the lines here, it seems that on receiving news that d'Erlon was moving to support him, Ney flew into a rage and facetiously or satirically ranted that 'he did not need anyone sending', by which we assume that Ney needed 1st Corps. Ney's rage is all too obvious in the letter. Importantly, this account, written days after the incident, predates anything from d'Erlon. Indeed, d'Erlon contradicts this account—are we dealing with false memory? It would seem to be the case, or at least for the accounts to be so different, we must question the reliability of both and wonder what the missing portion of d'Erlon's diary actually said.

The 'who did what, why, and when' is one of the great controversies of the campaign. The courier sending the 3.30 p.m. order to Ney would have encountered d'Erlon on his line of movement from Ligny to Quatre Bras before arriving with Ney.

It seems that the courier passed on verbal instruction to d'Erlon about the importance of his move to Ligny as well as the written order. This is where the emperor's plans started to go wrong. General d'Erlon requested confirmation of his orders from his commander-in-chief (Ney) and, if Ney's response is taken as genuine, no doubt took the view that the order from the emperor took priority: an imperial order outweighed those of a marshal.

About the episode of receiving the order, d'Erlon writes nearly fifteen years later:

> Towards eleven o'clock or midday, Marshal Ney sent me orders for my corps to take up arms and move towards Frasné and Quatre Bras, where I would receive subsequent orders. My corps set off immediately, after giving the general commanding the head of column the order to move quickly. I went ahead to Quatre Bras to see where Reille's corps was engaged.
>
> Beyond Frasné, I halted with the generals from the Guard,[7] where I was joined by General de La Bédoyère, who showed me a note in pencil which he carried to Marshal Ney, which ordered the marshal to send my corps to Ligny. General de La Bédoyère warned me that he had already given the order for this movement and the head of column had changed its direction, and he indicated to me where I could join it. I immediately took this route and sent my chief-of-staff, Delcambre, to the marshal, to warn him of the change of destination.[5]

He adds more information, writing in 1844:

> The 1st and 2nd corps went to Gosselies. The Emperor and the other corps marched on Ligny and Fleurus, where the Prussians seemed to be concentrating. It has often been said, and wrongly, that the day before the Battle of Ligny, Marshal Ney should have made himself master of the important position of Quatre Bras; but out outposts were pushed only as far as Frasné, and that it was not until the next day, about eleven o'clock, that the two corps marched on Gosselies, which of course was too late to seize this position, on which the enemy had time to gather forces which increased each moment. Besides, the occupation of Quatre Bras had no other purpose than to occupy the English army, in order to prevent it from making detachments towards the Prussian army. The 2nd Corps formed the head of the column; the 1st Corps was on the second line, and was destined (according to what has been known since) to act

according to circumstances, either at Quatre Bras or on the right wing of the Prussian army ... Although several writers, who invent history, have written, that the Emperor never intended to deliver two battles the same day. Thus Quatre Bras ... was feebly occupied on the eve of the battle of Ligny, which was reinforced by the enemy, to such an extent that the whole of 2nd Corps was faced with the most obstinate resistance, and which grew stronger every minute; finally, in spite of great efforts, the 2nd Corps could not seize it.

I ask the reader to read carefully the following paragraph because it is important that the truth be finally known ... The Emperor, strongly engaged at Ligny, sent an orderly officer to Marshal Ney, to tell him to direct the 1st Corps on Ligny, in order to turn the right wing of the Prussian army. This officer met the head of the column of the 1st Corps, which reached Frasné, and, before having transmitted the orders of the Emperor to Marshal Ney, had this column taken to the direction of Ligny. About four o'clock, having gone forward, without any knowledge of the new direction which my army corps had just received, and after having indirectly learned it, I immediately hastened to re-join it, and sent my chief of staff to Marshal Ney, to announce to him the new movement being made. Marshal Ney, being at the moment being pressed back at Quatre Bras, had not taken into account the orders sent by the Emperor, and recalled my army corps. It was an unfortunately a very great fault, which prevented the battle of Ligny from having the results which the Emperor expected, and which completely paralyzed the 1st Corps, which could not take part in any of the two affairs, by the marching and counter-marching that last during the whole day. I hope this explanation will make all that has been told and written to lie about my inaction in this day. There is no doubt that if the Emperor had addressed his orders directly to me, as it is said in several relations of this battle, they would have been punctually executed, and that this battle would have had much more important results. Waterloo would probably not have occurred. It's my opinion; the more I think about it, the more I am inclined to believe it. Back with my army corps ahead of Frasnés, I took the outposts to relieve the 2nd Corps, which had suffered a lot. We learned during the night that the battle of Ligny had forced the Prussian army to retreat.[6]

With clear written orders, and no doubt verbal instruction, d'Erlon headed off to Ligny and we know from Chéron had sent a written and verbal dispatch to Ney, via Delcambre, to inform him of his movements. For d'Erlon, there was no ambiguity in the order—Ney was to hold the allied troops in check and to wheel around towards Ligny. Ney, however, took a markedly different view to his orders, choosing to ignore them to hold the allies and prevent Wellington from linking with Blücher. Ney had committed all his available troops in a full frontal and futile assault. Rather than blocking Wellington from moving to Ligny, Ney chose to try and defeat Wellington: his plan of operations relied on d'Erlon. Ney had failed to grasp his mission objective and committed a greater error in countermanding the emperor's orders.

The sequence of events of that fateful afternoon was perhaps as follows: we propose Ney met Chéron on the field of Quatre Bras and was handed a copy of the 3.30 p.m. order from Imperial Headquarters regarding his new mission objective. This, we think, occurred sometime before 5.30 p.m. Ney, having been unable to secure the crossroads as ordered, had been expecting the arrival of three, if not four, infantry divisions from 1st Corps to enable him to do so. Now he was being told—after the fact—that his much-needed reinforcements were now marching towards Ligny. Ney had clearly forgotten the portions of the orders from the emperor telling him that Kellermann's cuirassiers and at least a division of infantry were to be at the disposal of the emperor for service at Ligny. He totally misunderstood the situation and his mission objective. At some stage, Ney sent a recall order to d'Erlon as he notes fifteen years or so later:

> Marshal Ney sent ... definitive orders to return to Quatre Bras, where he was hard pressed, and was relying upon the co-operation of my corps. I thus decided that I was urgently required there, since the marshal took it upon himself to recall me ...
>
> I therefore ordered my column to counter-march; but despite all the effort I put into this movement, my column only arrived at Quatre Bras at dusk.[7]

It seems d'Erlon sent word of his actions to Soult. In response, Soult's own aide-de-camp, Baudus, claims he was tasked with making the tactical situation clear to Ney and recalls the meeting with him which he says took place after Kellermann's charge:

> Soon, I found Marshal Ney at the point of most danger, in the midst of a terrible fire. I passed him the emperor's orders, but he was so agitated that I felt he was unlikely to execute them. In fact, he had a good reason to be agitated, for in his attack at Quatre Bras, he had not hesitated to commit all three divisions of General Reille's 2nd Corps, because he was expecting the co-operation of 1st Corps commanded by Comte d'Erlon ... the marshal was desperate at having no reinforcements to support his divisions that had only been committed because he thought he had 20,000 men in reserve.[8]

Baudus further adds:

> I insisted with the greatest force to the marshal not to oppose the emperor's orders; I thought I had succeeded; but after the events of the day as I returned to the rear, I observed that the Comte d'Erlon had returned.[9]

This implies that the meeting took place around 7 p.m. and cannot have lasted very long, which places the arrival of Quiot and 1st Division at 8 p.m., if Baudus (writing decades later) is to be believed. Heymès, aide-de-camp to Marshal Ney, writes:

> General d'Erlon arrived in person around nine o'clock in the evening, having completed his journey and received orders from the marshal. The corps was to take up bivouacs in the rear of Frasné, and was to spend part of the night to march to this location and to establish a rally point.[10]

Marshal Ney continues the narration of the battle as follows:

> Frasné, 16 June, 22.00
>
> Monsieur, I attacked and moved against the English in the positions of Quatre Bras with the greatest of vigour, but a wrong movement by Comte d'Erlon deprived me of a good victory, for at that moment the 5th and 9th Divisions of General Reille were totally cut up. The 1st Corps marched to Saint-Amand to join the left wing of Your Majesty, but at that critical moment the corps began to retreat to re-join myself, thus not a single man was of use.
>
> The division of Prince Jérôme acted with great valour. His Highness was slightly wounded, so I in reality only had three divisions of infantry, a brigade of cuirassiers and the cavalry of General Piré. The Comte de Valmy performed a very good charge. Everyone did their duty except the 1st Corps. The enemy lost a lot of men, for our part we took a cannon and a flag. We have lost perhaps 2,000 men killed and 4,000 wounded.
>
> I have asked the Generals Reille and d'Erlon to submit reports to Your Excellency.[11]

Reille's report exists, but d'Erlon's report, if he ever sent one, is missing from archives in France. We suspect d'Erlon simply never wrote a report about his actions that day, but was the 'wrong movement' heading to Ligny? Ney implies to some degree that it was, and that it robbed him of victory at Quatre Bras. Ney, however, is totally silent about recalling 1st Corps and who sent the order. About this incorrect movement, Napoleon wrote the following dispatch to Ney on 16 June:

If the Comte d'Erlon had carried out the movement to Saint-Amand as the emperor ordered, the Prussian army would have been totally destroyed, and we would perhaps have had 30,000 prisoners. The corps of Generals Vandamme and Gérard and also the Imperial Guard were always united; we are exposed to setbacks when detachments are compromised.[12]

The emperor was perfectly correct to vent his wrath at d'Erlon. His inaction at Ligny turned what could have been a complete victory into a bloody stalemate and contributed to the events of the 18th. The tide of the war had been turning against the French since the Mons debacle; d'Erlon now tipped the balance ever stronger in favour of the allies by his bungling on 15 and 16 June. Many seek to blame Grouchy for the defeat at Waterloo, yet the seeds of that defeat were sewn by d'Erlon's fatal perambulations and his failure to keep his corps concentrated. Yet the blame for his appointment rests with the commander in chief, the emperor. He appointed d'Erlon knowing full well his mediocre track record of success, therefore the blame by and large rests with him. He sowed the seeds of his own downfall, then blamed others for his mistakes.

5

Durutte Attacks at Ligny

With 1st Corps heading back to Quatre Bras, d'Erlon had left a cavalry division and an infantry division at Ligny. There was still a chance that some form of flank attack be initiated and the Prussians crushed. For this to be achieved required a quick-thinking field commander, willing to take risks to exploit the situation he found himself in on the flank of the Prussians. The emperor's intention of taking the Prussians in the rear and turning a stalemate into an out-and-out victory was still possible.

Sadly, General Durutte was not such a general. Any other general would have jumped at such a golden opportunity—to attack the exposed flank of the Prussian army. Where d'Erlon and Delcambre were gullible and easily swayed by a marshal of France, Ney was truculent and behaved at times like a spoiled brat with a 'teddy tantrum' over d'Erlon. The situation could still have been saved, but the man on the ground, General Durutte, was not the man to do so; he was timid and unimaginative—hardly skills one needed in a field commander at the head of four regiments of infantry.

Napoleon's plan of operations had always been to post an infantry division at Marbais. Of the four infantry divisions in 1st Corps, Durutte's was the closest geographically to Gosselies, the 'right hand most division' (to quote Ney's 11 a.m. order) and, therefore, we suppose it was Durutte's division that Ney anticipated was to head to Marbais in accordance to his 11 a.m. orders. Yet Durutte and all other eyewitnesses from the 4th Infantry Division seem totally ignorant of that in their writings on the campaign. Did Durutte get the order? If not, why not? If not Durutte, then who was ordered to Marbais? Certainly, it was not Quiot with 1st Division or Marcognet with the 3rd, leaving Donzelot and Durutte as likely candidates.

Given Durutte was the head of column for 1st Corps when it headed to Ligny, we assume that it was indeed Durutte who was, in theory, to have been at Marbais. So, the question is: why did Durutte not arrive there? Was his staff in such chaos that the entire division was paralysed since Gordon had deserted? It does seem so. Clearly, there must have been a fundamental breakdown in the chain of command, or a change of order, for d'Erlon to not act on the 11 a.m. order, unless Ney impressed on him the importance of not sending a division to Marbais. There is no evidence to back up this statement, but something had clearly gone wrong, or orders had been changed, for a major part of the 11 a.m. order not to have been carried out in accordance with the emperor's wishes or Ney's own orders. If such an order was issued, it no longer survives. It is more likely that the division's staff was in meltdown, and the division was totally incapable of operations until the afternoon.

Ney never knew the truth of course, as Durutte did his best to cover up the defection of an officer who had served with him since 1807, lest guilty fingers be pointed at him. Certainly, it threw Durutte into some kind of stupor and he was rendered a mere automaton, unable to take the initiative if not directly ordered to do so. Most histories of Waterloo speak of de Bourmont almost as an afterthought in that it did not affect the outcome of the campaign. The truth is that the army was shedding officers like a tree's leaves in autumn. Not only was 14th Division paralysed, but so were 4th Division and the *Carabiniers-à-Cheval*.

Be that as it may, history tells us that the cavalry division of Jacquinot and Durutte's division remained at Villers-Perwin on the night of 16 June, with only Marcognet and Donzelot moving back to Quatre Bras to join Quiot. According to d'Erlon himself, Durutte and Jacquinot were placed to guard against a possible Prussian attack coming between Ney and Napoleon, as Durutte's son explains:

> General Durutte observed that an enemy column could emerge onto the plain which was between Brye and Delhutte Wood, and which would completely cut off the emperor's wing of the army from the command of Marshal Ney, he [General d'Erlon] concluded to leave General Durutte in this place. Besides his own division, d'Erlon placed under his command three [actually four] regiments of cavalry commanded by General Jacquinot.
>
> General Durutte, when leaving General d'Erlon, asked him if he should march on Brye. D'Erlon replied that in the circumstances he could give him no orders and that he was to rely on his own experience and judgement. General Durutte directed his cavalry towards the road running from Sombreffe to Quatre Bras, leaving Wagnelée and Brye on his right, but still moving towards these villages. His infantry followed the same movement.

General d'Erlon had told him to be cautious because things were going badly at Quatre Bras. This resulted in General Durutte to thoroughly reconnoitre [sic.] Delhutte Wood, for any retreat of Marshal Ney would place the enemy behind General Durutte.

When General Jacquinot arrived a cannon-shot away from the road between Sombreffe and Quatre Bras, he was assailed by an enemy formation, with which he began an exchange of musketry and artillery fire which lasted for three quarters of an hour. General Durutte advanced his infantry towards him in support. The enemy troops who were exchanging cannon fire with General Jacquinot retired and General Durutte, receiving no news about the left wing, marched on Brye.

By the movement of our troops he presumed that we were victorious on the side of Saint-Amand. His sharpshooters engaged Prussian light troops who were still at Wagnelée. He seized the village and when the day began to end, and being assured that the enemy was in full retreat, he sent to Brye two battalions, who on arriving there found a few Prussian stragglers. During the night, General Durutte was ordered to move to Villers-Perwin.[1]

So much for the official line of what happened. Several other eyewitnesses, including Durutte's deputy, totally disagreed with Durutte's account when it was published. Captain Chapuis, of the 85th Regiment of Line Infantry, notes:

The 85th, marching at the head of its division, was followed in its movement by the other divisions of the 1st Corps, which on the morning of 16 June, received the order of the emperor, brought by Colonel Lawrence [sic., Laurent], attached to the headquarters of the army, to change our direction of march to the right. It was made when we were marching towards Quatre Bras.

We abandoned our movement from Marchiennes-au-Pont, and we established ourselves on the new route with celerity, the column formed by divisions was to be established behind the right of the Prussian army. The position was one of great importance.[2]

When the column had arrived at Wagnelée, Chapuis notes an officer from Marshal Ney ordered that the column was to march back to Quatre Bras. It was now that General Durutte began a ponderous and slow attack on Wagnelée. Battalion Commander Rullieres of the 95th Regiment of Line Infantry notes, 'The voltigeurs of Durutte's division began to fire against Prussian scouts, it was about eight o'clock at night.'[3] Chapuis continues the narration:

Located a short distance from the hamlet of Wagnelée, which was close to the village of Saint-Amand, we were waiting for the order that would have us march on Wagnelée; we were all convinced 1st Corps had been called to play a great part in the struggle that was engaged … Our position at Wagnelée gave us the absolute assurance that a few minutes would suffice to place the whole of the Prussian right wing between two fires, and not one of us there, soldier or officer, who could not see that acting with vigour and promptness the safety of the enemy would be totally compromised.

This order on which we expected to gain such favourable results arrived, but it was not executed, as General Drouet and d'Erlon had left to join Marshal Ney at Quatre Bras, under whose orders were the 1st and 2nd Corps and that General Durutte did not dare to give the order for such a movement, refusing the responsibility as he was a divisional commander and not the commanding general of the 1st Corps. In consequence of this, he sent an officer to Quatre Bras carrying this order and demanding instructions that others put in his situation would not have hesitated to carry out.[4]

This can in no way be considered the strong flank attack that Napoleon desired. If d'Erlon was guilty of splitting his command, then Durutte was guilty for not attacking when he had the chance and for not using his initiative rather than waiting for orders from d'Erlon who, at Quatre Bras, could make no valid contribution to the action at Ligny. Surely Durutte knew this? Or was he so incapable of independent field command, as we noted before, that he was a mere automaton that had to do everything by the book? D'Erlon should have issued clearer instructions to Durutte, but Durutte should have been able to judge the situation for himself; if not, he was not fit to command the division. Both generals were at fault for the fiasco that unfolded between the battlefields of Ligny and Quatre Bras. About the lack of action, Chapuis adroitly notes:

Whilst this position was being taken, an angrier scene was taking place between our divisional commander, Durutte, and General Brue, our brigade commander. The latter was frustrated at the caution of his superior and criticised him loudly. He shouted, 'it is intolerable that we witness the retreat of a beaten army and do nothing, when everything indicates that if it was attacked it would be destroyed'.

General Durutte could only offer the excuse to General Brue, 'it is lucky for you that you are not responsible!' General Brue replied, 'I wish to God that I was, we would already be fighting!'

This episode was overheard by the senior officers of the 85th that were at the head of the regiment … for those that witnessed the scene and reflected upon it, that a major error had been committed in employing certain commanders, for whom the words of 'glory' and *'La Patrie'* were no longer of the same significance as to their subordinates.

This suspicion was further confirmed when we learnt that on the next day, 17 June, Colonel Gordon, the chief-of-staff of 4th Division, and Battalion Commander Gaugler, the first aide-de-camp to General Durutte, had passed to the enemy the previous morning and had been concealed from us for twenty-four hours ... The desertion of these two men, in positions close to General Durutte, and his hesitation a few hours earlier to execute orders, which should have been done quickly, produced such a bad impression on the 85th that it took all the efforts of the officers to restore the morale of the men.[5]

Clearly, there was no trust between regimental officers and higher-ranking staff officers. General Brue, commanding the 2nd Brigade of Durutte's division (formed by the 85th and 95th Regiments of Line Infantry), notes:

If General Durutte had attacked the defeated and retreating Prussian army at Ligny, this army would have been annihilated; all those who were not killed would have been forced to lay down their arms and would have been captured.[6]

General Brue was perfectly correct in his assessment of Durutte's failure; he reproached his superior with the following words: 'It is unheard of to march with shouldered arms in pursuit of a defeated army, when all indications were that we had to attack it and destroy it'.[7] Brue further lambasted Durutte as a traitor and stated that Durutte's failures on 16 and 18 June led to the loss of the campaign—a fairly accurate summation of Durutte's catastrophic failure to seize the initiative at Ligny.[8]

Napoleon's flank attack had been derailed by Ney, and then at the vital moment when the 4th Infantry Division (with Jacquinot's cavalry) could have dramatically intervened at Ligny, General Durutte seemingly panicked and did nothing. Even more alarmingly, the sudden appearance of a large column of men on the French left caused panic to spread. Parts of General Lefol's command wavered, falling back from the attack, and men fled, believing they were outflanked. The most badly affected regiment by this panic set in motion by Durutte was the 64th Line, which took over an hour to rally. This caused a fatal delay to Vandamme's attack, which contributed to Ligny being a stalemate rather than an outright victory. D'Erlon's blunderings and Durutte's timidity had major repercussions. Durutte's motivation or lack of it owed a great deal to his loyalties. Colonel Gordon, who rode off to join the allies that morning, gives us a vital insight into Durutte's mental state that day:

I unfortunately found myself employed with the army along with general Durutte, who like me had come to detest Bonaparte, but he was too timid to make the decision to leave the army along with me. I had declared to him my intentions.[9]

Clearly, Durutte knew very well that Gordon and others were preparing to desert, and it seems he was of the same mind, but his lack of decision-making ability or a sense of loyalty to the army meant he remained in his post. Certainly, Durutte was far from 'reliable' in his loyalty to the emperor; a secret police dossier kept on him reported that 'this officer who had a command in the Army of the North showed through his conduct his fervour for the Royalist cause at the time of the return of Bonaparte.'[10] Without a shadow of a doubt, Durutte was a man of torn loyalties, which in turn impacted on how he conducted himself during the campaign. The responsibility for Durutte's failure rests with those who gave him a command beyond his ability, especially when he clearly reluctantly took up the position.

Durutte's lack of ability and drive was symptomatic of the army as a whole: it is clear that from marshal down to private, the French army of 1815 lacked something vital—it had no soul or desire to fight. The burning ambition to follow the emperor to glory had, it seems, evaporated. Durutte failed spectacularly to exploit the situation. We admit that the conflicting orders of Ney and Napoleon judiciously affected the outcome of the battles of Quatre Bras and Ligny, which, if d'Erlon had intervened in strength earlier at either battle, would have tipped the balance decidedly in the favour of the French. Ney blundered badly in recalling d'Erlon based on his understanding of his orders. Durutte could still have changed the outcome of Ligny in a more decisive victory, yet the timidness of Ney and d'Erlon seems to have been infectious, and Durutte dithered and dallied with much hand-wringing until the vital moment had gone, then attacked ineffectively and too late. The bulk of d'Erlon's troops were uselessly tied down.

The emperor had very good reasons to blame Ney and the senior officers of 1st Corps for the debacle that had unfolded, but he, too, is to blame for not making his intentions better known through more precise and clearer orders. Napoleon had appointed Ney, d'Erlon, and Durutte, and in choosing these men seemingly not fit for high command, he was ultimately to blame for the mistakes that took place on 16 June. Be that as it may, Ligny was not a clear-cut victory for the French, and it had badly mauled the Prussian army, which Napoleon believed was now in full retreat back to Namur and would take no part in the campaign. Napoleon then turned his attention to the troops of Wellington. Napoleon was wrong in his summation of the results of the battle.

6

17 June

The Prussian I Corps had its bivouacs around the villages of Tilly and Gentinnes and at around 4 a.m., just as day was breaking, the first elements of the corps began to move north. The Prussian II Corps left its position around 6 a.m. and followed behind I Corps. Thielmann began his moves on 16 June. The corps reached Gembloux around 6 p.m., some six hours or so before Grouchy began his pursuit. Pajol had been on the road since daybreak but had headed towards Namur, thus Thielmann could retreat unmolested. Napoleon's action plans for the morning of the 17th were to find out where the Prussians had gone to, since contact with them had been lost during the night, and to drive them away from Wellington; secondly, he wanted to find out how Ney had fared and to send him help if he needed it. As the sun rose, Pajol had been sent off to Namur to look for Prussians: he never found them. Simultaneously, d'Erlon wrote to Ney:

> Frasné 17 June,
> Marshal, conforming to the orders of His Majesty, the 1st Corps is holding the line astride the Brussels road, the 1st Cavalry Division is covering its front and flanks.
> I have the honour to inform Your Majesty that the 1st Cavalry Division undertook a number of successful charges and captured a number of wagons and prisoners.[1]

Thus 1st Corps, less Durutte, was now in the front line, with 2nd Corps behind. By the morning of 17 June, General Roussel d'Herbal's command had arrived at Mellet.[2] The division had marched 80 miles in two days and had arrived at Quatre Bras sometime between 9 and 10 p.m., or at least Donop's brigade had. Thus, only by the morning of 17 June had all of Ney's command become concentrated. If a battle was coming with

Wellington, the emperor needed as many fresh troops as possible. The 1st and 6th Corps had seen little action on 16 June, along with the bulk of 3rd Cavalry Corps, the Young Guard, and the 1st and 2nd Grenadiers and *Chasseurs à Pied*. It made perfect sense to swing around to Quatre Bras with 6th Corps, Milhaud's cavalry corps, and the Imperial Guard, then head north with 1st and 2nd Corps to face Wellington. Clearly, the emperor wanted to conduct any forthcoming battle against Wellington in person. Who could he trust to lead the pursuit against the Prussians? Ney had proved himself incapable of independent command. Given the major shortage of senior field officers, the emperor had no option but to employ Grouchy on this mission. General Baudrand explains how Grouchy was given his orders:

> June 17, 1815, the day after the battle of Fleurus, Napoleon mounted on horseback about nine o'clock in the morning, and went beyond the village of Ligny and alighted on the ground that the day was occupied by the centre of the Prussian army.
>
> Most of the people who accompanied the Emperor, also dismounted from their horse, I was of this number, and found myself with three people, who unfortunately are no longer living, the two commanders of artillery and engineers MM. Generals Ruty and Rogniat and their Chiefs of Staff, General Berge and myself.
>
> There arrived in succession with the Emperor several general officers of the staff, who probably came to report what had happened during the night or in the morning, and came to ask for orders or instructions.
>
> Then you came, Marshal, and after a few moments of conversation, as you became separated from Napoleon, he told you in a loud and clear voice, so as to be easily heard at the distance of twenty or thirty feet where we were: 'Mr. Marshal, you will take the 3rd and 4th corps, a division of the sixth, the cavalry ... etc., and you will enter tonight in Namur', and when you were at some distance, the Emperor added in a loud voice: 'I recommend to you, Marshal, do not take many prisoners.'
>
> You immediately departed, the Emperor mounted his horse after traveling the battlefield which was covered in dead and wounded Prussians, by sending these words of consolation, Napoleon ordered that the headquarters was transferred from Fleurus to Marbais. He then turned quickly to Quatre Bras, and taking with him the very small number of troops he had at hand, he began to pursue the English who withdrew on the Mont-Saint-Jean.[3]

The order was as follows:

Repair to Gembloux with the Cavalry Corps of Pajol and Exelmans, the Light Cavalry of the Fourth Corps, Teste's Division, and the Third and Fourth Corps of Infantry. You will send out scouts in the direction of Namur and Maestricht, and you will pursue the enemy.

Reconnoitre his line march, and tell me of his movements, that I may penetrate his designs.

I shall move my head-quarters to Quatre Bras, where the English still were this morning; our communication will then be directed via the Namur road.

Should the enemy have evacuated Namur, write to the general in command of the Second Military Division at Charlemont to occupy this town with a few battalions of National Guards.

It is important to discover what Wellington and Blücher mean to do, and whether they meditate uniting their armies to cover Brussels and Liege by risking the fate of a battle.

At all events, keep your two Infantry Corps continually together, within a mile of each other, reserving several ways of retreat place detachments of cavalry between, so as to be able to communicate with Head-quarters.[4,5]

It is clear, however, that Napoleon's instructions left Grouchy with some degree of freedom for independent action. Furthermore, the order sent Grouchy's forces off in the wrong direction. The Prussians were heading north-east, but Maastricht was altogether in the wrong direction, as this would entail a more easterly line of march via Liege. The French headquarters had no idea where the Prussians were going, and until Grouchy had found this out, he could do very little. Unless the Prussians stopped to engage Grouchy, there was nothing he could do to catch them. Had Grouchy not taken the initiative, which many historians claim he was not capable of, and sent out scouts both north and north-east, he would have happily marched to Namur or Maastricht and have been of no use at all on 18 June. In such a scenario, the defeat at Waterloo would have been even more total as it would have freed up 19,000 Prussian troops.[6]

About the course of the 17th, d'Erlon writes:

During the morning, all of the 1st Corps was assembled in a position in front of Frasnés, straddling the main road, level with the first houses of Frasnés. A brigade of the 2nd Division and several squadrons were holding the outposts placed at the level of Gémioncourt, and extended their right to Pierpont.

There was no engagement during the morning, each side observed each other. There was a great deal of movement undertaken by the enemy army, but the woods and the hazards of the terrain that exist at the hamlet of Quatre Bras, did not allow us to observe them well. The woods were strongly occupied by skirmishers and the enemy had considerable masses of infantry on the left. These disappeared around 2 o'clock in the afternoon. At 3 o'clock the 1st Corps began its advanced, and having reached the fork in the Namur Road, it was joined by 6th Corps, and went immediately along the Brussels road; the Emperor arrived at Quatre Bras and ordered Comte d'Erlon to take the head of column; a brigade of cavalry under the orders of General Colbert was at the front, entered the defile of Genappe. The enemy artillery and cavalry held positions in front of this small town, at the house of Courtte Botte. He [the enemy] made a very strong fire from the defile; the General Colbert wanted to charges these guns and returned to Genappe; the cavalry of 1st Corps turned to the right, crossed the small river at Wais.[7] The infantry debouched from the defile and formed promptly. The light artillery was placed in battery, supported by a battery of 12-pdr. Having been established behind Genappe, the enemy left their position and continued its retreat [illegible] the terrain was appalling, and our artillery could only advance on the main road with the infantry on either side. Our cavalry was long distance in front and arrived at a hamlet near Plancenoit by half past seven in the evening. The Emperor stopped the movement and ordered that positions be taken up. The General Milhaud went forward with his cavalry, and having assembled level with La Belle Alliance, was received by extremely lively artillery fire and was obliged to withdraw.

The 1st Corps was established as follows: the 1st Division supporting its right on the main road at the fam of Rossome; the 2nd Division in front of Plancenoit, the 3rd Division between them, supporting its left on the main road and extending its right to Plancenoit. The 4th Division occupied the woods at the extreme left of the line, close to the Nivelles road—where there is an old telegraph. The cavalry cleared this road and was established at the farm of Mont Plaisir; an infantry regiment and two squadrons were established at Bonne Alliance. The line of our vedettes were [sic.] posted within pistol shot of the enemy vedettes. [inserted line mostly illegible] This house was occupied by a company of our infantry; four companies of infantry were sent to hold the small wood close to the farm of Hougoumont. They arrived there after nightfall having found it occupied by enemy troops, and despite their number, the established themselves within half musket range. The headquarters of Comte d'Erlon were established at the farm of Rossome. The night was atrocious, the rain fell in torrents, the soldiers were not able to bivouac.[8]

It is clear from what he says that 1st Corps and the cavalry were all the troops to hand. The 2nd Corps was miles behind, as was 6th Corps and the Guard. His account of the day's actions does fit with those recorded by other eyewitnesses and his own letters from that June day. Therefore, his account is consistent with it being written by a witness to these events and is a very credible description of the day's events. He wrote this in 1844:

> The Emperor, wishing to give battle to the English, composed a corps of about 40,000 under General Grouchy, and charged him to follow the Prussian army closely, and to ascertain to what extent she would be retiring. He came next, with the rest of his army, to join Marshal Ney at Quatre Bras, who were somehow already evacuated by the English. The Emperor found me in front of this position, and said to me with the tone of deep sorrow, these words which are forever etched in my memory: 'France has been lost; Come, my dear general, put yourself at the head of this cavalry, and strongly push the rear-guard of the English.' The Emperor did not leave the head of the column, and was even engaged in a cavalry charge, debouching from *Jemappes*. The pursuit continued until before *Plancenoit*. On reaching the left of the road, on a little height, from which one could discover the position which the enemy wished to take, the Emperor placed himself there to observe their movements, and thinking that he continued to retreat he said to me, 'Keep following them'. It was already night. At this very moment, Milhaud's division, of heavy cavalry, arrived on the ground, which, when it formed itself into line of battle, in advance of this position and to the right of the road, was strongly fired upon. The Emperor said to me: 'Make the troops take up positions and we will observe'. The night was terrible, the rain was falling abundantly, which had soaked the ground so as to impede the movement of the troops.[9]

D'Erlon's two accounts are robustly similar in the main details, the handwritten account being more detailed. By midnight, d'Erlon's men were in their muddy bivouacs. Durutte and Jacquinot were nowhere to be seen. Chapuis of the 85th Line relates:

> On 17, the 4th Division Wagnelé left to join the other three divisions of the 1st Corps, which had left the evening of 16 to Quatre Bras. This meeting could not be effected, the 4th Division had been ordered to stop behind the headquarters of the Emperor.
> Delayed in our journey by rain, mud and the many columns that were advancing towards the same point, we came so late in the position

we had been designated, it was impossible for our soldiers to take any shelter from the bad weather.

Beaten by a constant rain, without any fire, the night was the most cruel.[10]

The Prussians

The Prussian army had been badly bloodied at Ligny two days earlier, and contrary to what his field commanders reported, Napoleon felt that the Prussians were a spent force and could not take to the field. Yet the emperor had to make sure the Prussians were neutralised. As a result of the action at Ligny not being a conclusive action and the French 3rd and 4th Corps being fought to an exhausted standstill, the Prussian 1st and 2nd Corps headed north and had its bivouacs around the villages of Tilly and Gentinnes. At daybreak, around 4 a.m., the two corps began to move north towards Wavre. At the same time, the Prussian 3rd Corps, which had remained on the field, together with 4th Corps, moved off east and reached Gembloux around 6 a.m. Clausewitz notes:

> The 1st and 2nd Corps reached Wavre at midday on the 17th and then took their positions on both sides of the Dyle, having left part of their cavalry as a rearguard a few hours' march behind them. The 3rd Corps remained at Gembloux until 2 p.m. and then proceeded towards Wavre, where it did not arrive until evening. The 4th Corps spent the night of the 16th in Haute- and Bas-Bodecé, two hours' march behind Gembloux, and then during the 17th went to Dion-le-Mont, where it deployed to receive the other corps.[11]

Captain Fritz, commanding a squadron of Westphalian *Landwehr* cavalry, attached to Jagow's infantry brigade, writes:

> In very bad weather we set off again in the morning to cross the Dyle. The mood of the troops was certainly grave, but not in the least disheartened, and even if one could have detected that we were on a retreat rather than a victory march, the bearing of all but a few isolated units was very good. 'We have lost once, but the game is not up, and tomorrow is another day' remarked a Pomeranian soldier to his neighbour who was grumbling, and was quite right. The firm bearing of the army owed not a little to the cheerful spirit and freshness of our seventy-four-year-old field marshal. He had had his bruised limbs bathed in brandy and had helped himself to a large schnapps; and now, although riding must have been very painful,

he rode alongside the troops exchanging jokes and banter with many of them, and his humour spread like wildfire down the columns. I only glimpsed the old hero ride quickly past, although I should dearly have like to have expressed to him my pleasure of his fortunate escape.

Even my Westphalian *Landwehr* riders did not lose their good bearing. But in the rain many new saddles swelled, and the troops, as young riders often do, sat unsteadily and lolled about during the march, with the unfortunate result that I soon had a number of horses with saddle sores. I carried out a thorough inspection and anyone who had a horse in this condition was ordered to dismount and carry his portmanteaux on his back, and then go splashing through thick and thin on foot beside us.[12]

The whole aim of Napoleon's strategy had been to crush the Prussians and prevent them from interfering with his attack on Wellington. He had found Blücher ready to fight at Ligny and he had beaten him, but had not delivered the terminal knockout blow he needed due to the blundering of Ney and dithering of d'Erlon. Allowing Blücher to retreat with fighting power left in his army was to be avoided at all cost: the advantage of vigorous pursuit with all the available cavalry and Lobau's corps would have been enormous. But no attempt was made to hinder the retreat of Zieten and Pirch. Thielmann maintained a firm hold on Sombreffe, but he did not cover Brye or the roads to Tilly. Thielmann's rearguard did not begin to retreat until after sunrise, and when day broke the French were still in their bivouacs and the vedettes had not noticed any untoward movement by the Prussians. There seemed to be a fixed resolve to let the Prussians go free. Grouchy's 10 a.m. report to Napoleon states:

> Sire
>
> I will not lose a moment in sending you the information I have gathered here. I regard it as definitive, and so that Your Majesty receives it soonest, I am sending Major de la Fresnaye with it.
>
> Blücher's I, II and III Corps are marching in the direction of Brussels. Two of these corps marched either through Sart-lez-Walhain or just to the right of it. They are marching in three columns more or less abreast. Their march through here lasted six hours without interruption. Those troops passing through Sart-lez-Walhain are estimated as being at least 30,000 men with 50 to 60 cannon. An army corps came from Liege and has joined up with these corps that fought at Fleurus. Enclosed is a requisition form which proves this. Some of the Prussian troops in front of me have headed in the direction of the plains of Chyse, which is on the road to Louvain, that is north of Wavre, and two and a half leagues from that town. They seem to want to mass there, either to offer battle to any

troops that pursue them there, or to join with Wellington—a plan about which their officers spoke. With their usual boasting, they maintain they only left the battlefield of the 16th join up with the English army in Brussels.

This evening I will be standing before Wavre *en masse*, and in this way, be situated between Wellington, whom I assume is falling back before Your Majesty, and the Prussian army. I require further instructions, whatever Your Majesty chooses to order, as to what I should do. The terrain between Wavre and the plain of Chyse is difficult to pass; it is broken ground and boggy. I will be able to get to Brussels easily along the Vilvoorde road quicker than any troops who go over the plain of Chyse, especially if the Prussians make a stop there. If Your Majesty wishes to send me orders, I can still receive them before starting my movement tomorrow.[13]

Napoleon knew when this arrived with him that the bulk of the Prussians were heading north, but were they heading to join Wellington? Grouchy suspected this may have been the case. Some twelve hours later, Grouchy sent more news to the emperor:

Gembloux, 17th June, 10 p.m.

Sire,—I have the honour to report to you that I occupy Gembloux and that my Cavalry is at Sauveniere. The enemy, about 30,000 strong, continues his retreat. We have captured here a convoy of 400 cattle, magazines and baggage.

It would appear, according to all the reports, that, on reaching Sauveniere, the Prussians divided into two columns: one of which must have taken the road to Wavre, passing by Sart á Walhain; the other would appear to have been directed on Perwez.

It may perhaps be inferred from this that one portion is going to join Wellington; and that the centre, which is Blücher's army, is retreating on Liege. Another column, with artillery, having retreated by Namur, General Exelmans has orders to push, this evening, six squadrons to Sart á Walhain, and three to Perwez. According to their report, if the mass of the Prussians is retiring on Wavre, I shall follow them in that direction, so as to prevent them from reaching Brussels, and to separate them from Wellington. If, on the contrary, my information proves that the principal Prussian force has marched on Perwez, I shall pursue the enemy by that town.

Generals Thielmann and Borstel (?) formed part of the army which Your Majesty defeated yesterday; they were still here at 10 o'clock his morning, and have announced that they have 20,000 casualties. They enquired on leaving, the distances of Wavre, Perwez, and Hannut. Blücher has been slightly wounded in the arm, but it has not prevented him from continuing to command after having had his wound dressed. He has not passed by Gembloux.—I am, with respect, Sire, Your Majesty's faithful subject, Marshal Count Grouchy.[14]

With the arrival of Grouchy's report, it was now evident to Napoleon that Blücher was seeking to link with Wellington. Many historians say that the arrival of the Prussians came as a shock to the French; clearly, this is not the case. At the same time as Grouchy's dispatch was winging its way to headquarters, the whole of Blücher's army (except two divisions—the 9th and 13th—and the reserve cavalry of Thielmann's corps, which were posted as rearguards to the III and IV Corps) had reached Wavre and its neighbourhood. The 2nd and 3rd Corps bivouacked on the left bank of the Dyle, beyond Wavre, and the 1st and 4th on the right bank. Pirch was between Saint-Anne and Aisemont; Bülow was at Dion-le-Mont. The rearguards were posted at Vieux-Sart and Mont-Saint-Guibert; these troops fell back the next day as the French advanced. On Blücher's left, patrols scoured the country towards Namur and Louvain; on his right, they watched the Dyle and its approaches. Limale was held by a detachment from Zieten's corps to protect the right flank, and cavalry patrols rode to and fro all over the valley of the Dyle. The reserve ammunition columns with supplies reached Wavre in the afternoon of 17 June, thus munitions for the artillery and infantry were replenished; it speaks well for the Prussian arrangements that these supplies should have reached Wavre at so important a moment when, on account of their unexpected retreat to Wavre, all previous arrangements had to be cancelled.

The Mission of General Domon

Wary of the Prussian advance, sometime on 17 June, General Domon was ordered to reconnoitre in front of the army. The following order is a copy made by Comte du Casse in June 1865 and may be an exact transcript of a now lost order to Marshal Soult that is also missing from the correspondence registers of both Soult and Grouchy:

Order of the emperor to Marshal Grouchy
    Order General Domon to return from the field of Marbais. He is currently under orders of Comte de Lobau and is to send a detachment, via Quatre Bras, to traverse towards Brussels and to reunite with the troops of our left wing, the 1st and 2nd corps, which this morning are currently occupying the village of Frasné, which are to march from there to Quatre Bras against the English who are supposed to be there.

Order General Milhaud to move to Marbais. There he will find the light cavalry of General Domon. He will follow the movements of the corps of Comte Lobau and the Guard.
Ligny 17 June
Dictated by the emperor in the absence of the major-general
The grand marshal
Bertrand.[15]

According to an eyewitness, Domon's objective was to establish the nature of the Prussian threat; on the night of 17 June, a reconnaissance patrol that had been sent to Wavre returned:

> Since Quatre Bras, the division of Domon was detached to scout along the left bank of the Dyle, along to the Brussels road; the 4th regiment of Chasseurs passed the bridge at Moustier, where his skirmishers opened fire with their carbines at the Prussian cavalry. With the onset of night, the division returned and bivouacked to the right of Headquarters.[16]

Moustier is now called Mousty. It is 13 km due east of Belle Alliance. It is roughly an hour's trot away for the cavalry from the field of Waterloo. Regimental muster lists confirm Berton's observations that Domon ran into trouble that day.

On 10 June, the 4th Chasseurs mustered 306 other ranks. General Domon records six chasseurs wounded and seven troop horses killed at Ligny and one officer's mount.[17] Casualties for the 4th Chasseurs on the 17th were as follows:[18]

	Killed	Died of Wounds	Wounded	Prisoner of War	Missing
Total	2	0	0	4	4

In total, ten men were lost—nearly double those sustained on the 16th at Ligny. Clearly, the unit had run into trouble as General Berton notes.

Brigaded with the 4th were the 9th and 12th Chasseurs. General Domon notes that at Ligny, the 9th Chasseurs had two chasseurs mortally wounded, two wounded, three troop horses killed, and one troop horse wounded.[19] The regiment's muster list confirms Domon's report: two men wounded in 1st Squadron, two wounded in 3rd Squadron, and two men missing. Casualties for the 9th Chasseurs on the 17th was a single man, recorded as prisoner:[20]

	Killed	Died of Wounds	Wounded	Prisoner of War	Missing
Total	0	0	0	1	0

Due to water damage at the French Army Archives at Vincennes, the paperwork for the 12th Chasseurs was not able to be consulted by the author at the timing of researching and writing, so we are not able to offer any comments on the losses of the regiment.

Clearly, based on the casualties recorded, Domon had found Prussians, exchanged gunshots, and reported back to headquarters. The Prussians were closing in on the French right flank on the night of 17 June. We do not have any report that the chasseurs sent back to headquarters—if these documents could one day be found, they would transform our understanding of the battle. Without these reports, based on later intentions, it seems the emperor believed the Prussians were retreating and were no immediate threat. Yet he was to be proven to be totally wrong.

7

18 June

Sunday 18 June began in torrential rain. Over the course of the early morning, 2nd Corps slowly arrived, as would have a flow of couriers and messengers bringing reports to Soult. Napoleon's headquarters were set up in the small farm at Le Caillou. The little walled orchard that was on the northern side of the complex had been commandeered as a bivouac for the 'duty battalion', which comprised the 1st Battalion, 1st Chasseurs under Duuring's command. The first room on entering the building was reserved for the duty officers, and in the rooms on the first floor were bales of straw for the staff offices. The well-known story of the battle states Jérôme Bonaparte and General Reille had found lodgings at the Hotel du Roi d'Espagne in Genappe. During the night at around 2 a.m., Napoleon received a dispatch from Marshal Grouchy that the Prussians were withdrawing either to Wavre or Perwes. He never replied to this dispatch and let Grouchy continue with his movements; ergo it seems Napoleon was in agreement with Grouchy's course of action.

The sun rose at 4 a.m. The French army was strung out along the road from Genappe to Waterloo. Only the leading elements—mostly 2nd Corps, Milhaud's cuirassiers, Domon's cavalry, and elements of 1st Corps—had been at Waterloo since the 17th. All of 6th Corps, Kellermann's cavalry corps, and the Imperial Guard were between Genappe and what was to be the field of battle. Napoleon's army mustered perhaps 74,000 men with 256 guns. The 2nd Corps formed the left wing and 1st Corps the right. The reserve was formed from the two cavalry corps of Milhaud and Kellermann. The guard was deployed flanking the Brussels road.

It was still raining and there was no prospect of the rain ceasing. Only some elements of the army were at Waterloo, and the army strung out between Genappe and La Belle Alliance. Soon, the French army hit the road, marching to Waterloo some time later, even though many regiments had yet to join Napoleon. Eyewitness to the events, writing very soon after the battle, General Drouot recalled that 'at break of day, the Enemy was perceived in the same position. The weather was horrible, which had ruined the roads.'[1] The *Journal de Rouen* reported, 'The 18th. At this moment, 6 hours in the morning, the cannon can be heard; the army will force its entry into Brussels and Belgium will be in our hands.'[2] That morning, the emperor breakfasted and in the pouring rain reconnoitred the battlefield as Mameluke Ali noted:

> The next day, the 18th, the Emperor rose fairly early. He breakfasted with the Grand Marshal, the Duke of Dalmatia and some other persons, and then mounted his horse, followed by the Major General, the Duke of Dalmatia, the Grand Marshal, General Fouler, and all his suite. He went to the advanced posts to reconnoitre the positions occupied by the enemy and laid out the order of battle.[3]

It was at this pensive meal that the emperor upbraided Soult for lacking his optimism 'because you have been defeated by Wellington, you consider him to be a great general. I tell you he is a bad general … it will be as easy as eating breakfast'.[4] Such overoptimism would cost the French dearly as he told his brother, 'The Prussian army is completely beaten. It cannot recover in a matter of two days. I shall attack the English army and I shall defeat it'.[5] With the meeting over, the emperor issued his orders timed at 5 a.m.:

> The Emperor orders the Army to be ready to attack at 9 o'clock in the morning. The commanders of the Army Corps will assemble their troops, see that the soldier's weapons are in good order and allow the soldiers to prepare a meal and consume it. By 9 o'clock in the morning precisely each Army Corps will be formed up in line of battle, along with their artillery and ambulances, in the same positions as indicated by the Emperor in his orders of yesterday evening.
>
> The Lieutenant-Generals commanding the Corps of the Army of Infantry and Cavalry are to send field officers to the Major General to tell him of their positions and to carry orders.[6]

Despite the rain and mud, Napoleon was preparing to fight, just as he had done at Dresden three years earlier with mud on the shoes of his soldiers, and wet greatcoats on their backs. One of the great tales of Waterloo is that mud delayed the start of the battle. This idea does not stand up to much scrutiny. The waterlogged ground or at least the rain that was falling in the early hours of 18 June was commented upon by Hugue-Bernard Maret, 1st duke of Bassano (who also held the title of secretary of state and was a peer of France), as he sat at La Caillou that morning in a letter to the minister of foreign affairs in Paris:

> In the current situation of the Army, communications are easy from one Army Corps to another, but this situation is likely soon to Change….. The campaign started with great success. The victory of Ligny in Fleurus is of very high importance. The right and centre of our Army crushed the elite of the Prussian Army. The morale of this Army will be adversely affected for a long time to come. Our left has not obtained results as decisive, but they were also important. Lord Wellington commanded in person the struggle for the position of four roads between Sombreffe and Nivelles. The English, especially the Scots, were badly mauled. Their killed and wounded is estimated at 4,000 men. Our Army is as good as it was in our more prosperous times. Although the weather thwarts us. We will soon have more news for you.[7]

At the time of the 5 a.m. order being written, there was no prospect of any improvement in sight for the weather. The French and allies had no idea when the rain would stop. We only know it did with hindsight. At the moment that the weather actually did improve, ironically about 9 a.m., there was no prospect for the fields to dry up to such an extent that troops could be moved with relative ease a few hours later. Napoleon did not know the rain would stop, nor that the field of battle would dry. He made plans accordingly to attack, regardless of weather. The rain the previous day had not stopped operations at Genappe or Waterloo. As far as either army commander could tell, 18 June may have been one of continual rain based on the evidence they had to hand. Battles had been fought in torrential rain, or deep snow, so rain would not have meant the battle would not have taken place. Neither Napoleon or Wellington knew when the field of battle would be dry enough to move troops upon it.

The Prussians

The French were not the only soldiers with mud on their boots. The Prussian headquarters were at Wavre, where plans were being made to join battle later that day. Bülow received his orders at midnight to move to join Wellington:

> Wavre, 17th June, midnight. According to a report just received from the duke of Wellington, he has taken up the following position: the right wing on Braine l'Alleud, his centre near Mont Saint Jean, his left

wing near La Haye. The enemy is in front of him, the duke expects to be attacked and has asked us for our assistance. Your Excellency will therefore depart at daybreak from Dion le Mont with your IV corp, march through Wavre and take the direction of Chapelle Saint Lambert, where you will take up a covered position in case the enemy is not yet strongly engaged with the enemy; in case he is, you will throw yourself briskly on the enemy's rightflank. The II army corps will directly follow Your Excellency in order to support you. The I and III Corps will hold themselves also into readiness to follow, if needed. Your Excellency should leave an observation detachment near Mont Saint Guibert, which, in case it is driven, slowly falls back upon Wavre. All baggage, trains and everything which is not strictly needed for military actions, has to be sent to Louvain.[7]

The Prussians were heading to Waterloo to aid Wellington. All Wellington had to do was to 'buy time' till the Prussians arrived in overwhelming numbers to destroy the French. The French had marched into a trap set by Wellington, which became all too clear to the French as the day drew on. Yet, retreat was not an option. Not secure in his position, the French emperor had to win at all costs. Defeat meant he lost his reclaimed throne. Desperation rather than tactics drove the event planning for the French. As the new day dawned, Bülow issued orders as follows:

The IV army corps is to move off immediately through Wavre to Chapelle Saint Lambert, marched off to the right, and in the following order: The brigade of Von Losthinas will form the vanguard, accompanied by the of regiment Silesian hussars and a battery 12 pounders, the first marching in front, the latter in front of the last battalion in the 2nd column; next is the brigade Von Hiller, the brigade Von Haak, then the reserve-artillery, and upon this one the reserve-cavalry, to which the 2nd Neumark Landwehr cavalry regiment is attached. The brigade of Von Ryssel forms the extreme rear-guard, except for the detachment led by Lieutenant Colonel Von Ledebur, which is to remain near Mont Saint Guibert, and if pressured by the enemy, to fall back upon Wavre. I will be with the vanguard. All baggage trains will move towards Louvain; Lieutenant Colonel Von Schlegel will organise their departure from Chapelle Saint Laurent [sic.], no waggon is permitted in the column. The men must be provided with as much food as possible. Any outposts which cannot be pulled in swiftly are to attach themselves to the brigade Von Ryssel. The brigades have to turn their front units on the road for Wavre right away, and thus break up one after the other, without any intervals. Those regiments which have perhaps not yet received supplies will have to do so immediately.[8]

Well fed—unlike the French—despite the mud, the Prussians set off to link with Wellington. For those who had served in the campaigns of the previous year, it must have all seemed eerily familiar. Yet unlike 1815, when the French emperor with a small army beat off allied armies that often outnumbered it, the battle to come was a return to the crude tactics of Wagram or Borodino in a 'slogging match' between two armies, with artillery dominating the proceedings. The vanguard of the Prussians reached Wavre about 6 a.m. Crossing the river Dyle at the Pont du Christ, the next objective was Saint Lambert. Shortly before 11.30 a.m., Bülow sent word to Muffling:

> In the event that the middle or the left wing of the Marshal Wellington is attacked, General Bülow will be willing to pass the Lasne defile with the corps and to occupy the plateau between La Haye and Aywiers and thus attack the enemy in his Right flank and rear. My plan is that another Prussian corps will pass through Ohain in order to be able to support the most threatened point of the English position as the circumstances dictate. A third Prussian corps is to proceed via Maransart and Sauvagemont to cover the left flank and the rear of the IV Army corps. The rearmost troops of IV corps will be established as a reserve at Couture.[9]

The trap around the French army was slowly starting to close.

As the Prussians were moving off, south-west of Wavre, having perhaps spent a sleepless night, Grouchy sent a report of the situation to Napoleon in a letter dated Gembloux, 18 June 1815, timed at 6 a.m.:

> Sire,
> All my reports and information confirm that the Prussians are falling back on Brussels, either to concentrate there or to offer battle once united with Wellington. General Pajol reports that Namur has been evacuated. Regarding I and II Corps of Blücher's army, the I corps appear to be moving on Corbais, the II Corps on Chaumont. Both are said to have moved off from Tourinnes and marched all night. Fortunately, the weather was so bad, that they are unlikely to have gone far. I will move off to Sart-lez-Walhain immediately, and intend moving on Corbais and Wavre. I will send you further reports from one or the other places.
> I am with respect your humble servant.
> Grouchy
> PS Conforming to your orders the General Commanding the 2nd Military Division at Charlemont de Loire has occupied Namur with several battalions of National Guards and numerous artillery pieces have been transferred from Charlemont.

To ensure communication with your majesty I have 25 horses at my disposal.

The corps of infantry and the cavalry under my command still have a full provision and a further half in reserve in the case of a major action. When we are close to using our reserve ammunition it will be necessary your Majesty to make contact with the artillery depots you indicated to obtain replacements.[10]

We cannot be certain when this arrived, but it was sometime before 10 a.m., as this was when Marshal Soult sent orders to Grouchy:

Monsieur Marshal, the Emperor has received your last report dated Six o'clock in the morning at Gembloux.

You speak to the Emperor of only two columns of Prussians, which have passed at Sauvenière and Sart-lez-Walhain. Nevertheless, reports say a third column, which was a pretty strong one, had pass [sic.] by Géry and Gentinnes, directed on Wavre, reported by Milhaud's cavalry before they left.

The Emperor instructs me to tell you that at this moment His Majesty has decided to attack the English army in its position at Waterloo in front of the forest of Soignes. Thus, his majesty desires that you are to continue your movement to Wavre, in order to approach us, to put you in our sphere of operations, and to your communications with us, pushing before you those portions of the Prussian Army which have taken this direction, and which may have stopped at Wavre, were you ought to arrive as soon as possible.

You will follow the enemy columns which are on your right side with light troops, in order to observe their movements and pick up their stragglers. Instruct me immediately as to your dispositions and your march, as also to the news which you have of the enemy; and do not neglect to keep your communications with us. The Emperor desires to have news from you very often.[11]

Of key note is the passage 'pushing before you those portions of the Prussian army which have taken this direction'. Clearly, Soult and Napoleon knew that only parts of the Prussian forces were going to be at Wavre. No reply is listed as being sent or received to this order by either Grouchy or Soult. Grouchy's operations are described at length in two books by the author. The column observed by Milhaud was the Prussian I Corps. Gentinnes and St Gery are due north of Sombreffe and are clearly marked on the 1777 map. From Gentinnes, the troops would have headed to Vilroux, Hevillers, and Mont-Saint-Guibert, heading towards Wavre or Louvain.

From Mont-Saint-Guibert, the next point of destination would have been Baraque. There is no doubt that this column, observed by Milhaud, was the Prussian I Corps, which had placed its bivouacs around the villages of Tilly and Gentinnes. It was followed by the Prussian II Corps. This was vitally important information that could and should have been passed to Grouchy the day before. Prussian II Corps had moved out at 6.30 a.m. Why Napoleon did not transmit this news we can only guess at, and it had catastrophic consequences. The troops Grouchy had in front of him was Prussian III Corps with IV Corps beyond. From Grouchy's intelligence, the emperor knew the Prussians were heading to Brussels: were they linking with Wellington? Or were they a spent force retreating to cover Brussels? Domon's reconnaissance patrol had not brought clear answers, so a new patrol was sent out, led by Marcelin Marbot.

With Grouchy's dispatch, headquarters now had intelligence of the Prussians still on the right bank of the Dyle at Moustier. About the difficulties the Prussians faced in linking with Wellington, Bülow reports:

> The cohesion of the marching column had been greatly disturbed by the halt at Wavre and by the soft ground, so that only the 15th Brigade reached St. Lambert at 10 a.m. and the bulk of the corps only at noon. The 14th Brigade, which had been forced to march from Vieux Sart, did not reach the main body until 3 p.m. According to orders, the IV Corps was to remain at St. Lambert until the enemy's intentions were clarified.[12]

Another Prussian eyewitness, Reich, confirms this:

> The march to the battlefield was extremely difficult. Bottomless mud and paths that intersected with deep defiles had to be passed; the terrain was almost completely wooded on both sides, so it was not possible to avoid them, and the march could only go very slowly, all the more so because in many places people and horses could only be got through one by one and the bullets were extremely difficult to get through. This caused the solo soldiers to disperse greatly, and where the terrain permitted, their troops had to stop so that the detachments could gather again.[13]

Despite the mud and slow marching pace, the Prussians slithered slowly to Waterloo. Bülow noted:

> In order to come into as close contact with the English army as possible, the very arduous defile of St. Lambert and Lasne had to be passed, which could not be done with certainty until it was known with certainty whether the enemy was against our own left flank movements have

started or not. In order to clarify this point, I sent two strong cavalry detachments in the direction of my left flank for reconnaissance, *viz.* Witowsky of the 2nd Silesian Hussar Regiment to Maransart (halfway between St. Lambert and Genappe), which place was found occupied by the enemy,—and the other detachment under Major V. Falkenhausen to Cerour (close to Maransart), from where he sent a dispatch to Colonel-Lieutenant V. Ledebur at Mont St. Guibert. The reports of both staff officers showed that the enemy let the movement be so close to him: fortunately, along the creek had not fallen directly against our left flank, and so Se [*sic*]. Your Highness the Field-Marshal, that the IV Corps of the Army should pass through the Lasne defile and secure the forest of Frichemont (or Bois de Paris). First two battalions and the Silesian Hussar Regiment were stationed in this forest, then the 15th and 16th Brigades followed with the reserve artillery and the cavalry. These troops were deployed in a broad front and closely spaced out on both sides of the road in the woods, the artillery in the way: all in readiness to be able to debouch immediately against the available free height of Frichemont at the opportune moment. The reserve ravalry stood behind the forest, in order to follow the infantry at once. The enemy didn't seem to care about our existence. The 13th and 14th Brigades had not yet passed the Lasne defile; the 2nd and 1st army corps had not yet approached when the field marshal ordered them to break out of the forest at 4.30 p.m.[14]

He adds that a corps was to arrive via Maransart and Sauvagemont, to control the vulnerable right flank of IV Corps. Two brigades from IV Corps headed to Couture, having arrived at Saint Lambert at 4 p.m. This body of Prussians had been observed by Grouchy's men heading to Wavre earlier in the day, and precautions were made as necessary. Thielmann tells us the Prussian reserve cavalry was to head to Couture with the 9th Brigade. The Prussians arrived at Frichermont about 3 p.m when Von Witowski of the 2nd Silesian Hussars wrote a short pencil-note for Blücher:

> The enemy is on the left at the height of Plancechenoi [*sic*.] and the English on the height of Mont St. Jean. Frischmont [*sic*.] seems vacant. Enemy cavalry and artillery has moved up.[15]

The French Response

The movement of thousands of men did not go unwitnessed as General d'Erlon notes:

At break of day, Comte d'Erlon reconnoitred the enemy position. Everything suggested that they intended to defend it; at 8 o'clock an officer from the Emperor brought the order to put the columns in motion to follow the enemy, who according to reports were retreating, it was said by the Brussels road. The Comte d'Erlon immediately sent his chief of staff to make it known that the reports were incorrect, and that far from abandoning their position the enemy [illegible] was making preparations to defend it. The Emperor indicated that the movement was to be suspended, and the men were to return to their camps, to let them eat their soup, and clean their weapons which were in poor condition because of the rain during the night. One of the outposts stopped a peasant (the owner of the house called the Bonne Alliance), who, having served as a guide during the night to a Prussian column that was headed to Wavre, and had managed to escape, announced that many Prussian troops were at Wavre and that all of the English Army was before us, and wanted to defend themselves.[16]

D'Erlon comments that this episode took place before 9 a.m., around 8 a.m. If we believe d'Erlon, and we have no reason not to, it was clear that the Prussians were heading away from Wavre to Waterloo. Any notion that the arrival of the Prussians came as a surprise to the French is clearly wrong. Napoleon knew that the Prussians were coming to aid Wellington: whatever plans he made on the field of Waterloo to address the Prussian threat, he failed to tell Grouchy any of this. Grouchy would only learn of Waterloo by early evening. Napoleon was planning to fight both Wellington and Blücher and felt so confident of victory with the troops to hand, he either forgot Grouchy or felt he had no need of his support. This error of judgement was fatal.

Clearly aware now of the Prussian threat, d'Erlon tells us:

At 11 o'clock the Emperor came to reconnoitre the position and left his chief of staff and entourage behind the Bonne Alliance, and carried himself with the Comte d'Erlon, the General Bertrand, Prince de la Moskowa and a few other officers to the line of our outposts, to the right and very close to the main road. He ordered the Comte d'Erlon to make preparations to attack the enemy from the left, and to form for this purpose each of his divisions into column by battalion and to march in echelons, directing the one on the right to attack the enemy at Smohain, taking care to mask the movement for as long as possible; the light cavalry of General Subervie was to be united with that of General Jacquinot, and these two divisions were to take themselves to the right accompanied by three pieces of light artillery and a strong battalion of infantry to observe and overlook the terrain between Frischermont and the Abbey of Aywiers, the first place to be occupied by the light artillery.[17, 18]

This episode likely took place before Soult issued orders to Ney, so approximately 10.30 p.m. In his assessment of where to deploy troops, the emperor was perfectly correct, had clearly reconnoitred the terrain, and had a good map with him (perhaps the Ferrari's map). Certainly, a copy of this map at 1/8460000 that belonged to Durutte and used by him during the campaign housed at the Royal Army Museum in Brussels is of a scale as to show the abbey. Napoleon had correctly identified here that the Prussians would link with Wellington, but crucially not when or in what strength: and yet some historians tell us the French were surprised by the arrival of the Prussians. Clearly, this was not the case.

For those unfamiliar with the battlefield, Aywiers Abbey is on the route to Moustier—indeed, the *Rue de l'Abbeye* is the modern route to the village. The abbey is gone in 2023, but the imposing gatehouses remain. Then, as now, the abbey was concealed in dense woodland, set in a shallow valley with a flood plain to the north of the abbey site. It was the least likely place to be occupied by cavalry. We wonder if the cavalry was sent in the direction of Moustier? Certainly, from the abbey, the French had no clear vantage point for observing oncoming Prussian troops. The huge *Bois de Palante* blocked any route to Moustier and provided excellent cover for any troops in the area. The abbey controlled any approach to Plancenoit from Maransat or from Lanse: it was a key objective for the French to hold at all costs along with Maransart. Frichermont and Smohain—Marache today—were also key objectives to be held. The Prussians also realised this as we shall see. At the same time as d'Erlon was making his preparations, orders were sent to Lobau:

> The English are amassed on Mont-Saint Jean, that is in front of the forest of Soignes. If the Prussians retreat behind the forest of Soignes you must send a thousand cavalry behind them, and come with your troops to join us. If one finds they intend to come in front of the forest at Mont Saint-Jean, then make a screen and bar the route. Ney.[19]

This dispatch from Ney to Lobau, which was sold at an auction house in Canada, if authentic, implies that the corps was to head off towards Grouchy to contact the Prussians. It also means that Grouchy was never expected to march to Waterloo if he was being sent reinforcements as many historians assume. Grouchy was never ordered to be at Waterloo—and indeed had been sent to Maastricht and by disobeying orders had found the Prussians—as the author has discussed in two other books. Indeed, based on Grouchy's dispatch, Napoleon knew that Grouchy would soon be engaging the Prussians and could not easily break off an action once it began. It also seems clear that Napoleon felt Grouchy's forces were insufficient for the task assigned to him. Indeed, 3rd and 4th Corps had suffered casualties of around 40 per cent on 16 June, and thus Grouchy had no more than 20,000 men, far below the 30,000 often quoted. Indeed, until 4th Corps arrived, Grouchy was outnumbered at Wavre by the Prussians.

Based on what we know about the movements of the Prussians, if a strong force had been sent towards Chapelle de Saint Lambert and environs, as the Prussians moved off from Wavre, they would have been caught between Grouchy and Lobau, in essence cutting off the Prussians from Waterloo, or at least retarding their advance till the following day, by which time Wellington would have been defeated or contained by 1st and 2nd Corps and the *Garde Impériale*. In essence, Napoleon was planning to fight two battles on the same day by dividing his army even more by sending men to Grouchy. Operationally, this made a lot of sense. Napoleon knew the Prussians were a threat and sought to contain or neutralise that threat.

8

Marbot's Patrol

As d'Erlon remarked, French headquarters since 8 a.m. had been aware that the Prussians were heading to Waterloo. It was sensible precaution to send out patrols to assess the situation on the ground: it would allow an estimation of the strength of the Prussian force, its direction of travel, and likely time of arrival at Waterloo to be made. Domon had gone off at first light. In order to ascertain the threat posed by the Prussians, General Brue reports:

> I had in the morning detached the 7th Hussars to keep in communication with General Domont, and I was placed on the extreme right of 1st Corps with the 3rd Chasseurs which consisted of three squadrons.[1]

So, the 7th had, if we believe the brigade commander, been sent to link with Domon, so where was Domon? This confirms that Domon had headed off on patrol, and he was arguably somewhere towards Saint Lambert. What of Subervie? Where was he? Arguably, Domon and Suberbvie were strung out from Frichermont perhaps as far as Moustier. *Général de Division* Marie Joseph Raymond Delort, commander of 14th Division of General Milhaud's 4th Cavalry Division, recalls:

> At 11 o'clock in the morning were perceived in the direction of Saint-Lambert troops who were moving towards the left flank of the English Army. Our spirits were raised in hope. Were these troops emerging those of the detachment of Marshal Grouchy or were they the rear guard of the Prussian Army? However, we remained uncertain, a Prussian hussar carrying a dispatch to the English was made prisoner by the light cavalry that was posted between Wavre and Plancenoit, and said that the Corps of Bülow, a force of 30,000 men was coming. This Corps was intact

and redoubtable as it had not taken part in their defeat at Ligny. Their advance was later confirmed by Generals Domon and Subervie, and their divisions of light cavalry moved forward immediately to their right.[2]

Clearly, Domon and Subervie already in position on the French extreme right by the time the prisoner came in about 1 p.m. Delort's time of 11 a.m. seems plausible as it corroborates Marbot of the 7th Hussars. For four regiments of light cavalry to be sent off on reconnaissance with artillery and infantry support shows that as the morning of the 18th wore on, Napoleon was becoming increasingly concerned about his right flank and the Prussians. What was he thinking? Was he convinced that the Prussians were heading north or was he already contemplating the inevitable that he faced both Wellington and Blücher?

Having not heard from Domon or Subervie—indeed, neither men write a single word about their involvement in the battle that can be found in archives or published formats—and no doubt increasibly worried about the Prussian threat to this right flank, more cavalry patrols were sent out. About his operations, Marbot, the dashing colonel of the 7th Hussars, recalls:

> The 7th Hussars, of which I was colonel, was part of the Light Cavalry Division attached to the 1st Corps forming, June 18, the right wing of the Army that the Emperor commanded in person.
>
> At the beginning of the action, about 11 o'clock, my regiment was detached from the division along with a light infantry battalion, which was placed under my command. These troops were established as a reserve at the far right, behind Frischermont facing the Dyle.
>
> Specific instructions were given to me from the Emperor by his aide-de-camp, General Labédoyère, and an aide, that I cannot remember the name of, specified that I was to leave most of my troop always in view of the battlefield, and I was to take 200 infantry into the woods of Frischermont, established a squadron in Lasne, moving towards the positions at Saint-Lambert with another squadron, place half at Couture, and half at Beaumont, which were to send out reconnaissance patrols along the Dyle, and towards Moutiers Ottignies. The commanders of various detachments had to leave quarter of a mile between each out post forming a contiguous string along on the battlefield, so that by means of hussars, galloping from one post to the other, the officers on reconnaissance might inform me quickly before they met the vanguard troops of Marshal Grouchy, who were to arrive on the side of the Dyle. I was finally ordered to send directly to the Emperor all the reconnaissance reports.

I executed the order that I was given, it would be impossible, after a period of 15 years, to determine which you ask for, the time at which the detachment arrived at Moutiers. Especially as captain Elon who commanded had been instructed by me to proceed in his march with the utmost caution, but noting that he started at 11 o'clock from the battlefield, and had not more than two miles to go, one must assume that he did so in two hours.[3] Which would set his arrival in Moutiers at one o'clock.

A note from Captain Elon that I was promptly handed from the intermediate stations, told me that he found no troops in Moutiers, nor at Ottignies, and the inhabitants assured him that the French left on the right bank of Dyle, were crossing the river in Limalette and Wavre.

I sent this letter to the Emperor with Captain Kounkn, acting as adjutant major, he returned accompanied by an aid, who said to me, from the Emperor, to keep the line at Moutiers, and to send an officer and detachment along the defile of St. Lambert, and to dispatch the various parties in the directions of Limale, Limalette and Wavre.

I sent this order, and even sent a copy with my Detachment Chief at Lasnel Saint-Lambert (his name is no longer in my memory, but I think it was Lieutenant Municheffer).[4]

One of our platoons having advanced to a quarter of a mile beyond St. Lambert, encountered a picket of Prussian hussars, of which we took several men including an officer! I informed the Emperor of this strange capture, and sent him the prisoners.[5]

Marbot's times are hugely problematic to reconcile with Prussian sources. Yet, we are sure that Marbot was sent on such a mission and reached Chapelle-Saint-Lambert and Moustier, but much earlier in the day. I feel Marbot set off at first light and got to Lasne and Moustier before the Prussians, and that in reality, the Prussians he found were in fact the advance guard of Bülow's IV Corps. If he encountered the Prussians heading to Saint-Lambert as he states, he must have been there before 10.30 a.m. Given the prisoner had arrived at headquarters by 1 p.m., the prisoner must have left Saint-Lambert an hour or more earlier. It is very likely, given the place names he gives, that Eloy went via the rue d'Anogrune and thence to the rue de Lasne, passing through Couture, Lasne, Chapelle-Saint-Lambert, and then swung south-east along the rue des Ottignies—a journey of 10 miles. Marbot infers it took two hours to get to Moustier, Chappelle-Saint-Lambert is midway, so for the prisoner to get back to Waterloo for say 12.30 p.m., he must have been on his way to headquarters an hour or more earlier. It is very possible that Marbot was at Chapelle-Saint-Lambert as the Prussians arrived, and it was these

Prussians he found at 10.30 a.m., from which he made a prisoner. If so, this places Marbot leaving Waterloo by 9 a.m. to get to Chapelle-Saint-Lambert before the Prussians. If Domon had been at Moustier on 17 June and had spotted Prussians, it made sense for another patrol to be sent out, backed up with infantry to double check what Domon reported to confirm the Prussian threat on the right wing. The Prussians had been at Moustier. General Excelmans notes:

> On 18 June, my troops were ordered to march in the morning. I was ready to move at about half-past seven o'clock, but with no light cavalry it was not until about nine o'clock I found behind Mazy the rearguard of the Prussian army, on the road to Wavre at the height of Moustier, and almost simultaneously observed a convoy escorted by a few thousand men near the tavern *A Tous Vents*, which appeared to be heading towards Louvain, but I was moving as to bring all my attention on the Dyle. I formed my troops in a wooded ravine to the left, near the farm of Plaquerie, and the right on Neufsar.[6]

It was this body of troops at Moustier that Domon had sent to confront some time earlier, and would advance to Plancenoit from the south, almost totally surrounding the French army. In returning to Marbot's narrative, if Captain Elon got to Moustier, he would have done so before Excelmans arrived, perhaps the same time as Pont Bellanger had done, as they both sent the same information back to their respective headquarters staff, and thus must have left by the time Excelmans went into action about midday. In this way, we can reconcile Marbot's account with the known events at La Baraque. In viewing the events that Marbot wrote about as real, but occurring a lot earlier, it helps to corroborate Berton's observations. If Domon had been at Moustier on 17 June and had spotted Prussians, it made sense for another patrol to be sent out to confirm the Prussian threat on the right wing. Given that on the night of 17 June Domon had found Prussians at Moustier, and by 10 a.m. on 18 June, if not earlier, no Prussians were at Moustier as reported by Captain Elon, the logical conclusion was that they had crossed the Dyle at Wavre and were heading to Louvain and onto Brussels.

Indeed, Grouchy's aide-de-camp, de Blocqueville, comments that at daybreak 18 June, Squadron Commander Bellanger, with some of Grouchy's escort, headed north, ostensibly to follow up on Vandamme's reconnaissance reports about the Prussians moving to Wavre.[7,8,9] Bellanger, we are told, moved to the left of the main column of the army and arrived at Moustier. Here, he interviewed local inhabitants who told him that no enemy troops had been seen, other than a column heading to Wavre.

Once sure of the fact he had found the Prussians, he reported the news back to Grouchy.[10] Sénécal, another of Grouchy's aides, reports the same story in 1829.[11] *Officer d'Ordonnance* Leguest writes that Bellanger was informed that several Prussian columns had passed through Moustier on the night of 17–18 June towards Wavre. He reported this news back to Grouchy, at Sart-lez-Walhain.[12] This was the information Grouchy sent to Napoleon at 10 a.m. What did Napoleon make of it? Did he expect all or just part of the Prussian force to arrive? Whatever he was thinking, it is undeniable that Napoleon failed to transmit his strategic planning to Grouchy, who was operating in an information vacuum from his commander in chief. He relied on his own reconnaissance: if he had known of the intelligence from Waterloo, Grouchy would no doubt have changed his strategic objectives. As it was, two French armies were operating with almost no knowledge of what the other was doing: that fault lies with Napoleon, who never replied to Grouchy with any sense of urgency.

Napoleon, according to Berton, and Gérard (in 1830), became obsessed with the Prussians crossing the Dyle at Moustier and not at Wavre to head cross-country through wooded terrain to Waterloo.[13,14] Moustier was the obvious crossing point of the river.

Prussian Prisoner of War

One of Marbot's patrols stumbled into some Prussians, and both Delort and Marbot speak of a Prussian POW being taken to French headquarters for interrogation.

This is confirmed by Napoleon himself. The Elite Gendarmes of the Imperial Guard brought in a Prussian prisoner from the 2nd Silesian Hussars to the French headquarters, made by Marbot, who were then questioned by the staff. He revealed that he was carrying a dispatch from Bülow, commanding the Prussian IV Corps to Wellington, saying his command had just arrived at Chapelle-Saint-Lambert. This intercepted letter is reported in an order Napoleon sent to Grouchy sometime between 1 and 1.30 p.m.:

> A letter which has just been intercepted, which says General Bülow is about to attack our right flank, we believe that we see his Corps on the height of Saint-Lambert. Lose not an instant in moving towards us to join us, in order to crush Bülow, whom you will crush in the very act.[15]

This places the hussar being captured perhaps an hour earlier. The Prussian IV Corps was the strongest of the Prussian corps as it had not been involved in the Battle of Ligny. This made the urgency of sending Lobau to Chapelle-de-Saint Lambert all the more important. It is clear that Grouchy was not expected at Waterloo if the order to send Lobau to his aid is correct. Certainly, Napoleon wrote on 24 June that 'VI Corps with the cavalry of d'Aumont [Domon ed.], under the orders of Count Lobau, was designated to move to the rear of our right to oppose a Prussian corps'. Clearly, the Prussians were expected and knew this before the battle started, yet Napoleon's own account is often disregarded. So a strong force was sent off to delay or prevent contact with Wellington. Where Napoleon's plans went awry was that Lobau was still at Genappe at 8 a.m. and would not arrive in force till the early afternoon. Grouchy had not yet gained Wavre, and plans were being formulated to stop him. Thielmann began his predations to head north in the wake of I and II Corps. Carl Von Clausewitz notes:

The Prussian III Corps arrived at Wavre on the evening of the 17th, where it was re-joined by the previously detached 1st Brigade of the Reserve Cavalry. Three brigades, the 10th, 11th, and 12th, as well as the Reserve Cavalry, went through Wavre and then encamped at La Bavette. The 9th Brigade remained on the far side of the river because it had arrived too late. Together with the 8th Brigade of the 2nd Corps it now formed the advanced guard against Grouchy. On the morning of the 18th, as the IV Corps marched towards Saint-Lambert, General Thielmann received orders to form the rear guard for the other three corps. If no significant enemy force showed itself, he was to follow the others by taking the road via Couture, while leaving several battalions behind in Wavre to prevent any French patrols from causing problems on the road to Brussels while the armies fought at Waterloo. But if a considerable enemy force showed up in front of Wavre, General Thielmann was to occupy the strong position on the Dyle there and cover the rear of the army.

The departure of the II and I Corps from the position at Wavre took until around 2 p.m. Since nothing at all had been seen of the enemy up to that time, the Prussians were even more convinced that Bonaparte had turned his whole force against Wellington. General Thielmann therefore formed his corps into columns and was about to lead it down the Brussels road when a lively engagement began against the 9th and 8th Brigades, which were still on the left bank of the Dyle. General Thielmann therefore halted his troops until the situation became clearer. In the meantime, the 8th Brigade of the II Corps left altogether. The I [Corps], which had stopped for a while, recommenced its march but left behind a detachment of three battalions and three squadrons under the command of Major Stengel at the village of Limale.[16]

Losses

The 7th Hussars mustered thirty-seven officers and 415 other ranks with 500 horse on 15 June. Only one man was killed in the days leading up to Waterloo: Fourrier Chanalm, who was killed on 17 June at Genappe.[17] Thus, the regiment on the 18th was one of the strongest and freshest light cavalry regiments available to Napoleon. The regiment does not appear to have suffered greatly in the campaign as on 1 July, it mustered thirty-two officers and 348 men.[18] Marbot's men had been in action on 16 and 17 June. Presumably, the regiment fought at Ligny. Men lost that day were: MAT No. 70 Adrien Kapiot, corporal 8th Company, 4th Squadron, prisoner of war; MAT No. 464 Decadi Floréal Robine, trooper, 6th Company, 2nd Squadron, killed in action; MAT No. 466 Mathieu Denis, trooper, 5th Squadron, 1st Company, prisoner of war; MAT No. 529 Pierre François Debeuve, trooper, 5th Company, 1st Squadron, prisoner of war; MAT No. 566 Louis Jean Baptiste Alexandre Mercier, trooper 5th Company, 1st Squadron, missing; and MAT No. 970 Louis Besse, trooper, 4th Company, 4th Squadron, killed in action.[19]

At Genappe, the regiment incurred the following losses: MAT No. 67 Michel Muller, adjutant major, killed in action; MAT No. 75 François Joseph Romer, trooper 1st Company, 1st Squadron, prisoner of war; MAT No. 163 Pierre Eustache Ricard, trooper, 7th Company, 3rd Squadron, killed in action; MAT No. 176 Pierre Marie Mallet, trooper, 2nd Squadron, 2nd Company, killed in action; MAT No. 370 Simon Batel, trooper, 5th Company, 1st Squadron, killed in action; MAT No. 411 Vincent Rougejean, trooper, 5th Company, 1st Squadron, killed in action; MAT No. 414 Jean Nicolas, trooper, 2nd Company, 2nd Squadron, killed in action; MAT No. 426 Joseph Royons, trooper, 8th Company, 4th Squadron, killed in action; MAT No. 457 Jean Bonesse, trooper, 8th Company, 47th Squadron, killed in action; MAT No. 475 Nicolas Remy, trooper, 2nd Company, 2nd Squadron, killed in action; MAT No. 503 Joseph Chanalm, fourrier, 6th Company, 2nd Squadron, killed in action; MAT No. 617 Louis Vangenotte, trooper, 8th Company, 4th Squadron, killed in action; MAT No. 632 Hypolite Joseph Bheilly, trooper, 8th Company, 4th Squadron, killed in action; MAT No. 656 Jean Baptiste Parsy, trooper, 8th Company, 4th Squadron, killed in action; MAT No. 660 Alexis Dermouval, trooper, 5th Company, 1st Squadron, killed in action; MAT No. 662 Jean Baptiste Beauvais, trooper, 5th Company, 1st Squadron, prisoner of war; MAT No. 779 Jean Louis Richepain, trooper, 8th Company, 4th Squadron, killed in action; and MAT No. 1123 Jean Antoine Ymonier, trooper, 8th Company, 4th Squadron, killed in action.

The loss of sixteen men killed at Genappe is a huge figure compared to the losses of some regiments at Waterloo of men killed in action. Clearly the fighting here was desperate and of an intensity not found at Waterloo. At Waterloo, the following men were casualties:

Squadron	Killed	Deserted	POW	Total
1	6	1	-	7
2	10	-	-	10
3	17	-	1	18
4	16	-	2	18
Total	49	1	3	53

The regiment records forty-nine men killed, very high when compared to other regiments in the division. When we look at legion of honour records, we find: Louis Ogi, wounded with a sabre cut at Genappe and another at Waterloo; Nicolas Joseph Celestin Ihler, wounded at Waterloo with a sabre cut to the left arm; and Legere Lespinasse, wounded at Waterloo with a gunshot to the left side of his chest and another to his left arm.[20]

None of these men are listed as wounded, which takes the tally to fifty-six men killed, wounded, or prisoner. The regiment had the following men in prison in England: Martin Neon; Auguste Barbe; Louis Castinet; Francois Peret; and Esutache Ricard.[21]

However, the regimental muster list records: MAT No. 163 Pierre Eustache Ricard, trooper, 7th Company, 3rd Squadron, reported killed in action 17 June, but was clearly a POW; MAT No. 230 Auguste Henry Barbe, trooper 1st Company, 1st Squadron, reported killed in action 19 June, but was clearly a POW; MAT No. 459 Martin Neon, trooper, 8th Company, 4th Squadron killed in action, but was clearly a POW; MAT No. 254 Louis Castinet, corporal 2nd Company, 2nd Squadron, reported killed in action 20 June, but was clearly a POW, 20 June; and MAT No. 217 Pierre Francois Peret, trooper, 4th Company, 4th Squadron reported killed in action, but was clearly a POW.[22]

Therefore, the men reported as killed is a cover-all term for men made POW, deserted, and killed, so we cannot be certain of its accuracy. Dealing with line of sight reckoning for the loss of men in the woods at Saint Lambert meant some men who were wounded from a musket ball or had their horse shot under them and were wounded on hitting the deck and made POW were listed as dead; no doubt it would have looked like this. Overall, the regiment did have a very high attrition rate of men killed. For whatever reason, the wounded men are not recorded in the regimental muster list. In the wooded terrain to Saint Lambert and Moustier, one can imagine how a picket of hussars would have been easy targets for Prussian marksmen. The regiment was, it seems, also in action on 19 June, when the following men were lost:

MAT No. 230 Auguste Henry Barbe, trooper 1st Company, 1st Squadron, reported killed in action 19 June, but was clearly a POW; MAT No. 240 Charles Auguste Edu, trooper, 8th Company, 4th Squadron, deserted; MAT No. 273 Joseph Steland, trooper, 1st Company, 1st Squadron, killed in action; MAT No. 283 Charles Louis Devillet, trooper, 1st Company, 1st Squadron, killed in action; MAT No. 378 Joseph Regnier, trooper, 3rd Company, 3rd Squadron, killed in action; MAT No. 428 Pierre Philippe Branque, trooper, 7th Company, 3rd Squadron, deserted; and MAT No. 1169 Korn, trooper 4th Company, 4th Squadron, killed in action.

Some seven men were lost on 19 June and fourteen on 20 June; these losses are equivalent to the losses at Genappe on 17 June. In total, between 16 and 20 June, the regiment lost ninety-nine men. The lack of a high number of wounded makes us think that troopers were easy targets for Prussian marksmen, who simply shot the men out of their saddles. The Prussians state they took a sergeant-major prisoner who was interrorgated about the French movements. The only candidate is Sergeant-Major Lespinasse, who was wounded twice, but not made a POW. However, it seems possible that the group of POW in England were those taken by the Prussians, who then under interrogation informed the allies of the French intent. Yet what could these men had known? They would have seen the French troops stationed at Lasne, Couture. Perhaps on news that these places were occupied, the Prussians headed through the Lasne defile rather than risking combat with French troops of unknown strength? We shall never know, but the hypothesis is an intriguing one.[23]

9
Battle is Joined

Did the bells of Plancenoit church ring out that Sunday morning to call the faithful to service? Perhaps. What did the villagers make of the armies massed in their fields? How many were to perish? As the morning of 18 June wore on, it became clear to Napoleon that the situation was not developing the way he had accounted for in his mind. The planned confrontation had to be postponed as the concentration of the army was taking much longer than expected and this did not permit the action to commence at 9 a.m. Since first light, Durutte's men had been moving to join 1st Corps and 6th Corps was further behind.[1]

Order and Counterorder

D'Erlon speaks of an order from 8 a.m. No such order can be found today, unless it is the now lost 5 a.m. order. D'Erlon mentions two further orders; the originals are lost. In theory, Napoleon dictated the following order to Marshal Soult, addressed to Marshal Ney:

> Mont Saint Jean June 18th 11 o'clock.
> Once the Army is arrayed in line of battle, and soon after 1 o'clock in the afternoon the Emperor will give the order to Marshal Ney and the attack will commence on the village of Mont-Saint-Jean in order to capture the intersection of the roads. To this end the 12-pdr batteries of the 2nd Corps as well as those of the 6th Corps will be united with those of the 1st Corps. These 24 guns will fire upon the troops holding Mont-Saint-Jean, and Count d'Erlon will commence the attack first by launching his left-hand division and when necessary support it with the other divisions of the 1st Corps.
> The 2nd Corps will advance keeping abreast of the 1st Corps.

The company of engineers belonging to the 1st Corps are to hold themselves in readiness to barricade and fortify Mont-Saint-Jean as soon as it is captured.[2]

Marshal Ney subsequently ordered that 'Count d'Erlon is to understand that the attack is to begin on his left, instead of the right. Communicate this new provision to Commander in Chief Reille.'[3] The order is ambiguous. Did it confirm that d'Erlon was to advance from his left, sending Quiot's division up the Brussels road first, and then Donzelot, Marcognet, and Durutte were to move off at intervals? Or did it mean Reille and 2nd Corps was to attack first? History tells us Reille did move off before d'Erlon. D'Erlon's own words make this order make more sense as it inverts the sequence of attack for 1st Corps, and also the thrust of the attack. The initial plan had been to outflank Wellington, roll around his left flank, and cut him off from the Prussians. In this scenario, the attack at La Haie Sainte was to be a feint, while 3rd and 4th Infantry Division headed around the flank.

One eyewitness to the events was Octave Levavasour, one of Ney's aides-de-camp, remarks: 'Marshal Ney had just given the general the order to seize the farm at La Haye-Sainte [*sic*.] with about 3,000 men. The latter marched in tight columns towards the farm,' but notes that the 54th and 55th Line—no doubt seriously shaken after being routed by the Household Brigade—failed to capture the farm. He continues:

> The marshal, indignant at seeing the general's hesitation, sent me to tell him to take the position at a charge. I descend towards the road where I found two companies of sappers... The captain advances towards me and, handing me his card: 'Monsieur the aide-de-camp,' he exclaims, 'this is my name.' Then he beats the charge, his sappers run towards the farm shouting, 'Forward!' and, as I go to the general to give him the marshal's order, the sappers are already seizing the gardens, the hedges and flushing out the enemy who was pushed back, all in sight of the infantry, who then set off to support the attack.[4]

Among the engineers attacking the farm, one of the first to succumb to the garrison's musketry was Jean-Jacques Maignen. His death certificate reports that 'he died on the 18th June 1815 at two o'clock in the afternoon from a gunshot that pass[ed] through his chest whilst employed with his battalion to carry the farm at the foot of Mount Saint Jean which the enemy had fortified'. The engineer served as a captain in 5th Company of 2nd Battalion of 1st Regiment of Engineers. He was aged just twenty-five.[5] He may be the officer encountered by Levavasour. His time of death was exactly the moment that the Prussians began attacking the French positions at

Frichermont, assuming the time given correlates with that of the Prussians. Lieutenant Pierre Grille, formerly of the *Garde Impériale* engineers, tells us 'on the 18 June I was grievely wounded by a sun shot at the affair at Mont Saint Jean and left for dead on the field of battle, and in consequence abandoned by the regiment during the retreat'.[6] It is interesting to note that the 1st Battalion of the 1st Regiment of Engineers was held back from this action. An officer from the battalion tells us on '18 June ... we were charged by Prussian cavalry. I recieved during the charge 12 wounded and was left for dead on the field of battle, where I remained for 24 hours.'[7]

The attack on Hougoumont was to be a holding action and not, as a lot of history tells us, a diversionary attack to draw Wellington's strength from the centre and his right. The plan was for 1st and 2nd Corps to operate together, 1st Corps attacking first, and the 2nd Corps subsequently advancing in support. This means that the 2nd Corps was supposed to advance to the left rear of the 1st Corps, with the division of Jérôme Bonaparte covering the left flank by occupying the low grounds around the complex of Hougoumont.

The action did indeed start on the left with Piré's light cavalry, and Jérôme did indeed move forward. For an inexplicable reason, when d'Erlon advanced, Foy and Bachelu appear to have done nothing. Why did Jérôme attack before any plans for the artillery bombardment of Wellington's centre had been completed?

The lack of clear source material and sources that at times are contradictory makes analysing what happened difficult. Jérôme is blamed by modern historians as the instigator of this fiasco on the French left. Another writer blames Guillaminot. Reille himself says little and blames no one. Prince Jérôme's actions at Waterloo have often been described as reckless and that he needlessly destroyed his division and that of Foy. However, it seems on balance that the charges against Jérôme do not stand up to much scrutiny. Napoleon—who blames Ney, Grouchy, and Guyot for losing him the battle—blames no one for what occurred. Therefore, this means that the action was initiated in common consent. This makes sense of the way in which Reille describes the role of the division of Jérôme, *i.e.*, as covering the left flank of the grand attack by occupying the low ground around the complex of Hougoumont. Until more archive source material can be found, the most logical explanation of the preliminary attack on Hougoumont is that close proximity of the complex in relation to the grand attack was to ensure the left flank of the attack was not threatened from the troops at Hougoumont. Thus, the decision was taken to neutralise this outpost and to attack immediately. In the same vein, due to the lack of source material, we may never know why Foy and Bachelu did not advance in support of 1st Corps.

Perhaps, d'Erlon—seeing the action unfolding at Hougoumont, and depending how one reads Ney's amendment to the 11 a.m. order—could have taken this as a signal for him to attack, pushing Quiot forward as planned, expecting Foy and Bachelu to move up, reading the order to mean that Reille and 2nd Corps would attack first. In reading the order as d'Erlon was to move off from his left and then be supported by Reille and 2nd Corps, once d'Erlon was in motion, why Reille did nothing is a mystery, or seeing he was not supported, why did d'Erlon press on? Instead, Ney sent forward the cuirassiers, perhaps to fill the gap caused by Reille's inaction. Perhaps Reille's caution about Wellington's position delayed his advance, and also perhaps his forward movement was blocked by the cuirassiers or the allied cavalry attack occurred at the moment that Reille was to move off.[8] We simply do not know why the attack did not go to plan.

The French Artillery

In accordance to the emperor's 11 a.m. order, as the precursor to d'Erlon's attack, the French drew up a battery of guns on their right flank to bombard the allied lines. General Baron De Salle, commanding the artillery of 1st Corps, writes:

> About ten o'clock, the Emperor made advance the 1st Corps and the 2nd Corps which occupied the left of the road to Brussels. We occupied the right of this road, cashed in on this point. Two divisions of the 6th Corps and the guard formed the reserve. I was with the Count d'Erlon when Mr. Labédoyère, General Aide-de-Camp of the Emperor, came to tell me of him he gave me the he had given me command of a battery of eighty guns, which consisted all my 6-pdr batteries, the 12-pdrs of my reserve, and also the reserve batteries of 2nd and 6th corps which actually formed only fifty-four guns, twenty-four of them being 12-pdrs. I had to order all the guns placed into battery in the position we occupied, halfway up the slope, on one line, and begin firing all at once to astonish and shake the morale of the enemy.[9]

Colonel Bro of the 4th Lancers, attached to 1st Corps, narrates:

> The 18, we were given the objective of Mont-Saint-Jean, Napoleon after an inspection at the farm of Caillou, stopped and dictated at eleven o'clock the order to the left, once the army is ranged in order of battle, about one o'clock in the afternoon, (when the Emperor give the order to

Marshal Ney), the attack will begin to seize the village of Mont-Saint-Jean, where there was an intersection of roads.

To this end, the batteries 12-pdr of the 2nd corps and those of the 6th were convened with those of the 1st Corps. These fifty-four guns fired at the troops of Mont-Saint-Jean and the Comte d'Erlon begin the attack by bringing forward his left division and according to circumstances, brought up in support the remaining divisions of the 1st Corps. The 2nd Corps was able to advance to guard the flank of the Count d'Erlon.[10]

Napoleon claims in his report of the battle that the battery mustered eighty guns, almost double the number given by de la Salle and Bro. Bro tells us that the battery was formed into three elements and placed on the ridge of high ground running perpendicular to the Brussels road with the flank resting against La Belle Alliance. Colonel Bro also shows a battery to the west of the Brussels road, being flanked by infantry battalions and supported by cavalry.[11] The battery was comprised of one 12-pdr battery from 2nd Corps (eight guns); one 12-pdr battery from 6th Corps (eight guns); one 12-pdr battery from 1st Corps (eight guns); and four 6-pdr batteries from 1st Corps (thirty-two guns), for a total of fifty-six guns, assuming the guns from 6th Corps were on the field. The guns would have had to march along the paced road, with the infantry marching through muddy and boggy fields, so it is not impossible that the guns arrived in advance of the infantry.

Captain Eberhard von Brandis of the 5th Line Battalion King's German Legion served as the aide-de-camp to Colonel Baron Christian von Ompteda during the Waterloo campaign, and he described the French artillery opposed to the allied line thus:

> During the contest on our right wing the French also attacked the left of our line, where the Hanoverian Brigade commanded by Colonel Best was situated, but this attack was repulsed. Towards 2 o'clock it became our turn to be exposed to the cannonade which had spread along the whole of the front line, because Napoleon wished to accomplish his general plan and break through the British centre. For this purpose, he had positioned 80 cannon opposite our line, and these cannons raged with their full power against the two central divisions, those of Alten and Picton. At this time, Colonel von Hacke, whose regiment, the Cumberland Hussars, was just behind us, rode towards Colonel von Ompteda and requested permission move his regiment out of range of the cannon fire, which they could no longer endure. Ompteda directed him to Lord Uxbridge, the commander of the cavalry. Besides the regiment of Cumberland Hussars there were several English and Dutch cavalry regiments immediately

behind us that were suffering greatly from the cannon fire, like ourselves, but which maintained their designated position with the utmost courage and calm.[12]

Quite clearly, some of the shots from the battery were finding targets and inflicting losses on the allied troops on the reverse slop. The effects of artillery fire on human and horse alike could be terrifying. Artillery round shot, canister shot, or shell fragments were virtually guaranteed to cause casualties ranging from a slight flesh wound to the removal of heads and limbs splattering pieces of flesh, as well as items of equipment in all directions.

The Cuirassiers Attack

About 11.30 a.m., Prince Jérôme began his attack at Goumont. At the same time, Marshal Ney began to assemble the heavy cavalry as a prelude to the infantry assault. Ney's thinking was probably to bombard the enemy line, then attack with the heavy cavalry to exploit the situation. Aide-de-camp to Marshal Ney, Octave Levavasseur notes that he was on a reconnaissance mission for the marshal:

> Shortly before noon, the Emperor dictated the orders that Soult was writing in his notebook, the Major General then ripped the sheet off and gave it to Marshal Ney, who before handing it to me to communicate with commanders in chief, wrote in margin in pencil: Count d'Erlon is to understand that it is he who must begin the attack. I went galloping off to the left, and I arrived firstly with Prince Jérôme, whose troops are occupying a valley *en masse*, behind a small wood. I continued, but, before reaching the general d'Erlon, my horse fell and the paper, covered in mud becomes almost indecipherable, so that I am obliged to help his reading of the order. I Returned to Marshal Ney, who I found behind La Haye Sainte. Already the Count d'Erlon had started to commence his attack, the battle was joined.
>
> The Marshal summoned all the colonels of cavalry and ordered them each to send a squadron. These squadrons moved up from the rear, and he told one of his oldest aides, Crabbe, a retired brigadier general, who had only been a few days with us, to take command of the cavalry, and added: 'you will follow the left and sweep all that lies between the artillery and infantry, passing over the land occupied by the enemy behind La Haye Sainte.'
>
> Meanwhile, the Count d'Erlon advanced amid the shrapnel on the slope of plateau, but he failed to take the position. General Crabbe advanced

and penetrated into the valley; the Marshal turned and addressed me: 'Levavasseur, he said, go with that charge. I'm leaving and you, go join Crabbe at the front.' After passing the lines of enemy artillery, Crabbe formed in column by squadron and continued charge. We start pushing them back with the cries of '*Vive I'Empereur*! Forward!'[13]

With the fight for La Haie Sainte spilling out on the slopes of the plateau, the Lüneburg battalion presented an irresistible target for the cuirassiers, as Colonel Ordener narrates. Michel Ordener, commanding the *1er Régiment de Cuirassiers*, recounts the charge as follows:

Ney gave me orders to take an English battery placed near the farm of Mount St. Jean, whose fire was causing great havoc in our lines. I made my regiment advance at a trot, putting my regiment into column by squadron at large intervals The Hanoverian battalion of Lunenburg and the second light infantry of the Kings German Legion were placed in our way, and we fell on them with the corps. I killed with my own hand three officers, their flag came into our possession, we addressed in the same breath the English battery, and we captured the 24 guns and limber's that composed the battery and had the guns spiked, and I continued the charge that carried us to the edge of the forest of Soignes. Here I am ten feet away from of a square, when one face opened a murderous fire on us, my horse was killed struck by a bullet to the neck, protected by my armour, I can free myself, I leave my horse, and returned with my men to our lines, where after some quickly conducted first aide, I mounted a fresh horse and resumed my command.[14]

The cuirassiers attacked the King's German Legion of Ompteda. With the allied infantry broken up and dispersed, the British Household Brigade of Heavy Cavalry was launched against the intrepid cuirassiers. Carl Jacobi narrates:

The 5th and 8th Line Battalions advanced against the enemy infantry which had attacked La Haye Sainte. The battalion closed ranks and advanced to attack the enemy attack. But while advancing the enemy cavalry, which had been involved in the earlier attacks against the squares of the 1st Hanoverian Brigade on the heights, fell upon them. The 5th Line Battalion was supported just in time by the English cavalry which was falling back, and they suffered small losses. However, the 8th Line Battalion was completely destroyed as they endured the surprise attack which was eventually driven off by the English cavalry. The officer who bore the colour received three severe wounds and the Colour was lost.[15]

Under the swords of the cuirassiers, Ompteda's command was decimated. The brigade on the morning of 18 June mustered 1,527 officers and men. Of these, some 787 were killed or wounded and 207 were listed as missing—a total loss of 994 officers and men, equating to 65 per cent of effective strength being lost in the attack by the cuirassiers.[16]

D'Erlon Moves Off

Shortly before the cuirassiers moved off, both the French and allied armies were aligned in line of battle. What were the officers and men thinking? Following the bombardment of the allied lines, the infantry was ordered to the attack. However, it seems Napoleon's original point of attack was at Papelotte and La Haye, to outflank the allied lines, and not engage with a full-frontal assault. It seems the arrival of the Prussians at Saint Lambert changed Napoleon's original plans.

For the attack, d'Erlon formed his corps into vast attacking columns, termed *colonne de division par bataillon*, in essence being a column formed from an entire infantry division, each battalion being deployed in three ranks and approximately 150 files wide and twenty-four deep. This formation was neither new or unusual and had been used by the French before. The five-pace interval often cited as the course of failure of the French attack is, as far as can be ascertained, an invention by the strategist Jomini, later verified by later writers such as Battalion Commander Rulliers of the 95th Regiment of Line and Adjutant Gastineau of the 13th Regiment of Light Infantry. Marching such a concentration of troops, with this interval, across the difficult terrain would result in the battalions becoming mixed up, and there would be no way to restore order. If this had been the case, then when the columns attacked, the success that they achieved would in theory have not been possible.

Furthermore, with such intervals, the time taken to actually form the columns would have been both lengthy and very difficult to align. Based on the French 1813 infantry manual, it would be a much faster and more obvious way to form these columns with the twenty-four-pace interval by forming columns by section.[17]

About the attack, d'Erlon writes:

> According to the preparations made earlier, whilst all of 1st Corps was going to attack the left of the enemy, the 2nd Corps was to form on the main road, in order to attack the centre as soon as the troops of 1st Corps had succeeded in the capturing the positions on the right. All these arrangements had been made and the movement had commenced, the

Prince de la Moskowa came to the tell the Comte d'Erlon that according to new plans, the attack was to commence at the centre of the enemy and not the left; that the divisions would march in the order of columns already indicated, but the left hand echelon would take the lead, and was to take itself to the farm of La Haye Sainte, situated on the main road, and 80 artillery pieces would support our attack and that of 2nd Corps on the right of the enemy. The Comte d'Erlon hastened to execute the change that these new dispositions brought to the ones already under taken. He formed columns on the slope of the hillock to the right of the Bonne Alliance, the column on the left formed the 1st echelon which composed the 1st Division, next came the 3rd Division, the 2nd and 4th. The battalion which had been detached with the cavalry was recalled and the latter was ordered to draw nearer, to hold itself to the right, and position itself level with the infantry, and to follow its movements. 80 pieces of artillery, 36 of which were 12-pders, commanded by the Major Chandon were put under the orders of General de la Salle, who commanded the artillery of 1st Corps, which he established in a single line on the summit of the hillock behind which the infantry had formed, roughly along the road from La Belle Alliance to Ohain. As the line of guns was very long, and extended well beyond the space occupied by [illegible] column of infantry, a regiment from the 4th Division and sent to the extreme right in order to cover the artillery and defend it from all that may have come forward along the prolongation of the hillock that leads to Smohain.

At half past one, the Emperor who was standing close to La Belle Alliance sent the order to commence the attack. The 80 artillery pieces opened fire. The columns began to advance, the troops advanced on the enemy positions without any hesitation; the artillery supported the movement of the columns; the 1st column pushed along the main road, and having found the farm of La Haye Sainte embattled strongly occupied, as well as the road in the narrow defile being filled with an abatis the column divided, one brigade went to the positions above and to the left of the road, and the other to the right; the 2nd column had engaged and reached the enemy positions at the same moment as a charge took place against the troops of the 1st Division, and suffered heavy losses, and retreated in great disorder; the enemy cavalry had descended near the farm of La Haye Sainte at the foot of the position and closed to the flanks and rear of the 3rd Division as it was attacking the enemy position, which forced this division to fall back onto the 2nd which had immediately formed itself into square, and received a very strong charge by another mass of English cavalry which could not break them; another mass of English cavalry coming from the enemy's left charged the 4th

Division which also maintained itself in square. These two columns of cavalry having failed against our squares turned themselves against our numerous artillery, and did it the greatest of ills: men and horses were killed and dispersed.[18]

An eyewitness, Alexander Cheron, notes what happened next:

The soldiers displayed an enthusiasm that cannot be described, the cries of 'Long live the Emperor' merged with the sound of the guns. However, the enemy, concealed in an extremely favourable position, supported by a numerous and formidable artillery, did not seem to be impressed by our audacity. They opened fire so tremendously that the heads of our columns retreated in disarray.

10
The Allied Response

In their audacious attack, d'Erlon's men must be given credit, despite the heavy and accurate fire of allied canon and musketry, for reaching the very crest of the slope on the Anglo-allied left-centre. To make matters worse for Marcognet's men, upon cresting the ridge, they encountered a thick, 6-foot-high hedge. Marcognet got his men through this natural obstacle and they reached von Bijlandt's Dutch-Belgian brigade. Under the relentless pressure from the French, they had no option other than falling back, the retreat being recorded by men of Major-General Sir Thomas Picton's 5th Division as an inglorious route.

The myth of Waterloo castigates the brigade for its cowardice, but it ought to be recalled that it had been badly mauled at Quatre Bras and was therefore severely under-strength, and it had already withstood over an hour's artillery barrage at short range before the French infantry got up close and personal. Little wonder therefore it retired. If d'Erlon had been capable of consolidating his position on the crest of the ridge, he could have turned Wellington's flank. Marcognet's men were poised to break through the allies' beleaguered line. In the centre, at La Haie Sainte, Quiot's men had the satisfaction of forcing some companies of the 95th Rifle Brigade—whose musketry was far more accurate due to its employment of Baker rifles—out of the Sandpit to join the rest of their battalion behind the Wavre road. The 32nd Regiment of Foot had gotten to hand-to-hand fighting with the 28th Regiment of Line Infantry. For the French, the attack was succeeding.

Be that as it may, the lack of command and control in attacking with battalions deployed by company in line, lined up alongside one another, gave the French incredible firepower, but with hardly trained conscripts, keeping the dressing of the vast lines of attack was almost impossible, especially given the nature of the terrain the attack moved over.

Deep cloying mud under musketry and artillery fire made what was a parade ground manoeuvre almost impossible to maintain. That fault lies with whoever gave the order to attack in this manner: be it d'Erlon or Nety, it was the wrong formation at the wrong time. Given d'Erlon's experience against 'the thin red line' in Spain and the constant failure of attacking in column, one can see why d'Erlon or Ney chose to adopt, in essence, British tactics to overcome the lack of firepower of a column.

However, *l'ordre mixte* attacking with battalions in column with companies in line in the intervals between the columns would have given the hitting power of a column and a wide frontage for musketry, yet the use of a formation written into the 1791 drill book was, it seems, never considered. The attack formation and poor training of the officers and men contributed as much to the failure of the attack as to the allied cavalry. Be that as it may, the attack did cause serious disruption to Wellington's left.

In the firefight against Marcognet's men, Bijlandt lost 351 dead and wounded and 349 missing—in total, 700 men or 27 per cent of the men who had been in ranks at the start of the day being absent by the end. Bijlandt had lost 39 per cent of its starting strength at Quatre Bras already, while Kemp had lost 26 per cent. Standing alongside Bijlandt was the 9th British Brigade of General Pack. The brigade began the campaign with 2,173 men. At Quatre Bras, a staggering 957 men were killed or wounded—a loss of 46 per cent of effective strength.

On the morning of 18 June, the brigade had 1,216 officers and men under arms; 374 men were killed or wounded—a loss of 31 per cent of effective strength.[1] With losses of 39 per cent of Bijlandt's command, 36 per cent of Kempt's, and 31 per cent of Pack, we can see that the assault of 1st Corps was very effective indeed—little wonder Kempt and Bijlandt's troops had to be replaced in line of battle. With no time to spare, gone was the chance for a flanking movement. A sudden quick stroke was what was needed. The myth of the battle implies that Bijlandt's men ran away as cowards, and the musketry and artillery of the British smashed the columns before they opened fire. This understanding is totally at odds to French eyewitnesses and also, crucially, English and Dutch-Belgian accounts. Captain von Bronkhorst, a Dutch-Belgian officer, recounts:

> It was impossible to absorb the shock. We received orders to retreat behind the English troops who were in the second line. In those moments were suffered considerable losses. The French had reached the edge of the heights we occupied. Scottish troops were determinedly waiting for them.[2]

Lord Uxbridge's aide-de-camp Thomas Wildman describes what happened next:

The Life Guards & Blues distinguished themselves particularly & charged & overthrew the French Cuirassiers several times, our light cavalry was frequently engaged with the Lancers & I believe there was no part of the army that was not continually under fire & such a terrific fire as the oldest officers declare they never before experienced. Several times I believe all hopes were given up by everyone except the Duke of W. who only said we will beat them yet before night. This cavalry & Infantry were *enmêlée* [mixed] with our people, some of our guns in the midst of them & in our position, but were driven back with enormous slaughter.[3]

The two regiments of Life Guards—supported by the Blues and King's Dragoon Guards, led by Lord Somerset—hit the 1st Cuirassiers and Bourgeois column in the left flank and front. Almost simultaneously, the Union Brigade charged into the rest of 1st Corps.

The 2nd column had engaged and reached the enemy positions at the same moment as a charge took place against the troops of the 1st Division, and suffered heavy losses, and retreated in great disorder; the enemy cavalry had descended near the farm of La Haye Sainte at the foot of the position and closed to the flanks and rear of the 3rd Division as it was attacking the enemy position, which forced this division to fall back onto the 2nd which had immediately formed itself into square, and received a very strong charge by another mass of English cavalry which could not break them; another mass of English cavalry coming from the enemy's left charged the 4th Division which also maintained itself in square. These two columns of cavalry having failed against our squares turned themselves against our numerous artillery, and did it the greatest of ills: men and horses were killed and dispersed.[4]

Quiot's Division

On the extreme left of d'Erlon's attack came Quiot's division. An officer of 1st Corps, who, alas, remains anonymous, notes:

Count d'Erlon attacked the village of Mont St. Jean and supported his attack with 80 pieces of cannon, which must have occasioned great loss to the English Army. All the efforts were upon the plateau. A brigade from the 1st Division of Count d'Erlon took the village of Mont St Jean. The 2nd Brigade was charged by a corps of English cavalry which occasioned it much loss. At the same moment, a division of English cavalry charged the battery of the Count of d'Erlon by its right and disorganised several pieces; but the cuirassiers of General Milhaud charged that division, three regiments of which were broken and cut up.[5]

Another eyewitness participant in the charge was Dominique Fleuret:

> A mass of cavalry charged us and we jumped into the ditches. We did not have time to rally many. They were cut down by their sabres, and some others were made prisoners. The cavalry continued its charge, and we were then driven back by infantry. But as we stood in a depression, to our left, two regiments of French lancers came to our aid and saved us.... With the cavalry passed, we crawled on our stomachs to join our squares, which fired from their four faces into the English dragoons. The drums of the regiment beat the rally. We were re-united. The regiment was reduced to about 400 men.[6]

Louis Canler of the 28th Regiment of Line Infantry further notes:

> No sooner had we reached the plateau then we are received by the queen's dragoons who fell on us, uttering wild cries. The first division that did not have time to form square, it could not sustain this charge and was pressed back, then started veritable carnage. Each man found himself separated from his comrades, and fought only for himself. The sabres, and the bayonet opened a passage through the quivering masses, because it we were too close to each other to make use of our firearms.
>
> But the position was untenable for infantry fighting alone and surrounded by horsemen and I soon found myself an isolated unarmed prisoner.[7]

Marcognet's Division

Donzelot's column for whatever reason did not advance and instead formed square. *Maréchal de Camp* Baron Schmitz, commanding 1st Brigade 2nd Infantry Division of Donzelot, reports:

> [On] the 18th ... The division took up arms at 11 o'clock in the morning and was formed in columns by battalion in echelon behind the 3rd Division. At noon, when the signal was given for the attack, the Division followed in the order above the movement of the third and fourth divisions. The enemy cavalry charged and having routed these two divisions, the second division remained in the position where it stood, formed square by means of filling in the gap between

battalions by the platoons from the flank, and in this position repulsed the cavalry with considerable loss to them. The division had stopped and rendered null the impetuosity of the enemy, and saved the life of an infinite number of soldiers of the 3rd and 4th divisions which had been cut to pieces.[8]

It seems that as Marcognet's column advanced—and due to the difficulties in keeping the battalions formed in well-dressed lines—the companies began to drift apart laterally, and those on the left of the column had moved sufficiently far over to their left to impede Donzelot's movement. D'Erlon confirms this sequence of events when writing to Schmitz after the battle:

> [He was] distinguished by his courage and determination at the battle of Waterloo at the head of his brigade, most notably in the charge of the English cavalry against the 3rd and 4th Divisions and repelled the cavalry with considerable loss.[9]

Therefore, it seems as Schmitz states, Donzelot's column had to halt to avoid chaos of the 1st Division moving out of place and, in response to the cavalry, formed square, holding off the Household Brigade and elements of the Union Brigade.

In the centre came Marcogent's division, which was hit by the Union Brigade. General Antoine Noguès, a general of 1st Corps commanding the 21st Regiment of Line and the 46th Regiment of Line, narrates the day's events as he saw them in 1840:

> We advanced towards the enemy line with supported arms, without deploying sharpshooters or responding with a single shot to those of the enemy, when a body of cavalry at full gallop, fell on us, passed us, without threatening us, and turned on the battalions formed behind, one after the other, these battalions, they were not able to open fire and formed into circles, holding their bayonets over their heads to ward off sabre blows. The cavalry, having disunited the troops who had fallen under their first blows, continued to chase them to the tail of our column.[10]

About the attack, Jacques Martin of the 45th Line notes:

> Death flew from all around; entire ranks disappeared under the hail, but nothing could stop our march. It carried on with the same order, the same precision. Dead men were replaced on the field by those who survived; the ranks although thinner, were no less formed.

At last we arrived at the summit. We were about to receive the prize for such bravery. Already the English had started to bolt for it, already their guns were retiring at the gallop. A sunken road, lined with hedges, was now the only obstacle separating us from them. Our soldiers did not wait for the order to jump across; They charged, leaping over the hedges and leaving their ranks disordered to chase after their enemies. Fatal mistake! We had to enforce good order. We halted them to rally ... Just as I was pushing one man into his rank, I saw him fall at my feet from a sabre blow. The English cavalry charged at us from all directions and cut us to pieces. I just had time to throw myself into the middle of the crowd to avoid the same fate. The noise, the smoke, the confusion, all happening together, we could hardly see that on our right several squadrons of English Dragoons, having come down through a sort of ravine, had extended and formed behind us and charged us in the rear.[11]

In the melee, the eagle of the 45th Line and that of the 105th were taken by the allies. The French advance had been crushed and the first major French offensive have been stopped in its tracks. It would take time for the French to regain order from chaos: every moment of disorder brought the Prussians a few paces closer to destiny.

Losses

Losses for the 1st Infantry Division are below:

1st Infantry Division						
	Wounded	Wounded & POW	POW	Killed	Missing	Total
54th Line[12]	3	-	452	13	-	468
55th Line[13]	129	-	281	14	88	512
28th Line[14]	17	113	572	-	-	702
105th Line[15]	1	-	416	25	8	450
Total	150	113	1721	52	96	2132

The division had mustered 6,063 men at the start of the campaign and lost 2,132 men at Waterloo, or a loss of 35 per cent of effective strength.

In the 3rd Division, losses were as follows:

3rd Infantry Division						
	Wounded	Wounded & POW	POW	Killed	Missing	Total
21st Line[16]	95	263	278	5	-	670
25th Line[17]	8	-	733	-	-	741
45th Line[18]	45	-	-	2	732	779
46th Line[19]	10	-	198	12	125	345
Total	158	263	1209	19	857	2535

Marcognet's command had mustered 3,905 men at the start of the campaign, with 2,535 men being lost at Waterloo, equating to a staggering loss of 64 per cent of effective strength.

Due to water damage to the regimental muster lists for the 6th and 8th Foot Artillery, we cannot generate losses for the bulk of the battery. However, we do have losses for the 12-pdr battery from 2nd Corps. Regimental losses were as follows for Waterloo:[20]

Company	Army Corps	Killed	Died of Wounds	Wounded	Wounded & Missing	POW	Missing
7th	2nd Corps, Reserve	3	1	4	1	-	24
8th	-	1	-	1	-	-	-
16th	-	-	-	-	1	-	5
Total	-	4	1	5	2	-	31

Due to a shortage of manpower, 7th Company was bolstered with men from 8th and 16th Companies. The killed and wounded are likely to have been victims of either the Prussians or the Union Brigade. The missing are likely to have been lost during the route. The 7th Company, which was the reserve 12-pdr battery of 2nd Corps, was commanded by Michel Valnet. He was born at Rougermont les Cendrey on 22 December 1770. Enlisted in the 2nd Foot Artillery on 11 October 1790, he was promoted to fourrier on 1 June 1792, sergeant on 24 November 1792, and sergeant-major on 1 March 1798. Promotion to second lieutenant came on 22 February 1801, second captain on 13 July 1807, and captain on 12 October 1811. He was placed in command of 7th Company in August 1814.[21]

During the campaign, 7th Company—comprising of six 12-pdr and two 6.4-lb howitzers—lost far more men. At Quatre Bras, one gunner was killed and three were wounded. On the 17th, four men were lost.

At Waterloo, three gunners were killed, six were wounded, and nineteen went missing. The 7th Company at Waterloo was posted to join the artillery of 1st Corps on the right flank. It seems possible that the much higher losses from the battery can be partially explained by the fact the battery was charged by the Union Brigade in the first half of the battle, and then around 7 p.m. deployed with the troops of General Pégot in supporting the attack of the Imperial Guard. Given that General de la Salle who commanded the reserve 12-pdr batteries of 1st Corps tells us the reserves were not attacked but fired into the allied cavalry, the losses, therefore, seem to be primarily from the closing stages of the battle, when the allied cavalry charged the guns.[22]

The horse artillery of Jacquinot's 1st Cavalry Division, long said to have been part of the battery, was the 2nd Company, 1st Horse Artillery. The company lost two men as prisoners and one missing at Waterloo—a total of just three men.[23] In theory, they were not part of the grand battery that was posted a few miles south of the gun line. Clearly, the battery was not heavily involved in the charge by the Union Brigade, nor it seems came under fire from the Prussians later in the day. This seems to support d'Erlon's observations.

11

Durutte's Offensive

By the time d'Erlon had set off to the attack with the 1st, 2nd, and 3rd Divisions of his corps, the 4th Division had just taken its place in line of battle. The 4th Division had become detached on 16 June and only rejoined 1st Corps once the battle had started.

The 1st Brigade was commanded by General Pégot comprising the 8th and 29th Regiments of Line, a force of some 1,800 men. The 2nd Brigade was commanded by General Brue and comprised the 85th and 95th Line; we are told they had the same effective strength as the 1st Brigade.[1] Battalion Commander Joseph-Marcelin Rulliers of the 95th Regiment of Line—albeit in 1856 when his memories of the day have been altered by what he has read and been told later, so cannot be seen to be wholly reliable account—adds the following:

> The rain had started two o'clock in the afternoon and, soon drenched the ground and forced the Army to march on the main road, in one column. The general movement was slowed considerably. It was almost dark when the 1st Corps being formed in columns, arrived straddling the road, not far behind the Belle Alliance, where the headquarters of the Emperor had been established. It was raining heavily and the soldiers had mud up to their knees. It was impossible to light a fire to make soup. The night was very bad for the French Army. There, we learned that the British Army had taken position at some distance in front of the forest of Soignes where they had been sheltered by the trees of the wood and had been able to make fires.
>
> The rain ceased to fall at 4 o'clock in the morning, but on our side, the rain had so soaked the ground, it would have been impossible for Artillery, the Cavalry and even the infantry, to operate immediately, it was really only practicable at 11 o'clock.

At 6 o'clock, the Division of Durutte was ordered to go and establish itself on a hill to the left of the highway where the British had established for a while a telegraph. It arrived about 8 o'clock and immediately set about making soup and setting fires to dry clothing and equipment. From this height, which dominated all those around it, we could distinguish the French and British Lines. The British had their front crowned with a formidable artillery. Their main strengths of infantry and cavalry were slightly right flank, what of the centre in front of the forest, which was masked by elevations in the terrain. They occupied the strong point of Hougoumont, as well as the gardens and a small wood. Their left extended until Papelotte, in front of the woods.[2]

About the attack, Captain Camille Durutte notes the following occurred as soon as his father's command arrived with 1st Corps:

It was immediately announced that it was necessary that all divisions should form in columns by battalion, and we had to attack the enemy main force, starting with the left.

General Durutte perceiving that his right could be overwhelmed, and that a village, which was at the end of our line, was occupied by enemy troops, he observed that it was appropriate that he should deal with these troops. However, he was told that nothing could change the provisions of the Emperor, and he executed his orders as given when he saw the divisions of the left begin their movement.

The artillery of the guard was placed on the heights behind this division, and was bombarding the enemy, who were replying with a roughly equal number of guns. Some cavalry regiments were established behind the guns. General Durutte began his movement, and the cavalry placed on his right also followed this movement, but it did nothing. Persistence by the Emperor to keep each arm separate, and not to make the cavalry subordinate to the generals who commanded the divisions of infantry, was fatal and made this day very hard for us. The 4th Division was to have on its left Donzelot's 3rd Division [sic.], but we could not find them, they were probably further behind.[3]

Durutte adanced to the attack and assailed the Hanoverian troops under Best. What happened next was immortalised in paint by Lady Butler. Durutte's command was hit by the Scots Greys. Trooper James Armour of Captain Fenton's Troop Scots Greys writes as follows about this episode:[4]

Durutte's Offensive

When we got clear through the Highlanders, we were soon on the charge and a short one it was. A cross-road being in our way, we leaped the first hedge gallantly, traversed the road, and had to leap over another hedge. At this time the smoke from the firing on both sides made it so dark that we could not see distinctly. We had not charged many yards till we came to a column. As yet we had stuck pretty well together, although a great number had fallen about the cross-roads. In a very short time we were down upon the column making pretty clean work of them. Numbers by this time had dropped off; still we pushed forward, and very soon came upon another column who cried out 'Prisoners!' threw down their arms, stripped themselves of their belts, in accordance with French discipline, and ran like hares towards the rear. We pushed on still, and soon came up to another column, some of whom went down on their knees, called out 'Quarter!' in tone of supplication. Now, then, we got among the guns, which had so terribly annoyed us and paid back the annoyance in slaughter such as never before was witnessed; artillerymen were cut down and run through, horses were houghed, harness was cut and all rendered useless. Some who were good judges of such work reckoned we had made a very good job of it. I was engaged amongst six or seven guns, all brass, where almost all the artillerymen were cut down, and most, if not all the horses were houghed.

While at work amongst these guns, no thought had we but that we should have nothing to do when we were done but to retrace our steps. I admit I was much surprised when we began to return whence we came to behold great numbers of the cuirassiers and lancers pushing across betwixt us and our own forces. They were the first troops of this kind I had ever beheld in my life, and now they were cutting off our retreat. Nothing daunted, we faced them manfully. We had none to command us now. Lieutenant-Colonel Hamilton had been killed, and many of the officers killed and wounded. But every man did what he could. Conquer or Die! was the word. When the regiment returned from this charge, the troop to which I belonged did not muster above one or two sound men, unwounded, belonging to the front rank. Indeed, the whole troop did not muster above a dozen; there were upwards of twenty of the front rank killed and others wounded.[5]

The Scots Greys charged into Durutte's 4th Infantry Division. Durutte's division was partially overrun by the allied cavalry charge. About the movement of the 4th Division, Captain Camille Durutte writes:

Upon reaching the heights, General Durutte saw a column of cavalry was advancing on the second division, commanded by General Marcognet; the cavalry charged with great vigour entirely on that division. General Durutte advanced quickly towards this division with his column, but was soon forced to stop to receive the cavalry which was heading towards him. When the cavalry was within musket range, a discharge of musketry from the leading battalions stopped them, and he even believed that some leaders of this column were wounded; 150 riders not knowing how to restrain their horses, came up to his positions.

General Durutte had ordered the artillery of his division was to be established on a hill in front of the guard, whilst they were performing this movement, these horsemen arrived on them, sabred some of the gunners and others took flight. The drivers cut the traces of their horses and fled. The result was that the artillery of the division remained on the battlefield without horses.

After this event, General Durutte formed his division into two columns by brigade: one commanded by General Pégot, and the other by General Brue.

The division of General Marcognet was forced to go to rally behind our line.[6]

We are told that Pégot's brigade lost 300 killed or wounded and 200 captured. The prisoners were placed in the rear of the allied lines in a wood that covered the extreme left of the allied position.[7] It was perhaps now that Augustin Joseph Duquesnoy, commanding 2nd Battalion of the 29th Line, was wounded. He took a sabre cut to the inner thigh close to his groin.[8] In the melee, Sergeant-Major Jean Boijout of the 29th Line was lightly wounded and captured.[9] The same fate befell a fellow sergeant-major, Pierre Simon Joseph Laigle.[10]

Pégot's brigade and the two battalions of the 95th Line were caught in the open and did not or could not form square. Battalion Commander Jacques Bosse of the 95th Regiment of Line narrates:

> If we had formed square, I could have saved my entire battalion, while deployed in this fatal journey. I lost forty men killed or captured. The other battalions of the Division and Corps lost far more. If the attack had been well led and supported by the heavy cavalry, it would have given victory to the French Army.[11]

Battalion Commander Joseph-Marcelin Rulliers, also of the 95th Regiment of Line, notes, albeit in 1856 when his memories of the day have been altered by what he has read and been told later, so this cannot be seen to be a wholly reliable account:

> General Durutte had left behind his Division a regiment with no more than 800 men to serve as support if necessary. This regiment formed in square and successfully repelled the charges of the English cavalry.[12]

The regiment involved was the 85th Regiment of Line. Captain Francois-Claude Chapuis of the 85th writes:

> Established near the battery, with grounded arms, the 85th for several hours, experienced losses so sensitive that my grenadier company had 22 killed or wounded. Seeing these men fall horribly mutilated by the bullets, one might think that the morale of those left standing would be disrupted, but no one is wavering. Beautifully ordered, our soldiers were still at the height of courage and our General and our Colonel gave us fine examples. Also, in this time of sorrow, there were acts of such firmness, one would hardly believe such heroism and such abnegation.[13]

He further reports:

> Following their success, they arrived at the front face of our square, where a lively fire, well aimed, entirely paralysed the élan of the cavalry, which had appeared so great that it was incapable of being stopped. The ground was littered with red coats and grey horses, and our cries of *Vive l'Empereur* proved to them that it would not be easy to beat us. They whirled around us, and everything that our fire spared was soon destroyed by a regiment of our lancers and a regiment of *chasseurs à cheval* that had formed a short distance behind the 85th.[14]

In the centre, the charge carried on through the intervals between the French divisions, attacked the forward lines of the grand battery, and began sabreing the gunners and horses. The Scots Greys did not have everything their own way. In the ensuing melee, the French fought back. Sub-Lieutenant Kopp of the 1st Squadron of Artillery Train writes:

> The 18 June at the affair of Mont Saint Jean, the English cavalry charged my battery. I killed three English and wounded to others. I prevented with my action the enemy taking into their hands a howitzer and a 6-pdr.[15]

Kopp served in 5th Company, 1st Squadron of Artillery Train. The company was attached to 1st Infantry Division.[16] The reserves, the 12-pdrs, do not seem to have been attacked, only the more advanced 6-pdr batteries. General Baron De Salle, commanding the artillery of 1st Corps, writes:

> The infantry, pushed backwards by a great mass of cavalry, was broken. They arrived pell-mell with the enemy on the reserve artillery that could

not fire because they were paralyzed by the fear of killing our own men. I only had time to order a change of front, and to bring right wing back upon the guns placed on the left. I managed to open fire with my reserve of my own corps which was commanded by the battalion commander Saint-Michel, a brave officer full of sang-froid: but the others were meek and are driven along by the general disorder. The rest of the battery was in the middle of this cavalry, and were forced to flee. I mounted my horse, I pushed him to a gallop in the middle of the fray, to try and rally this alarmed multitude at my side, that is to say near the sunken road along which I had managed to arrange my reserve of twelve pounders. But vain efforts! No one listened to me! Moreover, the leaders and soldiers of the artillery and the train fled. I recommenced my fire from Saint-Michel's battery with a new energy: my officers that I had sent to the rear failed to rally a single battery although the charge had been repulsed and that men of honour would have had returned to their position, since no guns and no ammunition caissons had been taken by the enemy: there were only men and horses killed. This failure was serious.[17]

Napoleon's line had been brutally weakened by the Union and Household brigades; for many men in the ranks of the British cavalry, this was their first experience of combat, and instead, exhilarated by their success over the massed ranks of d'Erlon's hapless infantry, the Scots Greys (and no doubt elements from other regiments) charged disastrously onwards. Despite some success in cutting down some French gunners, Ponsonby's Union Brigade carried on the charge further into the French lines. Ponsonby and his staff's efforts were useless in endeavouring to rally their troops. The allied charge had disrupted Napoleon's plans and bought Wellington time to wait for more Prussians to arrive to tip the balance in the allies' favour.

12

Jacquinot's Counterattack

French retribution was swift and merciless. General Jacquinot himself states:

> At the battle of Waterloo, the division of cavalry commanded by the Lieutenant-General; Subervie which comprised the 1st and 2nd Lancers and the 11th Chasseurs was placed under my orders; during the course of the battle, I commanded the A Corps of cavalry composed of this division and that of the 1st Army Corp, which had been earlier placed under my command and was formed by the 3rd and 4th lancers, the 3rd Chasseurs and 7th Hussars.[1]

He notes in a second narration of that day:

> I commanded in 1815 a division of cavalry from the 1st Corps. Several hours after the battle of Waterloo began. The Emperor, via the Major General, ordered me to join to my command, the division of General Subervie. I therefore had two divisions under my orders. The corps mustered 58 squadrons and was composed of the 1st, 2nd, 3rd, 4th lancers, the 3e and 11th Chasseurs and 7th Hussars along with two batteries of horse artillery. The two divisions were supported by a brigade of cuirassiers from the division of Delort and commanded that general officer and totally destroyed the consecutive charges made by the English cavalry commanded by General Ponsonby. The division of Subervie remained under my orders till the end of the battle.[2]

Général de Brigade Gobrecht, who commanded the 3rd and 4th Lancers, remembers:

> With the two regiments of Lancers under my orders we vigorously [*sic*.] charged and totally pushed back the *Gendarmes of the Maison du Roi*[3]

and *Dragons de la Reine*[4] in a movement which disengaged the division of Durutte which was almost totally surrounded and cut up.[5]

As the French cavalry surged forward, the British cavalry had dispersed into small groups of a dozen or so men, attacking isolated groups of French soldiers as they fled or tried to rally. Any order among the British cavalry was lost and made any defensive action against a counter charge impossible. Lieutenant George Gunning of the 1st Royal Dragoons writes:

> General Ponsonby rode up to me by himself and said 'For god's sake, sir, collect your men, and retire on the brigade'. At this moment, the French infantry on our left advanced rapidly and fired a volley of musketry among the scattered cavalry. By this volley General Ponsonby was killed within twenty yards of me. I saw him fall from his horse at the bottom of the hollow way to the left of General Picton's division. The ridiculous story about the general's horse being unmanageable was all farce to please the lovers of the marvellous. I was severely wounded by the same volley of musketry and a few seconds afterwards my horse had his near fore leg hit by a cannon ball. I then made my way into the square of the 28th Regiment of Foot [General Picton's Division] with several other dismounted men, and remained their till evening before I could get a horse and go to the rear. I arrived in Brussels late that night.[6]

Colonel Bro of the 4th Lancers explains what happened to his regiment:

> Our infantry was cut up and dispersed; Drouet Erlon ordered the cavalry to charge. A boggy field did not allow us to operate at ease. I advanced my 4th Lancers.
>
> On the right was a little wood, we could see the English cavalry, who promptly reformed, they threatened to outflank the 3rd Chasseurs. I was at the head of the squadrons, crying 'Come, children, we must reverse this rabble!' The soldiers replied, 'Forward! Long live the Emperor!'
>
> Two minutes later, the attack takes place. Three enemy ranks were pushed in. We savagely attacked the others! the scrummage became frightful. Our horses crushed the bodies of corpses and the cries of the injured arose from all sides. I found myself for a moment to be lost in the gun smoke. When the smoke thinned, I saw British officers around Lt. Verrand, with our eagle.[7] Rallying a few riders, I came to his aid. Fourrier Orban killed with a lance General Ponsonby.[8,9] My sword mowed down three of his captains. Two others escaped.
>
> I returned to the front to save my adjutant. I emptied my second pistol when I suddenly felt my right arm paralysed ... Stunned, I was forced to

take hold of the mane of my horse. I had the strength to say to Major Perrot 'Take command of the regiment!'.[10] General Jacquinot, concurred when he saw the blood flood my clothes, supported me and said, 'Withdraw.' And he went to lead the charge. Major Motet cut my jacket and applied a bandage and lint on my wound, pronouncing: 'This is not fatal, but do not stay here.'[11] The rage in having to leave my squadrons brought tears to my eyes.[12]

In this melee, the 21st Regiment of Line were, we are told by its major, 'destroyed'.[13] When we look at the casualty records for the 21st Line, we see that standing out from the mass of data is that the porte-aigle Sub-Lieutenant Fleury was made prisoner of war and the 3rd porte-aigle was also captured. So, what happened to the eagle? It seems to have been captured by the Inniskilling Dragoons as Trooper Penfold relates:

After we charged, I saw an Eagle which I rode up to, and seized hold of it. The man who bore it would not give it up, and I dragged him along by it for a considerable distance. Then the pole broke about the middle, and I carried off the Eagle. Immediately after that I saw a comrade, Hassard, in difficulties, and, giving the Eagle to a young soldier of the Inniskillings, I went to his aid. The Eagle got dropped and lost.[14]

Therefore, it seems reasonable that the Inniskillings captured and lost an eagle. About this episode, Sergeant Orban of the 4th Lancers records that he was escorting a senior officer who had been made prisoner, and as he looked around, he observed English dragoons coming to the officer's rescue. Before they reached him, Orban observed an eagle under attack; in an instant, he says he killed the officer and rode forward to save the eagle. Orban said that he killed the horse of the dragoon taking the eagle away with a lance thrust to the left shoulder, and then killed the dismounted trooper. He then picked up the eagle and rode to the rear to present it to Colonel Bro.[15]

The rumour about the loss of the eagle prompted the regiment's major to write on 21 June that the regiment, despite being destroyed, did save the eagle. Clearly for him to have to say this in writing to Marshal Soult, rumours must have been rife that the regiment lost its eagle.[16]

Trooper Jean Armand Flotard of the 4th Lancers relate:

One of our soldiers said to our captain, pointing to a regiment of English dragoons against which we would charge: Upon my word, captain, these j ... f .... they have the nerve to wait for us!—Comrades, says Colonel Bro before we conducted our first charge of the day: at this hour I have only been at your head for only one month and I shall know it's an honour, and you will know in a moment whether I am worthy of it. this kind of challenge, delivered to our regiment, was enough to exalt in us fury, the desire to fight. At seven o'clock, at the time of the decisive attack of Blücher, we had three officers, two killed or wounded.[17]

Trooper James Smithies of the 1st Royal Dragoons brigaded with the Greys writes about the tactics of the French lancers as follows:

> We were next ordered to charge a whole regiment of French lancers, who looked if possible, a still uglier enemy than their coated bretheren. The lance was fastened to their boot and when we neared them, they sent it out with all their might; and if the man at which they aimed did not manage to parry the blow, it was all over with him.[18]

This was a tactic the French used elsewhere in the battle. Captain Fortune de Brack of the Light Horse Lancers of the Imperial Guard notes:

> At Waterloo, when we charged the English squares, one of our lancers, not being able to break down the rampart of bayonets which opposed us, stood up in his stirrups and hurled his lance like a dart; it passed through an infantry soldier, whose death would have opened a passage for us, if the gap had not been quickly closed. That was another lance well lost.[19]

In the melee, Captain Denis Gros suffered a gunshot wound to the left leg.[20] Captain Martial Lepage, who had joined the regiment in 1814, suffered at Waterloo a gunshot wound to the left shoulder, as well as a sabre cut to the left thigh and one to the right arm.[21] Lieutenant Francois Aubert was unlucky enough to be bruised by a cannon ball.[22] Squadron Commander Jean Theodore Dudouit was seriously wounded in the battle and was placed on half pay due to his infirmity resulting for his wounds.[23] Sub-Lieutenant Guillaume Dessaux was slightly wounded when his horse was killed under him.[24] Sub-Lieutenant Jean Francois de Saint Romain suffered the same fate.[25] Moving up with the Lancers were the brigaded 3rd Chasseurs. General Bruno states the following:

> I had the honour to serve under the orders of *Général de Division* Jacquinot commanding the 1st Brigade of cavalry, comprising the *3e régiment de chasseurs à cheval* of Colonel de La Woëstine and the 7th Hussars of Marbot.
>
> ... The enemy artillery fired at us and we lost an officer and some chasseurs, some distance behind us was an undulation in the terrain, that would protect us from the enemy's fire, into which we moved.

> The artillery stopped and there was a great silence. Our attention was quickly drawn to our left where there was a great cloud of dust [what happened to the mud? Or does the term refer to the clods of grass and earth kicked up the horse's hooves? Ed], I judged that though still some distance away, it was a charge of enemy cavalry against our infantry. Shortly after the column of cavalry composed of English Dragoon Guards and Belgian Lancers [sic.] attacked the squares, being unable to break the squares they headed directly towards us.
>
> Squadron Commander Pozac[26] commanding the first squadron of the regiment I ordered to charge the flank, and at the same time Colonel La Woëstine with the remaining two squadrons charged the English front.
>
> The charge was executed with the great energy and was entirely successful. The English column was shattered, and to avoid utter destruction, made a turn to the left and retired in great disorder.
>
> The *3e régiment de chasseurs à cheval* had saved Durutte's division from destruction. It was only when that they had already retreated a good distance, that I saw a new charge conducted by the cuirassiers, under the orders of General Milhaud.[27]

The Belgian cavalry mentioned were in fact the Dutch-Belgian cavalry brigade of General de Ghingy. De Ghingy's brigade was moved up along with the English Light Cavalry Brigade of Vandaleur at the request of Prince Saxon-Weimar, who was defending La Haye, Papelotte, and Smohain.

While the 3rd Chasseurs were attacking the allied cavalry, Chapuis of the 85th Line notes that if it was not for the proven courage of Colonel Masson and General Brue, the regiment would have been easily crushed. As Pégot's men fell back, contrary to Durutte but noted by Schmitz and Chapuis, in disorder, the 85th and 95th Regiments of Line Infantry began an offensive movement, and the rump of Pégot's brigade rallied behind the division of General Brue, which formed a 'living redoubt as at Marengo', with reference to the baptism of fire of the 1st Regiment of Grenadiers à Pied of the Imperial Guard. Pégot's division, we are told by Chapuis, was out of action for the remainder of the day.[28] However, Pégot's men were, according to Durutte, in action later in the day.

Losses

3rd Regiment of Lancers

The 'Lanciers du Dauphin' were formed in 26 August 1814 around a cadre of men from the former 3rd Lancers (some 307 men and thirty-eight officers), the 22nd Chausseurs à Cheval (some 367 men and forty-eight officers), and 7th Company 2nd Lancers of the Guard (some seventy-one men with forty-four horses and six officers). The 3rd Lancers on 10 June mustered twenty-seven officers and 379 other ranks. However, of these 379 other ranks, only 288 were mounted.[29]

The regimental muster list reports:[30]

3rd Regiment of Light Horse Lancers						
Squadron	Killed	Deserted	Wounded	POW	Missing	Total
1	2	1	1	8	12	24
2	4	-	-	14	23	41
3	2	-	-	9	18	29
4	1	3	-	20	41	65
Total	9	4	1	51	94	155

The regiment lost 155 men, or 40 per cent of effective strength at Waterloo, leaving 131 men potentially under arms on 19 June. What we do not have is equine losses. It could easily be that the regiment lost over 200 horses, leaving around 100 men in the saddle.

What does missing actually mean? It is reasonable to assume they were men that no one had seen since the battle and their fate was not known. Could it include dead and wounded? We can start to check this data by looking for the men held in POW in England against the regimental muster list. The 3rd Lancers had twenty-four POWs in England returned to France, which included:[31]

MAT No. 124 Aime Gentot, trooper, 2nd Company, 2nd Squadron, recorded POW 18 June

MAT No. 141 Pierre Guillaume, corporal 1st Company, 1st Squadron, recorded missing 18 June

MAT No. 172 Alexandre Joseph Gerradot, trooper 5th Company, 1st Squadron, recorded missing 18 June

MAT No. 237 Augustin Francois Dupa, trumpeter 1st Company, 1st Squadron, recorded deserted 18 June

MAT No. 607 Nicolas Martinet, trooper 3rd Company, 3rd Squadron, recorded missing 18 June

MAT No. 651 Antoine Bourot, 3rd Company, 3rd Squadron, recorded missing 18 June

MAT No. 685 Claud Nicolas Dufourd, trooper 6th Company, 2nd Squadron, recorded POW 18 June

Clearly, men recorded as missing or deserted were in fact POWs. We therefore assume a percentage of the missing were men who had been dismounted and became POWs. Indeed, the regiment records:[32]

MAT No. 336 Francois Richards of 3rd Squadron marked missing
MAT No. 375 trooper Leaonard Vasseur of 4th Squadron reported as POW
MAT No. 575 Nicolas Detrez of 4th Squadron marked missing
MAT No. 658 Antoine Martine of 2nd Squadron marked missing
MAT No. 787 Antoine Rousseau of 3rd Squadron marked missing
MAT No. 860 Adrian Abrhama Dusailly of 4th Squadron, reported as POW
MAT No. 867 Jean Boisseau, reported POW

All made their way back to the regiment on 1 July. Of comment, the regiment had a very high attrition rate of trumpeters lost at Waterloo:[33]

MAT No. 237 Augustin Francois Dupa, 1st Company, 1st Squadron: deserted
MAT No. 399 Nicolas Joseph Papey, 2nd Company, 2nd Squadron: missing
MAT No. 405 Constant Degrincourt, 5th Company, 1st Squadron: missing
MAT No. 423 Ciceron Turber, 8th Company, 4th Squadron: missing
MAT No. 455 Constant Pipart, 2nd Company, 2nd Squadron: missing
MAT No. 535 Secretain Joseph Muguet, 4th Company, 4th Squadron: missing

What made them easy targets? Were they wearing rose uniforms with green facings? Modern high-vis clothing is most effective when it is orange or pink—did their pink uniforms make them highly visible targets? Seemingly so. This helps us not in understanding the action the regiment took part in. We assume they charged with the 4th.

4th Regiment of Lancers

On 1 June 1815, the regiment mustered forty-eight officers and 490 other ranks. However, of the officers, only thirty-one were in the war squadrons, and of the other ranks, only 208 took the field, with just 145 troopers. The regiment left 134 other ranks in barracks. The regiment had a total of 356 horses. Of interest, the regiment had two cadet trumpeters and only six trumpeters in the war squadrons.[34] In terms of the other ranks, 90 per cent had joined in 1813 or later. Of these, 40 per cent had joined in 1814 from other cavalry regiments under the royalist reorganisation. These men in the main were all conscripts of the class of 1813. Overall, the regiment was experienced as the men had at least two years of combat experience. It was not a veteran regiment. The men were aged on average twenty-three. The officers of the regiment had been appointed in the main in April and May 1815, thus had not yet had the chance to build the bonds of trust and loyalty essential in any cohesive formation.

At Waterloo, one officer was promoted on the field for bravery:

Pierre Gabriel Moreau, born 3rd August 1775, admitted to the 12th Dragoons 7th April 1793, passed to the 9th Dragoons in 1799, which became the 4th Lancers in 1811. Successively promoted to 2nd Lieutenant on 27th September 1813. For conspicuous bravery on the field of Waterloo promoted to 1st Lieutenant by General Jacquinot in person.[35]

The regimental muster list reports casualties at Waterloo:[36]

4th Regiment of Light Horse Lancers				
Squadron	Killed	POW	Missing	Total
1	4	14	3	21
2	4	7	10	21
3	1	11	11	23
4	2	11	6	19
Total	11	43	30	84

Thus, Colonel Bro's regiment lost eighty-four men at Waterloo. In addition, twelve men were recorded missing on 20 June and two men were listed missing on 21 June. Presumably, these men were dismounted and left behind during the retreat. The relatively low number of fatalities broadly reflects the record for the 3rd. The largest loss was in horse-flesh and not manpower. Unlike the 3rd, we note three trumpeters, all sent to the rear as dismounted, so clearly, they are not as conspicuous a target.

3rd Regiment of Chassuers

The regiment began the campaign with twenty-nine officers and 336 other ranks; forty-two men were lost at Waterloo, representing a loss of 12 per cent of effective strength.[37]

Squadron	Killed	Wounded	Missing	Total
1	1	2	12	15
2	3	2	8	13
3	-	2	11	13
4	1	-	1	2
Total	4	6	32	42

The loss of forty-two men is far fewer than for the two regiments of Lancers. As Colonel Bruno reports, the regiment only engaged some of the Scots Greys, which the casualty data implies. In total, the three French regiments lost 281 men. Losses for Jacquinot's command were as follows:

1st Cavalry Division	Killed & Died of Wounds	Deserted	Wounded	Wounded & Missing	POW	Missing	Total
3rd Lancers	9	4	1	-	51	94	155
4th Lancers	11	-	-	-	43	30	84
3rd Chasseurs	4	-	6	-	-	32	42
7th Hussars	49	1	-	3	3	-	56
Total	73	5	7	3	97	156	337

The 3rd Lancers bore the brunt of the fighting. The missing and POW are very likely to be dismounted men who 'went home'. Horse losses would be perhaps double, if not treble, those of the men. If the 3rd Lancers lost its casualties in a single episode, it was rendered *'hors de combat'*. Some 155 men lost out of 379 men present represents losses of 40 per cent, easily 60 per cent or more when factoring in equine losses.

13

The Cuirassiers

With Jacqionot's light cavalry committed to the action, and the cavalry melee threatening to engulf the French right, moving up came the cuirassiers as d'Erlon tells us:

> The cuirassiers of General Milhaud that had formed near the main road, near to La Belle Alliance, as well as the Division of Jacquinot that was on our right, charged the English cavalry with such impetuosity that very few of them were able to return to their positions, and the terrain was strewn with men and horses; the 3rd and 4th cavalry corps were particularly distinguished. The troops having rallied in the squares of the 2nd and 4th divisions, order was re-stablished—these divisions did not take a single pace in retreat despite the heavy fire they were under.[1]

General Delort, with his cuirassiers, remembers:

> General Farine at the battle of Waterloo had three horses killed under him, was particularly distinguished in a charge made during that day against the brigade of cavalry of the English Royal Guard commanded by Lord Somerset, and that same cavalry was totally routed by the two brigades of the division, these being the 5th and 10th and 6th and 9th regiment of cuirassiers.[2]

Delort adds more detail, writing decades after the battle:

> The enemy sharpshooters were pushed back on all their points who abandoned their important positions, and the retreating English concentrated their forces on their left, and entire masses were exterminated by the terrible fire of the muskets and artillery. La-Haye-Sainte [*sic.*] was captured by the 1st Corps under the orders of General Reille [*sic.*—d'Erlon]

a great confusion reigned in the middle of their baggage, the convoys of the wounded all of which blocked the road to Brussels. The English General was in ... consternation about the immobility of his troops, the ardour of the French troops announced the total routing of the English Army. At this critical moment, the Duke of Wellington ordered to charge the brigades of Major-Generals Ponsonby and Somerset. The brigade was formed with the 1st and 2nd Life Guards, the Dragoon Guards, and the 1st 2nd and 3rd regiments of English Dragoons who fell with impetuousity [*sic*.] on the division of General Durutte. The division was put to the swords, dispersed they lost an eagle and their artillery.

However the division of Cuirassiers of General Delort was ordered to move forward, to profit from their disorder and push back the English cavalry which covered the plain, success was assured. In a moment the brigade composed of the 6th and 9th regiments led forward with *Maréchal de Camp* Farine, Lieutenant-General Delort and Lieutenant-General Dejean at their head, fell on the English cavalry, they were tumbled back, and the ground was littered with their dead. Two elite English regiments were totally destroyed in this vigorous charge, and due to their low number and disadvantage, the attack was a brilliant success. The curiassiers [*sic*.] lost not a single man, a few were wounded, the captured artillery was re-captured and the infantry promptly rallied.[3]

General Farine, who led the charge, tells us:

The 18th June at Waterloo, I was wounded by a musket ball and I had three horses killed under me; I was at the head of my brigade, and undertook several good charges against the infantry and cavalry. One of these charges was made to save the division of General Durutte from total destruction which had been charged in its flank by the English cavalry, which I scattered onto the plain in total disarray.[4]

In a letter written slightly later, Farine tells us that 'he charged with success against infantry squares and to repulse the cavalry which had put one our divisions into great disorder.'[5] Farine led forward the 5th and 10th Cuirassiers. David Regent writes as follows about the cuirassiers falling on to the Union Brigade:

The Cuirassiers and Polish Lancers [*sic*.] came to the rescue of the infantry; we attacked them right and left, and there was no such thing as mastering them but by downright strength. After some hard fighting they broke up and fled. However, we, the Greys, followed the French too far, and Sir William Ponsonby in trying to bring us back was killed in a ploughed field, to our left, by a troop of Polish Lancers, his horse having become fast in the clay. It was thus following the enemy that we lost our brave Colonel Hamilton: he was a brave man. The Enniskilillens [*sic.*] did all they could to save General Ponsonby, and sixteen of the brave fellow lost their lives in the attempt. I saw Shaw of the Lifeguardsman, the day after the battle: he was frightfully mangled, but had not a mortal wound about him: he died from loss of blood. I came off with three slight sabre wounds. My comrade, Wilson, parried a blow made at me and saved my life, but lost his own.[6]

Moving up after the light cavalry came the 7th and 12th Cuirassiers, as English Sergeant-Major Dickson writes:

You can imagine my astonishment when drawn below, on the very ground we had crossed, appeared at full gallop, a couple of regiments of Cuirassiers on the right, and away to the left a regiment of lancers. I shall never forget the sight. The Cuirassiers in their sparkling steel breastplates and helmets, mounted on strong black horses, with great blue rugs across the croups, were galloping towards me, tearing up the earth as they went, the trumpets blowing wild notes in the midst of discharges of grape and canister shots from the heights. Around me there was one continuous noise of clashing arms, shouting men, neighing and moaning of horses.[7]

General Milhaud's after-action report to Marshal Soult notes:

At the battle of 18th, the 4th Cavalry corps saved the right wing of the Count d'Erlon, and saved many thousands of our infantry and twenty guns from the hands of the English cavalry, which left more than eight hundred dragoons dead on the field of battle and more than one hundred and fifty horses in the hands of our brave cuirassiers.[8]

In the attack and throughout the course of the day, the 5th Cuirassiers lost the following men:[9]

5e Régiment de Cuirassiers					
Squadron	Killed	Deserted	Died of Wounds	POW	TOTAL
1	5	1	-	20	26
2	4	-	-	9	13
3	1	-	-	12	13

4	9	-	1	5	15
Total	19	1	1	46	67

Some twenty-eight men were lost at Ligny: five killed in 1st Squadron, two in 2nd, six in 3rd, and two in 4th. At Waterloo, the 5th Cuirassiers lost a total of two officers killed, one died of wounds, twelve were wounded, and twenty other ranks were killed. Colonel Gobert was wounded. He died of his injuries on 1 February 1816. Also wounded was Captain-Adjutant-Major Jean de Brouville, who suffered a gunshot wound to the left leg. Starting the campaign with 479 men, twenty-eight men were out of action on 16 June, and perhaps sixty to eighty horses, reducing effective strength to 400 men, give or take.[10] Presumably, the 1st and 4th Cuirassier, having been blooded earlier that morning against the King's German Legion and the attacking Household Brigade, were still in the fight to some extent when Farine's men galloped up.

Attacking with the 5th came the 10th. Officers killed in the 10th Cuirassiers at Waterloo were Squadron Commander Dijon and Lieutenant Collin. Furthermore, ten officers were wounded:

> Captains: Francois Louis Guinet with a gunshot to the right leg[11], Magnien
>
> Captain-Adjutant-Major Jean Ferdinand Fere with a gunshot to the kidneys having passed through his cuirass. He had joined the regiment on 6 August 1814. He had served in the Grenadiers à Cheval of the Imperial Guard from 6 July 1806 to 17 February 1811.[12]
>
> Lieutenants: Amand Antoine Scherb who had joined the regiment in 1804. Took two gunshot wounds, one to the chest, one to the left shoulder. He retired from the army with the rank of general[13], Chandebois, Lieutenant Pierre Francois Aubert was wounded with a sabre cut to the head.
>
> 2nd Lieutenants: Seguin, Sub-Lieutenant Hiacynthe Adnet was shot in the neck by a musket ball, Collas, Rousseau.[14]

Casualties for the 10th Cuirassiers at Waterloo were as follows:[15]

10e Régiment de Cuirassiers						
Squadron	Company	Killed	Wounded	POW	Missing	Total
1	1	1	1	2	6	10
	5	2	-	2	6	10
2	2	1	-	1	3	5
	6	-	-	2	1	3

3		1	-	3	7	11
	7	1	-	1	5	7
4	4	-	-	-	6	6
	8	-	-	-	2	2
Total		6	1	11	36	53

On the morning of 10 June 1815, the regiment had thirty-six officers and 327 other ranks. The regiment lost fifty-three men at Waterloo, representing a loss of 16 per cent of effective strength. It is likely three times this number of horses were killed or wounded. Even so, the regiment still had over 300 men on the morning of 19 June.[16]

At one stage in the attack, the 10th clearly got very close to breaking into a square, as General Delort records that Sergeant Aubert of the 10th took a colour from an allied square.[17] For this to have taken place, the 10th must have gotten into the centre of a square where the colours stood. Alas, we do not know which colour was taken by the 10th.

Moving up behind Farine came General Travers leading the 2nd Brigade of 13th Cavalry Division under the orders of General Watier. Michel Ordener, commanding the *1er Régiment de Cuirassiers*, whose father, Michel Ordener, had commanded the *Grenadiers à Cheval* of the Imperial Guard, recounts the campaign as follows:

> June 18, Milhaud's division was placed 300 metres behind the line that formed the corps of D'Erlon to our extreme right, from the castle Frichermont to the farm of La Haye Sainte; points occupied by the English. No sooner was the battle committed than the regiments of D'Erlon fell to Wellington's cannon balls and swords of the dragoons commanded by Ponsonby. Our infantry fall in their hundreds, and the enemy cavalry were cutting them down under the muzzles of our guns which they tried to capture. It was at this stage that the 7th and 12th Cuirassiers fell upon the dragoons of Ponsonby, swept them away and totally destroyed them. They then returned to their initial positions.[18]

To witness the episode, we assume he had pulled back from the fighting to reorganise his regiment. Among the officers killed in the 7th Cuirassiers were Lieutenant Forceville and Sub-Lieutenant Thervais. Squadron Commander Jean Antoine Loup suffered a gunshot to the lower abdomen and had his horse killed under him.[19] Sub-Lieutenant Gervais Hanin suffered a sabre cut to a shoulder.[20] One of the regiment's officers who came away from the field of battle was Major Desmot.[21] Casualties for the other ranks was as follows:[22]

7e Régiment de Cuirassiers

Squadron	Company	Killed	Wounded	POW	Missing	Total
1	1	-	-	-	7	8
	5	1	-	-	3	4
2	2	-	-	-	4	4
	6	1	-	-	10	11
3	3	-	-	-	12	12
	7	-	-	4	4	8
4	4	-	1	-	14	15
	8	1	-	-	8	9
Total		3	1	4	62	70

The regiment began the campaign with twenty-two officers and 158 other ranks and lost seventy other ranks at Waterloo. This represents a loss of 45 per cent of effective strength at Waterloo.[23] Of the wounded men, MAT No. 72 Jean Baptiste Gabrielle Cuenier, who had joined the regiment on 18 March 1807, was wounded with a sabre cut to the right buttock. MAT No. 481 Jean Pierre Leblond, who had joined the regiment on 17 May 1809, and was on the regiment's staff as adjutant-sous-officer, had his horse killed under him.[24]

The regimental history of the 12th states that at Waterloo, eighty-five other ranks were killed, wounded, made POW, or disappeared. The regimental history further records that some 150 had been killed, wounded, or dismounted at Ligny.[25] The regiment had mustered 234 men on 1 June. Losses from the regimental muster list is presented here in full:[26]

12e Régiment de Cuirassiers

	Killed	Wounded	POW	Missing	TOTAL
Total	17	3	24	75	119

Among the missing were no doubt men made POW as twenty-eight men were recorded as POW in England.[27]

Worthy of comment, recorded in Dartmoor Prison, was Sergeant Nicolas Mathieu. The regimental muster list records him as MAT No.

22 Nicolas Mathieu, POW on 25 June 1815. Also, in Dartmoor was Corporal Jean Baptiste Tavernier, recorded in the regiment as MAT No. 91, deserted 25 June 1815. Also, in Dartmoor was MAT No. 345 Leonard Augustin Mathieu, recorded by the regiment as missing 18 June 1815; MAT No. 333 Jean Pierre Roulingue, recorded as missing 18 June 1815; MAT No. 382 Jacques Francois Philippe Joseph Desmulliere, recorded deserted 25 June; MAT No. 345 Leonard Augustin Mathieu Gourbin, recorded missing 18 June; MAT No. 389 Jean Schaffer, recorded POW 18 June 1815; clearly men captured after Waterloo were also packed off to Dartmoor. The regimental muster list records MAT No. 225 Etienne Charlemagne as 'Killed in Action 18 June 1815', but he was recorded in prison in Dartmoor in August 1815—clearly, he must have been wounded rather than killed. Losses in 4th Cavalry Corps were as follows:

		Killed & died of wounds	Deserted	Wounded	POW	Missing	Total
13th Division	1st Cuirassiers[28]	4	7	4	88	5	108
	4th Cuirassiers[29]	9	-	29		54	120
	7th Cuirassiers[30]	3	-	1	4	62	70
	12th Cuirassiers[31]	17	-	3	24	75	119
	5th Coy 1st Horse Artillery[32]	-	-	-	6	-	6
TOTAL		33	7	37	122	236	423
14th Division	5th Cuirassier[33]	20	1	-	46	-	67
	10th Cuirassiers[34]	5	-	1	11	36	53
	6th Cuirassiers[35]	8	-	6		34	48
	9th Cuirassiers[36]	8	-	-	8	50	66
	4th Coy 3rd Horse Artillery[37]	1	-	2	-	-	3
TOTAL		42	1	9	65	120	237
RESUME		54	8	65	187	356	660

These figures are from the entire day's actions, just as those for the allied cavalry. The French lost perhaps 21 per cent effective strength in terms of manpower, half that of the allies who lost approximately 45 per cent of the men were killed wounded or missing at Waterloo. In total, the three French regiments lost 281 men, while the cuirassiers lost 309 men throughout the course of the day, some 590 men overall. In comparison, the Household and Union Brigades lost 991 men, with 1,305 men out of 2,407 out of action.

The 1st Royal Dragoons had eighty-six killed out of 400 men, 107 wounded, and 238 horses killed or wounded, representing losses of 50 per cent. The Scots Greys lost eight officers, four sergeants, seven corporals, one trumpeter, and ninety-five privates killed, and seven officers, seven sergeants, nine corporals, one trumpeter, and seventy-four privates wounded out of 444 all ranks. Further, 183 horses were killed and sixty-seven wounded.

The prisoner escorts would re-join as quickly as possible, broken equipment would be repaired, and dismounted soldiers remounted, so the brigades should have been fielding 1,400 men within a few days of the battle. The French lost perhaps 2,000 men from wounds, being captured or killed from 1st Corps. In addition, some twelve field guns were out of action due to loss of draft horses. Despite crippling losses, the allied cavalry charge had disrupted French plans and crucially bought time for the Prussians to arrive. Before the charge was ordered, Wellington knew the Prussians were coming to his aid.

14

Durutte's Second Attack

Aware of Prussian forces marching to aid Wellington, Durutte knew that controlling the vulnerable right flank was essential.[1] This is what Durutte set out to achieve with the battered remains of his division by sending one body of troops to Papelotte and La Haye and the second towards Smohain and Frichermont along with its adjacent houses and enclosures. These farms had been occupied by a portion of the 2nd Brigade of Perponcher's Division of the troops from the Netherlands since the night before.

The Orange-Nassau Regiment, consisting of two battalions, held Smohain and La Haye, while the farm of Papelotte was occupied by the Light Company of the 3rd Battalion of the 2nd Nassau Regiment. The 3rd and 2nd Battalion of this regiment, with four guns of Captain Byleveld's Dutch-Belgian Battery of Horse Artillery, were posted upon the rear slope, immediately under the brow of the main ridge and a little to the west of the lane leading directly up the slope from the farm of Papelotte.

The 2nd Nassau Regiment, the Orange-Nassau Regiment (28th Netherlands Line), and a volunteer Jägers company formed Prince Bernhard of Saxe-Weimar's 2nd Brigade of the 2nd Netherlands Division. Having fought the French at Quatre Bras, the entire brigade except for the 1st Battalion of the 2nd Nassau Regiment took position on the morning of 18 June in the Papelotte area. The 1st Battalion had marched off to Hougoumont at about 9 a.m. in order to reinforce its garrison of British Guards and Hanoverians. An advanced squadron of General Vivian's 10th Hussars had been stationed at Smohain village earlier in the day. About the deployment of the Nassau troops in this area, Captain Carl Rettburg, commanding the light company of the 2nd Battalion, 3rd Nassau Regiment, notes:

> The 2nd Regiment formed a brigade together with the Orange-Nassau Regiment under the command of Prince Bernhard von Sachsen-Weimar.

During the evening of the 17 June the brigade took its position on the extreme left wing of the line in front of the farms of Papelotte, La Haie and the village of Smohain. The 3rd Battalion commanded by Major Hegmann had the 2nd Battalion of the 2nd Regiment on its right and on its left, slightly farther away, the 1st Battalion of the Orange-Nassau Regiment.[2]

Carl Jacobi, who served at Waterloo in the Lüneburg Light Infantry Battalion, describes the terrain thusly:

There were hedges along the edge of the road on the slope of the height on the left wing that was standing, leading towards Papelotte, which constituted the extreme point of this wing; these hedges could be partly used as cover for the troops in line and partly for cover by the aforementioned Tirailleurs. Beside the thickets hedge ran a path leading from the road to Smohain, which formed a hollow way for quite a distance.[3]

Captain (*Hauptmann*) Friedrich von Jeckeln, Flanqueur Company, 2nd Battalion, 28th Orange-Nassau Regiment, writes:

On the 17th in the evening towards 5 o'clock there was a short cannon engagement, and the day ended with a tremendous downpour which lasted the whole night from the 17th to the 18th. It was the worst night of my life. Without shelter, up to my knees in mud, without food, and the ever-continuous rain. So, it was that the morning of the 18th began. At 9 o'clock the operations of the two armies commenced, and each took up their position and prepared for the forthcoming battle. Soaked to the core and suffering from hunger, as we had had nothing to eat for two days, we moved to the position which had been assigned to us. Our division stood with its right flank close to the road leading to Brussels, and with the left flank close to a village, which was of the utmost importance to both armies, as it served as the point of communication with Blücher's Army. Towards midday on the 18th the bloody battle began, and according to the statements of those present, it was even worse than the battle of Leipzig.[4]

It was vital that these three bastions were held. If the French took the position, any communication between Blücher and Wellington could be compromised. Further, with the French established on the allied left, with as yet three relatively fresh cavalry brigades and all of 6th Corps, Napoleon could roll up Wellington's flank, or at least draw off troops from other sectors, to weaken the centre. A major French presence across the Prussian line of advance would also delay the arrival of the Prussians, by which time Wellington may have been defeated.

The action began when the vedettes of the British 10th Hussars were withdrawn due to advance of the 7th Hussars as they moved off east. Behind came the 13th Regiment of Light Infantry and elements of Durutte's infantry. The 13th Regiment of Light Infantry seemingly pushed back the two Nassau battalions of the 2nd Regiment which were lining the valley road and which began threatening the second line of defences—the Hanoverians of Vincke and Best. Colonel Carl Best in the 4th Hanoverian Brigade observed the first attacks against the allied left:

> A detachment of enemy infantry, composed mostly of light troops (probably from Lieutenant-General Durutte's Division), and attacked our extreme left flank, and attempted to gain possession of Smohain and the farms of Papelotte and La Haie and also the Château of Frischermont; each of these were defended obstinately by the brave Nassau troops. The attack by this detachment was executed by several columns formed into line and was supported by artillery, with the Tirailleurs at the head. I cannot state if it was the enemy's intention to overthrow our left wing, because even though the enemy attacked furiously the division did not appear to be strong enough to achieve this task, despite being vastly superior in number to the Nassau troops.[5]

About the operations on the French right following the repulse of the Union Brigade and allied cavalry, Captain Camille Durutte writes:

> The Corps commanded by General Lobau placed its self behind the division of General Durutte who was forced to send sharpshooters out and face the enemy troops which threatened to outflank his right flank. He soon felt the need to send one or two battalions to Frischermont.[6]

We now turn our attention to the action around this fortified château.

Frichermont

Historian Pierre de Witt notes that Château Frichermont is first mentioned in 1250 in a document that concerns the donation of 1.75 hectares of land to Awywiers Abbey. The château as it stood in 1815 probably dated from the mid-sixteenth century. The buildings, comprising the château and a farm, formed in 1815 an irregular rectangular of about 80 × 50 m around a large courtyard. In its southwest corner was a huge barn.[7] The complex was dominated by a massive square tower, which based on contemporary engravings had only narrow lancet-type windows; this is no doubt made ideal places to fire from. This tower was situated in the northeast corner of the complex. The dilapidated state of the upper part of the tower forced the owner to demolish it in 1830, and the remaining farm complex was demolished in 1859. The ruins can still be found today, although they are heavily overgrown. On its north side the complex was bordered by a garden and a park. The whole complex was surrounded by high trees which formed a small, triangular wood. The château was garrisoned by the 28th Orange-Nassau Regiment. A member of the regiment, Sergeant Johann Heinrich Doring, writes:

> Our battalion was posted for several hours on the left wing of the plateau, at the farm of Frischermont, which was surrounded by a wall 3 to 4 feet high. We were able to defend this fairly important position for quite some time against the attacks of a regiment of Voltigeurs. They attempted several times to force the wall, each time with no success, until they were reinforced by the arrival of a corps of some 4,000 men. We then had to retire from this position in great haste and we continued our defence further back at the hamlet.... for us this was the day's most critical and dangerous moment as the French moved against us with ever more powerful columns. We were separated from the enemy by no more than half musket shot range. Due to the huge clouds of powder smoke which was blown into our faces by the wind, we could only discern the enemy from the flashes of his muskets. The turmoil became more general by the minute, and there could be no thought of some form of order. Without interruption, we loaded and fired into the enemy's ranks: there was no use in aiming at a particular target. As the enemy was forcefully pushing forward, gaining reinforcements all the time, we could have hardly withstood his attack much longer. Wellington moreover had pulled many regiments to his faltering centre. It was at this critical and decisive moment that the vanguard of Bülow's Corps descended.[8]

The fighting for the château of Frichermont was, we assume, bitter and conducted at close range. The sunken lanes, numerous hedges, and wooded terrain was ideal cover for the attacking and defending forces, especially for voltigeurs to operate detached from their parent regiment in the hollow ways and thickets. The voltigeurs were either the men Durutte ordered forward as sharpshooters, or more likely the 13th Light Infantry, and it is Durutte's troops (the corps mentioned by Doring), with the ever-larger columns he comments on being, no doubt, Lobau and 6th Corps. Captain Eberhard of the Orange-Nassau Regiment recalls:

During the night of the 17th to 18th, one of our companies occupied a village [Smohain] located in front of the battalion. Defending the village and maintain contact with the localities left and right was the battalions objective.

Our lack of ammunition was barely alleviated by cartridges being obtained from the Duchy of Nassau regiments. But before these supplies arrived, the battalion was already facing the enemy and his tirailleurs were engaged with our skirmishers. At first, holding the village seemed not to be overly difficult. But when in the afternoon, the French right wing started to press hard on our left wing, in support of his operations in the centre, our lone company was not able to withstand his attack's. It had to be reinforced first with the grenadier company, and then with No. 1 and eventually with part of No. 2 Company. The battalion nevertheless held onto the village.[9]

So desperate was the fighting that ammunition became a major worry for the defending troops. This led to an improvised means of obtaining more cartridges as Friedrich May, a former drummer with the 1st Battalion, 28th Orange-Nassau Regiment, explains for us:

As early as at 3 o'clock we realised that the ammunition was in very short supply, and we could not use the ammunition from the 2nd Battalion, because they have had French rifles and were using a different calibre. Therefore, I removed all of my leather accoutrements and ran back through the line of fire to the British troops, from whom I received sufficient cartridges to fill my haversack. Having returned to the battalion and distributed the cartridges, I ran back a second time, but on the way back I was struck just beneath the right hip by a spent musket ball (which I later found in my underwear). But this did not prevent me from returning a third time. However, when I returned on this occasion with my haversack full of cartridges I met Prince Sachsen-Weimar, and he asked me how many times I had been to collect ammunition in this manner, and then asked how many cartridges a haversack can hold. My having answered, he then told me that I would not have to return for more, because the men had enough cartridges, but that he would remember me. I put my leather accoutrements back on and picked up my drum. Now we were face to face with the French Guards, who received us with the utmost calmest, which forced us to retire a short distance. The Prince arrived along with Lieutenant Rath, and he ordered us not to retired a single step further. When I heard this I went to the front, and without having received any orders I beat the pas de charge, whereupon my comrades cried: 'Follow the little one, do not to leave him alone!' Under the heaviest fire imaginable, we advanced.

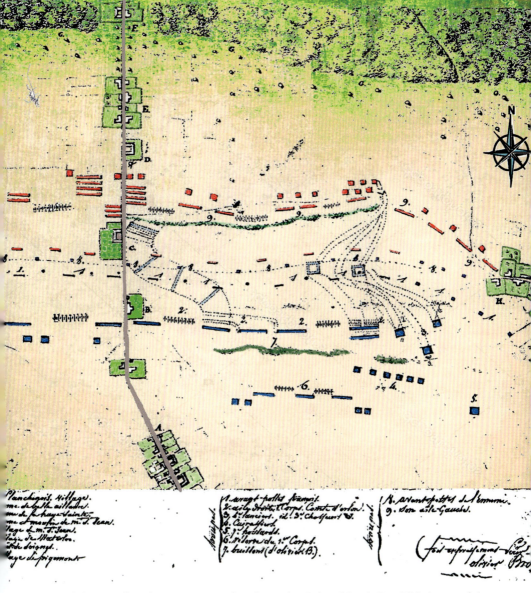

Map of the French right wing at Waterloo drawn by Colonel Louis Bro. This is one of the earliest depictions of the battlefield and can be found in the *Archives Nationales* in Paris. The map shows in great detail the movement of 1st Corps as Bro understood them to have been. He also shows numerous gun lines rather than a single mass battery. Of interest to us is that he shows elements of 1st Corps forming square to repel the allied cavalry.

Four views of the farm in La Haie Sainte, the key to the allied position. It was fought over throughout the day of 18 June and was eventually captured by the French towards 4 p.m.

Almost contemporary view looking towards Plancenoit and Papalotte. This is where the left wing of Wellington's army stood, and it was up the gentle slope that the French 1st Corps attacked. Here too was the charge of the Union Brigade.

Looking from the crossroads north of La Haie Sainte, which can be seen in the centre mid-ground. The depth of the banks either side of the Brussels road here is clearly evident, as well as the depth of the sunken road that heads off to join the Nivelles road to the right of the image. The 1st Life Guards had to negotiate this major obstacle before they could charge. Many writers on the battle forget two major obstacles: the abates blocking the Brussels road by La Haie Sainte and the sunken roads. It was no easy task for cavalry to traverse this ground.

Looking towards La Belle Alliance, middle foreground, and La Haie Sainte. This view from Wellington's right shows the French positions taken up on the mid-morning of 18 June. The great chasm beyond La Belle Alliance is where the Brussels road is sunken into the surrounding landscape. This major obstacle caused problems for the retreating French on the night of 18 June. One can also see the excellent field of view from Wellington's position and how the allied troops had chance to prepare themselves before the onslaught of the French cavalry charging up the slope. It was here too that the infantry of the Imperial Guard made the last attack at Waterloo to try and tip the battle in favour of the French.

Looking to the woods of Hougoumont, up this slope charged the French cavalry for four hours of attrition. The steepness of the slope is apparent in this view. The scene today is greatly changed as the allied ridge was dug away to make the lion mound, greatly altering the topography of the battlefield. The Prussian infantry steamrollered through the French right wing at Plancenoit and threatened the French army in the rear around 8 p.m. on 18 June. This attack spread panic and alarm through the French army, and was the beginning of the end for Napoleon. (*D. Troiani*)

The chateau of Papelotte, a key location in the fighting on the French right wing. (© D. Timmermans napoleon-monuments.eu)

Opposite above: Panoramic view of the approaches to the farm of Papelotte. This is where Durutte deployed the 85th and 95th Regiments of Line. (© D. Timmermans napoleon-monuments.eu)

Opposite middle: Panoramic view of the terrain around the farm of Papelotte. The terrain in 1815 was more heavily wooded than now, and its undulating nature provided ample scope for defence by the French. (© D. Timmermans napoleon-monuments.eu)

Opposite middle: The approach to Papelotte and La Haye from the Prussian line of attack. The field of Waterloo and Plancenoit are totally obscured by the ridge of high ground on which the two farms were built. (© D. Timmermans napoleon-monuments.eu)

Opposite below: The approach to the farm of La Haye, left of centre, with Papelotte to the right. The ground drops away beyond both farms towards Plancenoit. It made the ridge line an obvious line of defence. The woods around La Haye were present in 1815 and afforded cover to both the French and attacking Prussians. (© D. Timmermans napoleon-monuments.eu)

Above: The farm of La Haye. The farm was attacked several times by General Durutte during the day of 18 June. It is little changed from the time of the battle. (© *D. Timmermans napoleon-monuments.eu*)

Below: Looking south from Wellington's left flank. It was over this terrain that General d'Erlon attacked on the afternoon of 16 June. The ridge of high ground in the background provided an excellent defensive position for the French. The building in the centre of the image is Frichermont; centre left are La Haye and Papelotte. The hollow in centre ground is likely to be the place where the Scots Greys attacked the French infantry. The hollow ground is wet, even in high summer. The land around it all drains into this space. If General Ponsonby was killed on his horse trapped in mud, it is likely to have been here. The fields in this part of the battlefield have seen extensive work to improve drainage; even so, the hollow is still wet and muddy. (© D. Timmermans napoleon-monuments.eu)

Frichermont seen from the crossroads, the centre of Wellington's position.
(© *D. Timmermans napoleon-monuments.eu*)

Panoramic shot of Plancenoit. The steeply undulating terrain of the village is notable in this shot. (© *D. Timmermans napoleon-monuments.eu*)

Panoramic shot of the farm at Plancenoit. The farm buildings are unchanged since the battle and witnessed the bitter fighting on the streets of the village. (© *D. Timmermans napoleon-monuments.eu*)

Panoramic shot of Plancenoit. The buildings on the south side of the village, clustered around the church, are where the Old Guard led by General Pelet charged to retake the village from the Prussians. (© *D. Timmermans napoleon-monuments.eu*)

Looking north-east from Papelotte. The farm of La Haye is on the right of the image. (© *D. Timmermans napoleon-monuments.eu*)

The terrain occupied by the French right wing, the scene of bloody fighting on 18 June. (© *D. Timmermans napoleon-monuments.eu*)

Looking north towards the crossroads. La Haie Sainte is in the centre background. Across the terrain to the left of the image is where the Old Guard advanced supported by General Pegot's brigade from 4th Infantry Division and elements from 2nd Corps. (© D. Timmermans napoleon-monuments.eu)

Papelotte farm is remarkably unchanged since the battle. It is now used as a riding centre. The cupola over the main gate was built in the years after Waterloo.

The road that passes the site of the château of Frichermont is little changed since the battle. It is a deeply sunken road in the midst of woodland. It is through this thick cover that the French attacked the château, and through which the Prussians had to force passage at the close of Waterloo.

Across this landscape is where General Durutte led the men of his 4th Division to attack the farms of Papelotte and La Haye.

It is up this road, which is deeply sunken in many places below the level of the surrounding fields, that Durutte's men stormed to attack the farm of La Haye.

Looking south from Papelotte towards Plancenoit, standing midway between the two places. Even halfway across the French right wing, only the top of the church spire can be seen on the horizon. This ridge line totally obscures the village. The nature of the terrain clearly broke the French right wing into three distinct sectors, viz.,: around Papelotte and La Haye, in the valley between Frichermont and Plancenoit, and Plancenoit itself. It is in this valley that Lobau deployed his men.

Above: The church in Plancenoit was virtually destroyed in the fighting on 18 June. The church was rebuilt in 1816–1817 using much of the remaining masonry. It was this wall around the cemetery that the Young Guard was drawn up, the wall providing a handy firing step and cover.

Left: The church seen from the main street of the village.

The steeply sloping ground in front of the church, which is not evident on many maps, is clearly visible. It is evidence how the church and farm to the left of the image became redoubts for the French. Defence of the western side of the village was almost impossible due to the nature of the terrain. Once the church had fallen into Prussian hands, the village became an untenable position.

Looking north-west across the French right wing towards the French left, with lion mound in the centre of the image.

Le Caillou farm, Napoleon's last headquarters. It houses a small museum to commemorate this fact.

Here in 1815 stood the artillery of 1st Corps which bombarded the allied lines before General d'Erlon led his 1st Corps to the attack.

What remains today of the forest of Soignes, a very isolated patch of woodland north of the convent of Frichermont.

Watercolour of Plancenoit made in 1816–1817. It shows how close the woods came to the eastern side of the village.

A nineteenth-century imagining of the fighting in Plancenoit.

Papelotte farm in a watercolour painted in 1815–1816. It shows how damaged the farm was during the fighting on the eventful day of 18 June 1815.

The château of Frichermont. The farm had existed here since 1250. The enclosed nature of the roads around the château and the heavily wooded nature of the approach to the place is clearly in evidence in this lithograph published in 1817.

A rare photograph of the farm complex at Frichermont. All the buildings are now demolished. The buildings are worth comparing to the lithograph of 1817. The central building in both images is the same, seen from different angles. The gable of the roof to the left of the 1817 lithograph is the large barn in the left of the photograph. The large tower in the 1817 lithograph would have been to the right of the image. The complex was said to be demolished in 1859; if so, this image must date to just before this event.

A rare photograph of the farm taken between 1875 and 1880, published in 1880. The tower over the entrance way was added after the battle.

The Prussian approach area as seen from the French perspective and viewed from behind the French front line at what is called 'Napoleon's Observation Post' close to La Belle Alliance. The wood at upper left is the Frichermont wood; the blimp-shaped wood is technically part of the Frichermont wood and originally ran all the way (or almost all the way) across to the wood on the right. The Prussians debouched onto the battlefield approximately where the smaller clumps of trees are in the centre foreground.

Taken from beside the Prussian memorial above Plancenoit. The red roofs belong to the farm behind which the Prussians entered the village and arrived at the back of the church. Just out of shot (upper right) is the farm that was at the centre of Lobau's line in his final position before the Prussians outflanked him at the other end and took the village. This is, therefore, the view along the French line in its final position which is just 370 m in length.

This is the Prussian approach to Plancenoit. The wood (upper left) is Frichermont; the taller wood is the blimp which went almost right across to the right. Lob was approximately where the two brown fields meet halfway up the picture. The woodland hid the concentrating Prussians until they debouched on the skyline. The distance from the skyline to this point is 1,200 m and the skyline is about 8 m higher.

This is the view of Plancenoit that the Prussians would have had as they advanced towards the right-hand end of Lobau's last position (the white-walled farm with the red roof). The Prussian attack flowed around and through this farm. The church is clearly visible. The distance to the farm in this picture is 230 m.

Taken about 50 m from Plancenoit farm. The Prussian memorial is in the trees behind the farm. This is Lobau's last line of defence.

This is close to the farm looking back up the Prussian approach 1,500 m away.

The rear of the farm showing the back of the church 160 m away.

The back of the church (cluttered with vehicles) from where the lane beside the farm debouches into the place behind the church. As the French were well entrenched behind the graveyard wall (behind the orange lorry) and the Prussians were coming out of a one-vehicle-wide lane, this place would have become a killing zone.

This is the same view as the previous image but turned 180 degrees. It shows the narrow lane down which the Prussians entered the village.

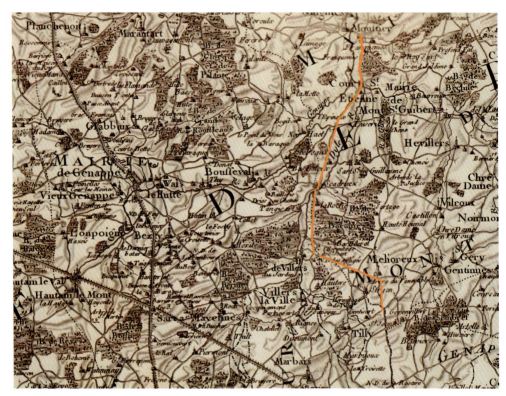

Map showing General Domon's line of march to Moustier undertaken on 17 June from the field of Ligny.

The church and green at Moustier. Domon arrived here late on 17 June, where he encountered Prussian troops marching to Wavre. Outnumbered and lacking infantry, Domon headed to the field of Waterloo. His intelligence report was passed to Grouchy over twelve hours later, by which time it was of no use to the marshal.

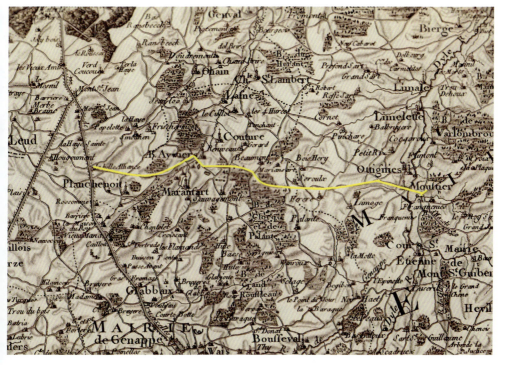

Domon's line of march to the field of Waterloo.

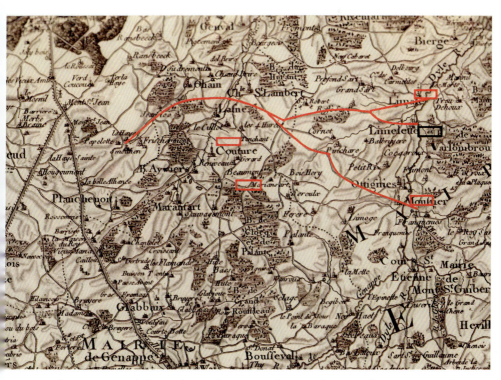

Marbot's supposed line of march to Limale, Limalette, and Moustier, and troop deployments of the 7th Hussars at Couture and Beaumont.

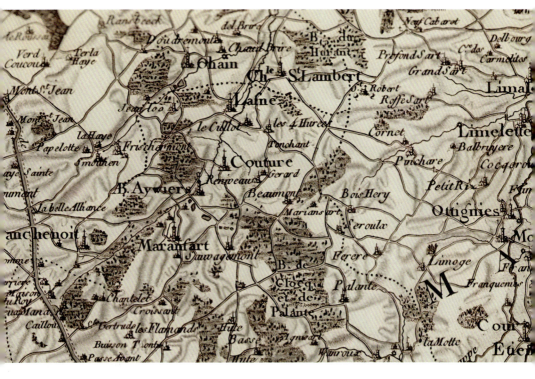

The map shows locations described in the text, notably Lasne, Couture, Saint-Lambert, Maransart, and Moustier.

The village of Couture, where Marbot left a squadron early on 18 June to guard against the Prussians, is ideally situated for defence. Yet Marbot initially had no infantry support until the arrival of the 13th Light Infantry. The village has changed little since the battle.

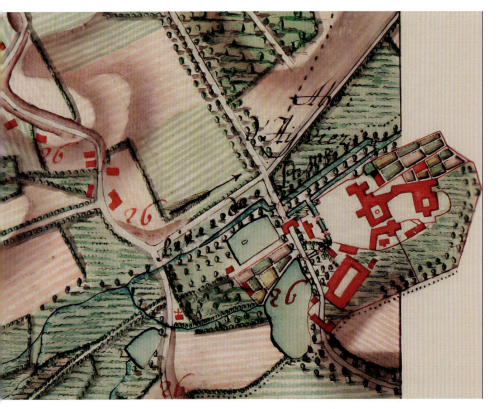

Aywiers Abbey was a Cistercian monastery. It is now demolished and replaced by a fine country château and riverside gardens. Some monastic buildings still linger. This ground plan from 1776 gives us a good idea of the scale of the complex.

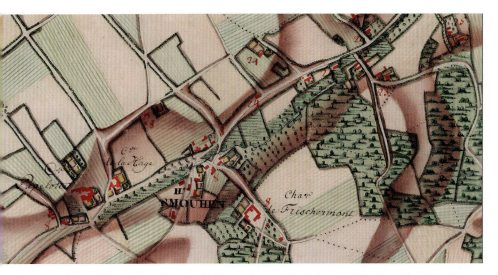

Map of the village of Smohain, which was key to the defence of the French right wing.

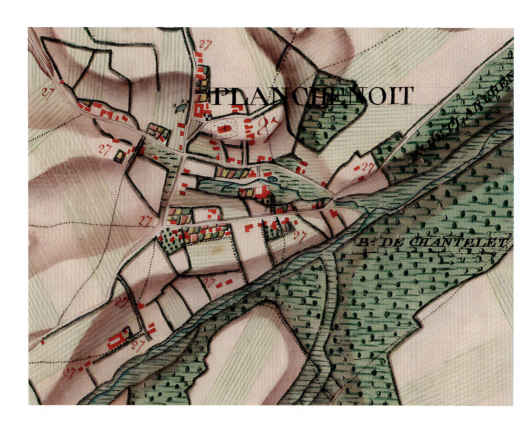

Above: Plancenoit village at the time of the battle, laid out in a map from 1776.

Left: Comte d'Erlon in later life. His command abilities during the 100-day campaign led to the failure of the Battle of Waterloo.

The reserves followed and the French subsequently retired. During this attack, I received a ball in the neck and collapsed. From this moment on I was unconscious for almost half an hour, and recall nothing which transpired.[10]

Ammunition and the lack of it was also a concern for Emil Bergmann. A report, dated 3 January 1816, from Captain (*Hauptmann*) Emil Bergmann, officer commanding the Nassau Jäger Volunteers, describes his role in the defence of the château and the major problems he had with ammunition supply:

Towards evening our brigade was ordered to deploy in the battle line. I believed that we would be engaged with the enemy's advance guard, and so I gave the order to those Jägers with ammunition to advance, while those Jägers without ammunition retired with 1st Lieutenant von Bierbrauer. I had been placed in an awkward position; I understood perfectly well that this decision was not entirely acceptable, but I moved with 2nd Lieutenant Schnabelius and between 10 and 12 Jägers to a position close to Frischermont [*sic*.], not far from the company commanded by Captain Bartmann of our regiment. Because of all I had witnessed I wanted to participate, but I was concerned that the fact I had ordered the Jägers to retire due to lack of ammunition would be doubted by those in authority. It was in this position, close to Frischermont, that I took part in the battle on the 18th, as skirmishers under the command of Lieutenant-Colonel von Dressel, and because of this behaviour, which was observed by the senior commanders, I received the Military Order of King Wilhelm.[11]

Johann Jost Holighausen, a former private with the 1st Battalion, 28th Orange-Nassau Regiment, writes:

It must have been towards 4 o'clock when we arrived at Waterloo; that same evening there was a terrible thunderstorm and the ground was turned to quagmire; we remained in our camp until the early morning of 18th June, when the enemy came so close that I thought—like so many of my comrades—that God needed to be with me and with us all. Fortunately, this happened. That morning Prince von Sachsen-Weimar came to us and told us to form square; it was thus ordered how we should fight. Shortly thereafter I once again became afraid. An advance guard was to be formed from the 3rd Company. Volunteers were called for, but no men stepped forward. Therefore, 10 sub-divisions were separated from the right wing, including myself. The cannonade shocked me.

I thought my God, what will become of me; we were then led into battle. I thought to myself, Lord, God, give me strength, help me to fight, so that I might receive the crown some day; and this happened, thank God, for when the battle was over we had been victorious with the help of the Lord Almighty. It was towards 4 o'clock in the afternoon when we heard Dutch Music, the Lord's Music.[12]

Johann Philipp Pinstock, Flanqueur Company, 1st Battalion, 28th Orange-Nassau Regiment, writes to his parents, brothers, and sisters in Eisemroth on 22 July 1815 recalling the events of Waterloo:

We held firm against the French from the 15th until 10 o'clock on the morning of the 17th, whereupon we had to retreat for 2 hours to Waterloo, because we had not received any assistance. In the evening, we had a position in front of the enemy once more. At 9 o'clock on the morning of the 18th our Army had assembled. Then began a battle which was terrible, and the cannon fire and musketry lasted until the evening.[13]

The fighting for Frichermont spilled out to neighbouring farms.

Papelotte and La Haye

The farm at Papelotte had been in existence since 1673, if not earlier, and in 1815 it was inhabited by Melchior Mathieu, who—according to the local tradition—did not leave the farm during the battle. As the farm was for a part damaged by fire, it was being restored not long after the battle. The farm was built around the sides of a rectangular enclosure. The north side of the farm was formed by the huge barn. Stables formed its east part as well as a part on the south side. Here the house of the farm could be found. Near the house was a well like the one which could be found at Le Caillou and the inn of La Belle Alliance. Apart from the fact that the old buildings have been reconstructed, some have been added after 1815. The wall on the west side has been expanded with stables and a large vaulted main entrance gate. Later, probably in 1860, this main gate was crowned with a small lantern-style tower.[14]

From the south side of the complex, the ground slopes steeply away to a narrow road. The networks of road present in 2023 is virtually unchanged since 1815, as are the sunken lanes, boarded by thick hedges. However, the approach to the farm is concealed by a low ridge which separates the farm complex, La Haye and Marache from the valley that slopes towards Plancenoit. It means that the French could use this ridge line as an excellent defensive position in case of Prussian troops emerging from the direction of Lasne. It also meant the French could move up troops without being immediately spotted by the allied garrison here. About the farm complex here at Papelotte, Carl Rettburg notes that 'The farm of Papelotte formed a square (quadrangle) built of stone and was surrounded by hollow ways and hedges; it was very well suited to a successful defence.'[15]

Less than 200 metres due east of Papelotte is the farm of La Haye. Pierre de Witt notes that the farm of La Haye dated from 1744. The buildings formed a rectangle, with a garden on the north side and one on the south, surrounded by a low wall which was covered in bushes. A gateway led into a barn from which access to the inner courtyard could be gained. There was also a small door leading from one of the gardens to the courtyard.[16] The farms were garrisoned by the 2nd and 3rd Battalions of the 2nd Nassau Regiment. Captain Inglby Royal Horse Artillery writes: 'Some Nassau troops were a little in advance, occupying the hedge rows in our front, and near the village of Papelotte, supported by the first of three or four guns.'[17]

General Baron August von Kruse writes as follows about the Nassau troops at Papelotte and La Haye for the 2nd Nassau Regiment:

> Towards 11 o'clock in the morning the 2nd and 3rd Battalions of the regiment moved into the line of battle. On their right stood Hanoverians, and on their left the 1st Battalion of the Orange-Nassau Regiment. Behind them was a column of light cavalry of the King's German Legion. The Flanqueur Company from the 3rd Battalion of the 2nd Nassau Regiment occupied Papelotte. Between midday and 1 o'clock an overwhelming mass of Tirailleurs forced this company to retire, and so Captain Rettburg, the company commander, was reinforced by a further four companies. With these he was able to recapture Papelotte, and to hold it until the end of the battle, despite several attacks by the enemy Tirailleurs. To attack the enemy in their position was not possible from Papelotte, as they were supported by artillery, whereas the Nassau troops were unsupported.[18]

These guns could well be the 12-pdrs that General d'Erlon sent over to General Durutte in the early afternoon. Durutte's divisional artillery had been caught by the Scots Greys earlier in the day, robbing the division of much needed artillery support.

Captain Reichenau of the 2nd Battalion, 2nd Nassau Regiment, writes:

> The 2nd and 3rd battalions of our regiment were stationed of the left wing of the English Army under orders to occupy a small village, called La Haie Sainte if I am not mistaken. Towards evening our entire battalion was posted there as skirmishers.[19]

About the fighting in this sector, Captain Carl Rettburg, commanding the light company of the 2nd Battalion, 3rd Nassau Regiment, notes:

> Between 11 and 12 o'clock in the morning the enemy artillery batteries deployed opposite our position along with their ammunition wagons. One of the first cannon shots injured Major Hegmann and Captain Frensdorf succeeded to the command.
>
> Between 12 and 1 o'clock the line of enemy artillery advanced towards Papelotte. Prince von Sachsen-Weimar sent me and my company, the 3rd Flanker, to confront them. Shortly thereafter, a detachment from the Orange-Nassau Regiment occupied the villages of Smohain and La Haie and I established communicated with this detachment. The farm of Papelotte formed a square [quadrangle] built of stone and was surrounded by hollow ways and hedges; it was very well suited to a successful defence. I succeeded in driving the enemy artillery back to the furthest hedge at the end of the grass valley, which separated our position from the enemy's, and I was able to occupy several small houses there.'[20]

In this account, Rettburg implies the French attacked in open order in waves of skirmishers. He also alludes to the fact he withdrew from Papelotte, as he had to move his line forward to reach Papelotte. The implication is he was either towards the Ohain road or La Haye. He also comments that Smohain and La Haye had fallen into French hands, leaving, we assume, only Frichermont in Nassau hands. Perhaps Papelotte was still garrisoned, but with the outbuildings being occupied by the French. A number of French writers, like Durutte, who were eyewitnesses to the event that day, state that La Haye and Smohain had indeed been taken by the French. Major Pierre Francois Tissot, officer commander the 92nd Regiment of Line Infantry, part of 2nd Corps, part of General Foy's 9th Infantry Brigade, notes 'the Count d'Erlon had seized the farms of La Haie and Papelotte'.[21]

This appears to corroborate what Rettburg says. Captain Carl Friedrich Frensdorf noted in a report dated Bussey 10 August 1815, concerning the part played by the 3rd Battalion, 2nd Nassau Regiment, during 16, 17, and 18 June 1815:

> On the 18th, towards half past eleven in the morning enemy infantry columns, supported by numerous artillery that fired at the 3rd Battalion, which at this moment was formed in line, showed themselves opposite the village. The second shot killed Major Hegmann and I, the undersigned, took command. I was ordered to form square because of an approaching cavalry column, which, however, was repulsed by our artillery fire. This is why their attack was unsuccessful; the enemy now tried to take possession of the village. I

ordered the flank Coy under command Capt. von Rettburg to the hedges and sunken lanes leading to the village, because of the growing numbers of enemy Tirailleurs, and due to the heavy losses sustained by his company I had to send the 12th, 11th and 10th Companies forward, one at a time, to augment this force, while at the same time, the 9th Company of Grenadiers maintained their ground under a continuous and heavy artillery fire, in a manner equal to that of skirmishing comrades under Capt. von Rettberg's command. The repeated efforts of the enemy to occupy the village were in vain, despite their endeavours, and they were thrown back each time with heavy losses. However, the various attacks resulted in the loss of our Colours.

With the arrival of evening the Prussians approached on our left wing. Some of the skirmishers from our battalion, not being informed of this arrival, considered them hostile, and rounds were exchanged, this, however was stopped immediately, when the error had been noticed.[22]

A few more details on the action can be found in a letter by Colonel (*Oberst*) Johann Friedrich Sattler, a former major with the 1st Battalion, 2nd Nassau Regiment:

On the 18th June at nine o'clock a Staff officer from the Duke of Wellington ordered the 1st Battalion of the regiment to move to the farm of Hougoumont, which was situated on the extreme right wing of the Army. The battalion, under the command of Captain Büsgen, immediately marched to this new destination, and defended the farmstead during the course of the battle, despite the fact that the buildings were totally destroyed by the enemy artillery fire. I advanced with the 2nd and 3rd Battalions some hundred paces, and at eleven o'clock, I moved from the position we had held during the night, opposite to the two farms of La Haie and Papelotte, and when I saw that an enemy infantry column had started to march to this side, I occupied the two with detachments of Tirailleurs, and strong reserves from both battalions. All of the attacks which the enemy made against these two farms during the day were steadfastly repulsed. The remainder of the two battalions, which had stayed in the line, were continuously shot at by the enemy artillery. Sattler.[23]

Losses

Can any more light be shed on the action here? Looking at the casualty data reveals some interesting points of comment.

8th Regiment of Line

Losses for the battalion from the regiment's muster role reveals the following losses (the following tables represent the formation of the regiment when in the field, when in line, with the Grenadier Company on the extreme right, but with probably the voltigeurs in open order, screening the battalion):[24]

	Volt Coy	4e Coy	3e Coy	2e Coy	1er Coy	Gren Coy.
Presumed POW	19	19	11	19	25	2
Presumed POW Wounded	-	-	1	2	2	1
Evacuated as Wounded	1	1	-	-	-	1
Total	20	20	12	21	28	4

The minimal losses of the Grenadier company are not explainable. Losses for the 2nd Battalion from the regiment's muster role reveals the following losses:

	Volt Coy	4e Coy	3e Coy	2e Coy	1er Coy	Gren Coy.
Presumed POW	15	19	14	12	19	10
Presumed POW Wounded	8	7	-	-	2	3
Total	23	26	14	12	21	13

The highest losses are with the 1er, 3e, and 4e Companies, suggesting an attack from both flanks. Losses for the 3rd Battalion were as follows:

	Volt Coy	4e Coy	3e Coy	2e Coy	1er Coy	Gren Coy.
Presumed POW	21	14	17	20	22	9
Presumed POW Wounded	-	3	3	-	3	3
Total	21	17	20	20	25	12

Discounting the Grenadier Company, the highest losses were the 1e, 2e, and Voltigeur Companies. The losses being far lower than the 1st and 2nd Battalions suggest parts of the battalion formed square. Total losses follow:

8th Regiment of Line			
	Wounded	Wounded & POW	POW
1st Battalion	3	6	105
2nd Battalion	-	20	89
3rd Battalion	-	12	103
Total	3	38	297

The regiment lost 338 other ranks at Waterloo. On 10 June 1815, the regiment had mustered 943 other ranks. The regiment lost 35 per cent of its men at Waterloo.

29th Regiment of Line
Losses for the 1st Battalion were as follows:[25]

	Volt Coy	4e Coy	3e Coy	2e Coy	1er Coy	Gren Coy.
Presumed POW	36	16	22	10	24	12
Killed	-	2	-	1	-	2
Presumed POW Wounded	-	-	-	-	1	-
Evacuated as Wounded	3	1	2	5	1	8
Total	39	19	24	16	26	22

Details of wounds inflicted on the other ranks of the battalion are below:

Grenadier Company
MAT No. 144 Charles Guillard, born 1791, admitted to the regiment on 13 September 1811, wounded with gunshot to left leg.

MAT No. 319 Barthelemi Latour, born 1793, admitted to the regiment on 17 December 1812, wounded with sabre cuts to both arms.

MAT No. 670 Gabriel Lavagne, born 1792, admitted to the regiment on 15 May 1813, wounded with a sabre cut to the left hand.

MAT No. 705 Francois Antoine Delprat, born 1793, admitted to the regiment on 23 May 1813, wounded with a sabre cut to the right hand.

MAT No. 706 Jean Pierre Constance Selmes, born 1787, admitted to the regiment on 23 May 1813, wounded with a gunshot, died of wounds on 21 July 1815.

MAT No. 1632 Francois Jublanc, born 1782, admitted to the regiment in 1804, wounded with a gunshot to the right hand.

2nd Company
MAT No. 399 Jean Verge, born 1793, admitted to the regiment on 11 March 1813, wounded with a sabre cut to the left hand.

Voltigeur Company
MAT No. 712 Francois Laurent, born 1789, admitted to the regiment on 23 May 1813, wounded with a gunshot to the right hand.

MAT No. 758 Laurent Mounede, born 1793, admitted to the regiment on 12 June 1813, wounded with sabre cut to the right hand.

MAT No. 1332 Vital Ade, born 1793, admitted to the regiment on 10 December 1812, wounded with a gunshot to the right hand, admitted to hospital on 21 June.

Losses for the 2nd Battalion are as follows:

	Volt Coy	4e Coy	3e Coy	2e Coy	1er Coy	Gren Coy.
Presumed POW	43	17	22	21	16	13
Killed	-	-	3	2	-	1
Presumed POW Wounded	-	-	-	-	-	1
Evacuated as Wounded	2	3	5	1	1	2
Total	45	20	29	23	17	17

Given the terrain that the regiment was fighting on, this made perfect sense. The voltigeurs suffered the highest losses. Details of wounds inflicted on the other ranks of the battalion are below:

Grenadier Company
MAT No. 234 Jean Martigues, born 1792, admitted to the regiment on 10 December 1812, wounded with gunshot to right arm.

1st Company
MAT No. 442 Jean Ferriere, born 1793, admitted to the regiment on 4 April 1813, wounded with a blow from a cannon ball.

MAT No. 1879 Jean Nicolas Henry, born 1792, admitted to the regiment on 26 December 1814, wounded with a gunshot to the right hand.

3rd Company
MAT No. 135 Jean Granier, born 1794, admitted to the regiment on 9 May 1811, wounded with gunshot to left arm.

MAT No. 593 Jean Dauch Dit Rattemillet, born 3 April 1794, admitted to the regiment on 4 May 1813, wounded with a canister shot.

MAT No. 1487 Jean Joseph Pradier, born 1791, admitted to the regiment on 26 May 1811, wounded with a gunshot to the right hand.

4th Company
MAT No. 336 Francois Dumouche, born 1793, admitted to the regiment on 17 December 1812, wounded with a gunshot to left hand.

MAT No. 339 Jean Baptiste Joules, born 1793, admitted to the regiment on 17 December 1812, wounded with a sabre cut to the left hand.

MAT No. 651 Guillaume Bernady, born 1787, admitted to the regiment on 12 May 1813, wounded with a gunshot to the right hand.

Voltigeur Company
MAT No. 420 Gregoire Anel, born 1791, admitted to the regiment on 2 April 1813, wounded with a gunshot to the right hand at Waterloo, served as Voltigeur 2nd Battalion.

Losses for the 3rd Battalion are as follows, with details of wounds inflicted on other ranks of the battalion below:

	Volt Coy	4e Coy	3e Coy	2e Coy	1er Coy	Gren Coy.
Presumed POW	40	19	23	21	15	5
Killed	-	-	2	-	-	1
Evacuated as Wounded	1	5	3	2	5	2
Total	41	24	28	23	20	8

1st Company
MAT No. 694 Matthieu Estrabaude, born 1790, admitted to the regiment on 23 May 1813, wounded with a gunshot to the left hand.

MAT No. Jean Georges Fine, born 1792, admitted to the regiment on 17 March 1813, wounded with a gunshot to the right hand, which removed the first fingers of the hand.

2nd Company
MAT No. 2031 Pierre Derrieux, born 1793, admitted to the regiment on 8 May 1815, wounded with a sabre cut to the left hand.

3rd Company
MAT No. 564 Jean Lafont, born 1794, admitted to the regiment on 28 April 1813, wounded with a sabre cut to the left hand.

Voltigeur Company
MAT No. 96 Louis Casimir, admitted to the regiment on 1 April 1809, wounded with a gunshot to the left arm at Waterloo.

In total, the 29th Line lost the following number of men at Waterloo:

29th Regiment of Line				
	Wounded	Wounded & POW	POW	Killed
1st Battalion	20	1	120	5
2nd Battalion	14	1	132	6
3rd Battalion	20	1	119	5
Total	54	3	371	16

The regiment lost 441 other ranks at Waterloo. On 10 June 1815, the regiment had mustered 1,106 other ranks. The regiment lost 39 per cent of its men at Waterloo. The brigade lost 38 per cent of its effective strength.

85th Regiment of Line
Losses for the 1st Battalion were as follows:[26]

	Volt Coy	4e Coy	3e Coy	2e Coy	1er Coy	Gren Coy.
Presumed POW	17	11	16	17	16	8
Killed	1	3	-	-	1	7
Wounded	-	4	-	-	2	3
Total	18	18	16	17	19	18

The grenadiers lost the most men, but no discernible pattern in losses can be made out.

The losses for the 2nd Battalion were as follows:

	Volt Coy	4e Coy	3e Coy	2e Coy	1er Coy	Gren Coy.
Presumed POW	19	14	13	8	19	9
Killed	3	-	1	1	1	-

Wounded	2	-	1	2	3	8
Total	24	14	15	11	23	17

The voltigeurs and 1st Company lost the most men, with the voltigeurs suffering the most killed and the grenadiers taking the largest number of wounded men.

The 3rd Battalion losses are as follows:

	Volt Coy	4e Coy	3e Coy	2e Coy	1er Coy	Gren Coy.
Presumed POW	17	15	14	15	24	6
Killed	-	-	1	1	1	3
Wounded	-	1	2	-	2	4
Total	17	16	17	16	27	13

The grenadiers lost the most men killed, but no discernable pattern in losses can be made out as, presumably, the battalion was amalgamated among the first two.

The table below gives the losses for the 85th Line:

85th Regiment of Line			
	Wounded	POW	Killed
1st Battalion	8	85	12
2nd Battalion	16	78	6
3rd Battalion	9	91	6
Total	33	254	24

At Waterloo, the regiment lost 311 other ranks out of 591 men, representing a loss of 52 per cent of effective strength. The regiment on 20 June 1815 mustered 280 men with twenty-five officers. On 26 June, the regiment mustered 180 men—a loss of 64 per cent of the remaining effective strength after Waterloo.

95th Regiment of Line

Unlike the detailed records for the other regiments in the division, those for the 95th Line are almost totally useless. The following table gives those losses:[27]

95th Regiment of Line Infantry			
	Wounded	POW	Missing
1	1	1	359
2	2	-	362
Total	3	1	721

At Waterloo, the 95th Line lost 725 men from an effective strength of 1,060—a staggering 68 per cent of the regiment's effective strength. At Ligny on 16 June, seven men were lost, making a total loss of 732 men. Some 328 men remained in ranks on 20 June 1815. On 26 June, the regiment mustered twenty-four officers and 239 men—a loss of eighty-nine men, representing a 27 per cent loss of effective strength. Nearly all men were listed as missing. Does this mean they surrendered or deserted?

The nature of the returns made by the regiment in 1815 relied upon men seeing what happened to their comrades. Therefore, we can only be certain of the fate of four men of the battalion. It is possible that with the allied cavalry surging down the field towards the squares, the square dissolved, and entire companies were rounded up and made POWs. It is, however, likely that the missing includes dead and wounded men, whose fate was not known, as no one remained in the regiment to say what happened to these men.

Comment

Combined, the division lost 1,818 men at Waterloo:

4th Infantry Division					
	Wounded	Wounded & POW	POW	Killed	Missing
8th Line	3	38	297	-	-
29th Line	54	3	371	16	-
85th Line	33	-	254	24	-
95th Line	3	-	1	-	721
Total	93	41	923	40	721

On the morning of 18 June, the division had mustered 3,700 men. Of this number, 49 per cent was lost at Waterloo, the vast majority being POWs or deserters. Presumably, the missing and POWs also included dead and wounded men. Clearly what happened to the 1st Brigade when it moved to the centre of the French positions, compared to the 2nd Brigade which deployed against the Prussians, was different. The data for the 95th Line is meaningless and comment on the losses can be made, whereas the losses of the 85th are lower than those for either the 8th or 29th Line. The lack of any clear data for the 95th hinders any comparison between the brigades. We do note that the losses are far lower than in the 3rd Division or the 28th Line from the 1st Infantry Division for the 8th, 29th, and 85th Line.

Moving up to support the Nassau troops came the Prussians:

> The 1 Battalion of the 18th regiment ... reached Frichermont and found the farm building to the left of the village occupied, it threw out skirmishes under *Kapitan* von Pogwash and attack the enemy positions. Their front line was taken with a very determined bayonet charge ... supported by the brigade battery and the 2nd Silesian Hussar Regiment under *Oberst* von Eicke, he forced the enemy to abandon the position. The Hussars drove back the enemy skirmish line posted to the left front of Frichermont and forced a chasseur regiment to retire.[28]

The French were losing their grip of the area, and only a timely charge by the 3rd Chasseurs stabilised the situation. Durutte needed more men and quickly.

15

The Prussians' Next Move

Due to the heavy rain from the previous night, the roads towards the battlefield were in poor condition—in essence, they were little more than a morass of ankle-deep cloying mud. The men of Bülow's command had had to pass through the congested streets of Wavre together with their eighty-eight guns. Crossing Wavre took time, and the last elements of the corps did not leave Wavre until around 10 a.m. It took a full six hours for the corps to cross through Wavre.

Behind IV Corps came the Prussian I and II Corps under Pirch and Zieten. Sensibly enough, the Prussians left a strong rearguard at Wavre to hold back the French pursuit conducted by Marshal Grouchy. Since Marbot had brought in his prisoner, Napoleon had been aware that a body of Prussians was marching to Waterloo. He knew from Grouchy's dispatches that the Prussians were in three columns and that Grouchy was in action with at least one. Therefore, Napoleon now knew that at least one, if not two Prussian columns were heading his way. Grouchy's operations are described at length in two volumes by the author, but we need to record that Marshal Soult sent the following order to Grouchy at 1 p.m. on 18 June 1815:

> Monsieur Marshal, you wrote to the Emperor this morning at six o'clock this morning, saying that you were marching on Sart-lez-Walhain, and that you planned then to move to Corbaix and to Wavre. This movement conforms with the dispositions of the Emperor which have been communicated to you.
>
> However, the Emperor orders me that you should manoeuvre in our direction and try to get closer to the army, so that you can link with us before another corps can come between us. I do not indicate a direction of movement. It is for you to see the place where we are, to govern

yourself accordingly and link with our communications, and to always be prepared to fall upon any of the enemy's troops who seek to annoy our right and crush them.

At this moment, the battle is won on the line the of Waterloo, in front of the Forest of Soignes, the centre of the enemy is at Mont-Saint-Jean, and manoeuvre to reach our right.

The Marshal, Duke of Dalmatia[1]

To defend the approach to the French right and to link with Grouchy, we remember that Marbot had left a picket of 7th Hussars at Chapelle-de-Saint Lambert and another at Lasne. Since the morning, Domon had been sent to Moustier and a detachment of the 13th Light Infantry had been posted to Aywiers Abbey. Bülow's objective was Plancenoit, which the Prussians intended to use as a springboard into the rear of the French positions at Plancenoit. At about 2 p.m., the advance guard of Bülow's IV Corps arrived on the field of battle. He reports:

According to the views expressed by the Duke of Wellington, the IVth Army Corps was to remain near Saint-Lambert until the enemy had shown his intentions. To be connected in a satisfactory manner with the English army, it was necessary to cross the very inconvenient defile of Saint-Lambert and Lasne; but this movement could not be executed with security until we had guarded ourselves against the presumed attempts of the enemy against our flank. Major de Falkenhausen's reports showed that the enemy, despite their proximity, fortunately did not undertake the direct movement against our left flank, along the Lasnes stream, which was so appropriate to the circumstances. His Serene Highness the Field-Marshal therefore decided that the IVth Army Corps would cross the defile of Lasnes and secure the wood of Fichermont. Two battalions and the regiment of Silesian hussars were first placed close together. green in this wood; behind this detachment marched the 15th and 16th brigades and the reserves of artillery and cavalry. These troops were deployed on a broad front on both sides of the road in the woods, the artillery on the road, all ready to debouch instantaneously on the open heights of Fichermont situated in front of the edge. The cavalry reserve was placed in the rear and very close to the wood, to be able to follow the infantry immediately.

The enemy had begun the attack on the English army around noon. He had been pushed back everywhere. Before 3 o'clock he had renewed his attack with fresh energy and made clear his intention of breaking through the left wing of the English and separating them from us. The moment was therefore very favorable to act against the right flank of the enemy, who showed themselves incomprehensibly negligent and seemed to pay no attention to our existence. As we had not yet crossed the defile of the Lasne, the field-marshal ordered that, to give aid to the English army, the available troops should move immediately to the attack; he correctly foresaw that the remainder of the IV Corps as well as the I and II Corps would arrive in succession and were to engage briskly as they arrived.

It was half past four when the head of our column debouched from the Bois de Fichermont. The 15th Brigade under the orders of General-Major von Losthin quickly deployed in massed battalions and launched its skirmishers forward: the brigade artillery as well as the artillery reserve followed immediately These troops endeavored to gain the height by in front of them; the brigade cavalry and the 2nd Silesian hussar regiment of the vanguard covered them provisionally. When they had gained sufficient ground in front, the 16th Brigade, under Colonel von Hiller, moved to their left and formed up in line: the front of the deployment thus extended from the ravine of the Abbey of Aywiers to the ravine of La Haie. The two battalions of the right wing of the 15th Brigade (the Riflemen of the 18th Infantry Regiment and those of the 3rd Silesian Landwehr Regiment), under Major von Kowsky, drove the enemy from the village of Fichermont and thus set about in liaison with the left wing of Wellington's army.[2]

Durutte's battered division, with the cavalry of Domon and Subervie, were all the troops available to defend the vulnerable French right flank. Another Prussian account reports:

Finally, it was about half past four, the Field Marshal and General Bulow, who had advanced through the forest for about an hour. Foom where they sootd, they could see the whole line, and to whom it seemed (as was the case) that the enemy had gained some ground to undertake the attack, although only two brigades were engaged. One of our battery's opened fired, and the duke was notified, so that the advance would immediately commence.

Beyond the forest, the terrain descends in terraces again into the valley where the village of Planchenoit lies.

An enemy cavalry detachment of about 150 horses came up the hill from the same just at that moment, probably to do some reconnaissance (for which it was admittedly a bit late now).

It might itself have been somewhat unexpected that so many of our troops had already debouched.

They hesitated and turned back, we followed, and soon the area opened up even more to us as we descended from the plateau.

We had Planchenoit close in front of us, beyond this place the terrain rises again up to the main road which leads from Quatre Bras to Brussels and whose direction was already clearly noticeable to us.

On this road was a beacon-like scaffolding near a dairy called Belle Alliance.

Here we could see dense masses of the enemy's reserves, namely all the Guards and the 6th Corps.

It was also from here that Napoleon had watched and directed the battle until then (and even later, until about 7 a.m.).

We were so close that we could mark the moment when the 6th Corps turned right to check our advance, set out on Planchenoit.

So, we were on the right flank of the enemy reserves and consequently in the rear of his engaged troops, whose line of fire was clearly visible to our right, albeit a little far off.

I believe that at that moment there was no enemy infantry in Planchenoit and that the 2 battalions standing closest could have been thrown in. But they would probably have been pushed out again by the enemy, since we had not yet been able to adequately shelter them. For the moment we were content to establish a strong artillery fire in the village which was just beginning to be occupied by the enemy.

Shortly thereafter, it might have been nearly 6 o'clock when our columns finally began to emerge from the forest in larger numbers, and received a less than pleasant message from General Thielmann that at the moment when he was preparing to follow our direction, was violently attacked by a significant enemy corps, so much so that the possession of Wavre was already being fought for and he accordingly asks for success.[3]

For the writer, the Prussians advanced almost totally unnoticed and observed Lobau moving up. We need to note that it seems likely that Lobau had not been long on the field of battle. As the morning of 18 June dawned, Lobau and his command were miles from headquarters. The 19th Division was camped in front of Genappe, with the 20th behind. A letter from Adjutant Deguin of the 10th Regiment of Line in the author's collection comments:

We camped as best we could in the fields of Genappe. Unable to lite fires, we spent a miserable night. Either by treason, or incompetence, we received orders at 9 o'clock to resume our march. The river had broken over its banks which made crossing the bridge precarious. The Brussels road after torrential rain and the passage of our army the day before had left it a quagmire of mud. We arrived at Mont-Saint Jean about 3 o'clock. Hardly had we any time to rest before we ordered to advance to support the troops of General d'Erlon and the troops from our Corps.

At 6 o'clock a failure happened along our line and we were forced to fall back successively, despite vigorous charges of cavalry and reinforcement by the Duhemse. By 8 o'clock we had taken refuge at Plancenoit.[4]

Confirming the time of the initial advance, *Le Moniteur Universal* of 21 June 1815 carries the following report by the emperor:

It was three o'clock in the afternoon. The Emperor advanced the guard to place it on the plain on the ground occupied by the first Corps at the beginning of the action: this body was already in front. The Prussian division, whose movement had been foreseen, then began to engage with Count Lobau's skirmishers, extending its fire all over our right flank. It was appropriate, before doing anything else, to wait for the outcome of this attack. To this end, all the means of the reserve were ready to come to the aid of Count Lobau and to crush the Prussian corps, when he had advanced.

Long discounted, this account is consistent with Prussian and other French eyewitnesses. Combes-Brassard of the 6th Corps reports:

It was three hours and half (3.30), when an infernal fire extended all along the line of the two armies. The 6th Corps completed its deployment in reserve on the right of the army, when, returning to the extreme right, I recognized heads of columns emerging from the direction of Vavres, by Ohain and Saint-Lambert.

These columns were Prussian. Their arrival occurred without the Emperor issuing any orders. We were turned.

Napoleon was the first to be aware of this danger. He ordered Lobau to cross the Brussels road and change direction to the right with his division, and move towards the Chapel of Saint-Lambert, and was supported by the cavalry of Domon and Subervie, who were also employed to reconoitre the Prussians.[5]

We have an eyewitness to what happened from the 13th Light Infantry, who reports Subervie trotting off to Saint-Lambert, the letter again being found in the author's collection. Lieutenant Jacques Combe, who had joined the 13e *légère* on 21 December 1796, promoted to sergeant on 16 November 1806, sergeant-major on 16 August 1811, and *sous-lieutenant* on 4 August 1812, thence lieutenant on 15 April 1813, writes:

I have never been as hot as on the plains of Fleurs or as wet as the night of Waterloo. At dawn we tried to make fires to dry our things. At 8 o'clock the colonel ordered us to stand too. We received orders at 9 o'clock to head to the Abbey of Aywars, with a battery of artillery, accompanied by the cavalry of Domon to link with Marshal Grouchy. The artillery was placed in the hamlet by the abbey [Couture ed.], and the 3rd battalion as you know was reinforced with men from the 4th, was placed in the village and Lasne. The cavalry of Subervie headed to four arms [Les Quatre Hueerees ed] and Domon headed in the direction of Moustier. We heard firing in the distance and about 1 o'clock dark masses emerged. Our voltigeurs made smoke for some time before falling back on Lasne. Forced back successively we retired to Abbey. Assailed from both sides, the Cavalry of Domon charged successively on the plain. Expending our ammunition, we fell back in disorder towards Genappe.[6]

Since Grouchy's dispatch had arrived, Napoleon knew the Prussians were 'out their [sic.] somewhere', and the best bet was that they were coming his way. The road which passes through Lasne was the most obvious line of approach—rue de Bois de Paris and Chemin des Hochequeues; this and via Beaumont were key routes to control. Marbot was occupying the Ohain road with Durutte; later, 6th Corps and the Young Guard deployed here from Frichermont, via Smohain, to control the western limit of the road.

Walking the ground around Couture and Lasne reveals these were fairly defensible locations: the churchyard of Saint Germaine Lasne affords commanding positions, and when filled with light infantrymen, it offered the French a formidable bastion to hold off the Prussian advance. The Ferrari map of 1775 shows the extensive flood plain of the river Lasne, which following the rain of the previous evening would have been swollen, limiting cross-country movement to paved roads on high ground. The village of Lasne at the intersection of two paved roads became strategically important. Likewise, Couture and the abbey, if held by the French, prevented the Prussians approaching Plancenoit from the north-east. The southern approach to the village was covered by the Bois de Chantelet, as well as a no doubt swollen stream and sodden flood plain. An officer of the Prussian 6th Hussars writes on 29 July 1815:

On the morning of the 18th we started marching, at the II. A.C. passing in Wavres, after the heights of St Lambert. I received with 70 pounds. the avant-garde. At 11 o'clock I arrived properly in St. Lambert. No enemy noticed me. I caught some French cavalrymen who had not suspected my nearness. A few cannon shots were heard to the left on the main Jemappe-Brussels road. In front of us a defile that absolutely had to be passed in order to get to the heavily wooded heights of Ohain and Lasnes, opposite St. Lambert.

I was ordered to proceed at once, to patrol the defile, and to pass by Lasnes, in order to learn if it was possible for the forest to the left of Lasnes and an old abbey in the valley which were occupied by the enemy. I moved to the left towards the abbey at the village of Lasnes, and learned that the right wing of the French reserve was stationed at Planchenois and between these villages and the forest beyond the Lasne defile. All the French troops stationed in that area turned their backs on me. I concluded from this that we were not expected here. So, I took off quietly, passed the Lasnes defile, and crept up the hill to the forest. Half of it was vacant. The unoccupied part lay towards Ohain, which was favorable to us; for from this place the I Corps was to make the connection between the left wing and the English and the IV Corps.

I went cautiously into the forest to a point where you could see an open field. In front of me on my left, at the height of Belle Alliance, was the French army in the rear, in full action with the English, which had already lost some ground by 1 o'clock in the afternoon. A General Staff officer who followed me shared my observations.

As my patrol meanwhile met no enemy in the woods, I left a few observation posts with instructions not to show themselves, and raced back to the heights of St. Lambert. Here I met all the generals. On my report and that of the General Staff officers, the IV Corps set out on the march, passed the defile at Lasnes and assembled, unseen by the enemy, on and in the forest. Before two brigades were united, the Field Marshal wanted to break out of the forest (towards the French). General Bulow, meanwhile, deliberately and rightly hesitated until at least 12,000 to 15,000 men were together. An adjutant now gave our regiment the order to break out of the forest and attack the enemy's reserve cavalry. This happened. An enemy skirmish line, which threw itself against us, was chased away.[7]

Clearly, the 13th, with Subervie's cavalry, pushed the Prussians into the Bois de Paris, but we are sure some headed towards Lasne as the casualty data shows. About the troops at Maransart and Couture, Pirch reports:

After 6 o'clock in the evening, the head of the army corps entered the woods situated on the reverse side of the Belle-Alliance battlefield. The cavalry deployed immediately forward, to give the infantry space to march past. The prince was informed of our arrival.

One of his officers brought the order to immediately detach a brigade by Caturiaux and Couture-Saint-Germain on Maransart, to cover the flank of the army which was advancing.

The 7th Brigade and the 4th Landwehr Cavalry Regiment of the Electoral March were designated for this mission. Meanwhile, the rest of the corps continued its march; at the request of General Count Bülow of Dennewitz, the entire cavalry reserve moved forward to reinforce the left wing. In front of this wing was Plancenoit, which was the fulcrum of the enemy battle line. The 5th and 6th Brigades followed and, as soon as they had debouched from the woods, formed up by brigade in columns at close intervals. took the same road as the 14th Brigade; the 6th followed immediately, a little behind, so as to be able to be employed, according to circumstances, towards the right or the left. The 8th Brigade was still at some distance behind, partly because of the rear guard fighting near Wavre, partly because of the 7th Brigade's dislocation from the column.[8]

Clearly it was these troops that came into contact with Domon and also the 13th Light Infantry.

Losses

Can the casualty data from the troops deployed here add any insights? The table below gives the losses for the 3rd Battalion, which mustered 269 men:[9]

	Volt Coy	4e Coy	3e Coy	2e Coy	1er Coy	Carab. Coy.
Presumed POW	3	1	-	1	1	-
Missing	26	6	6	6	5	3
Killed	3	1	-	1	1	-
Wounded	4	-	1	1	1	-
Evacuated as Wounded	-	1	-	-	-	-
Total	36	9	7	9	8	3

Looking at the data, the voltigeurs bore the brunt of the fighting. The 1st and 3rd Companines, superficially, seem to have been in action and suffered no casualties: were they deployed behind hard cover like garden walls and the churchyard, which was used as a redan, the men standing to fire, and then dropping down to reload? Possibly. The missing men perhaps were lost in the retreat to Plancenoit. The carabinier, 2nd, and 4th Companies took men wounded, which may suggest they did not have the luxury of a wall or similar structure to shelter behind. The 4th Company had the only men reported killed outright. In the 4th Battalion, losses were:

	Volt Coy	4e Coy	3e Coy	2e Coy	1er Coy	Carab. Coy.
Presumed POW	-	5	-	17	-	1
Missing	29	50	68	25	2	15
Killed	-	3	-	-	-	-
Wounded	10	7	-	4	-	3
Total	39	65	68	46	2	19

The largest loss of life was sustained by the 4th Company, with the voltigeurs we assume strung out in open order taking the highest number of men wounded. The missing will no doubt include men made POW, killed, and wounded.

Total regimental losses were:

13th Regiment of Light Infantry				
	Wounded	POW	Killed	Missing
1st Battalion	57	7	10	111
2nd Battalion	15	4	5	69
3rd Battalion	4	3	3	26
4th Battalion	24	23	3	189
Total	100	37	21	395

Combined, the battalion sent to Aywiers Abbey lost twenty-eight men wounded, six killed, and 206 missing. The 4th Battalion suffered losses overall of 57 per cent. We must also ask how many men were lost in Plancenoit or the retreat. We assume the casualties were all taken in combat, then the operations on the French right. The fighting in the centre was costly, with fifteen men killed and seventy-two wounded, and of a different intensity to that on the right wing, which was more exposed to enemy fire. We also note that the 682 men in the two battalions with three field guns could hardly hope to do anything other than slow down the Prussian steamroller. If more troops had been sent here, the outcome may have been different. As we shall see, it had been intended to send more men to this sphere of operations, but 'fate' intervened with the emperor's plans.

16

Domon and Subervie

Also strung out on the French right were the two cavalry divisions of Domon and Subervie, whose mission was to stop, or at least contain, the Prussian threat. Domon had been sent off to Moustier earlier that morning.[1]

Had he returned to the field of battle or was he constantly deployed at Moustier? If so, why does Marbot not mention him? In contradiction to Marbot's silence, General Brue reports:

> I had in the morning detached the 7th Hussars to keep in communication with General Domont, and I was placed on the extreme right of 1st Corps with the 3rd Chasseurs which consisted of three squadrons.[2]

With, we assume, Domon's men close to the river Dyle, this left just Subervie's command as yet uncommitted to the action. Marbot's pickets and the detachment from the 13th Regiment of Light Infantry at Saint-Lambert were too weak to offer much in the way of resistance; this perhaps explains the next move, as d'Erlon recalls:

> General Donzelot with the remains of his division and of the 1st was placed in front of the Bonne Alliance, on our right the troops of the 3rd and 4th divisions and the division of General Jacquinot, held the enemy columns in check that tried to debouche from Smohain and protected the artillery of the guard which fired on the English masses and did the greatest harm to them. The division of Subervie which had been detached behind our extreme right wing, had since the appearance of the first Prussian [illegible], was taking orders from Comte Lobau.[3]

Subervie's command of three regiments, as our eyewitness from the 13th Light Infantry tells us, was detached to the extreme, which *Général de Division* Marie Joseph Raymond Delort confirms:

Having been informed of the presence of the Prussian Army, our patrols could not discover the movements of Marshal Grouchy. The Emperor detached the Corps of Comte Labou along with the light cavalry of General Domon to contain the Prussians. Our spirits filled with confidence, with 10,000 French troops advantageously placed, filled with ardour and guided by their chief to whom they were devoted, we could resist at this point the troops of Bülow.[4]

Without infantry, what could Subervie actually achieve? Again, as our eyewitness from the 13th Light Infantry mentioned, and General Gourgand notes, Domon's cavalry was sent off to oppose the Prussians:

Great advantages were anticipated from the Marshal's coming upon the rear of Bülow's Corps. But, as that Corps appeared to be not more than two short leagues from the field of battle, it became necessary to send off a force to oppose it. Marshal Grouchy might delay passing the Dyle, or might be prevented by unforeseen obstacles. Lieutenant General Domont [*sic*.] was therefore sent forward with his light cavalry, and Subervick's [*sic*.] division of Pajol's Corps of cavalry, making altogether a force of nearly three thousand cavalry, to meet Bülow's advance guard; his instructions were to occupy all the passes, to prevent the enemy's hussars from attacking our flanks, and to send off couriers to meet Marshal Grouchy. Count de Lobau, with both divisions of his Corps [7,000 men], proceeded to reconnoitre his field of battle, in the rear of General Domont's cavalry, so that, in case General Bülow's movement should not be stopped by Marshal Grouchy, he might advance against the Prussians, and protect our flanks. Thus, the destination of this Corps was changed.[5]

De Mauduit goes on to note:

The count Lobau advanced his infantry and replaced his 1st Line with the cavalry of General Domon. The General Bülow emerged to his right on the heights and wood of Smohain, the left of which descended into a valley of the brook of Lasne, and thence the wood of Virer. The cavalry of the reserve made a movement in two columns, and debouched to the left, where Prince William of Prussia commended the battle.[6]

The total lack of any eyewitness recollections from Subervie, Domon, or the men he commanded means we can say literally nothing about what he was doing between 11 a.m. and 6 p.m.—some seven hours or more are missing. The same is true for Domon and also for the whereabouts of Jacquinot between 11 a.m. and 2 p.m.

We can only assume that the light artillery, the battalion of the 13th Light Infantry, and the action of the cavalry bought sufficient time to allow Durutte and Lobau's troops to set up a strong line of skirmishers. As the Prussian skirmish line engaged, they were charged and driven back by the French cavalry; these were classic and successful delaying tactics. On the slope from the wood of Frichermont, there was little cover and both sides suffered; the artillery fire was especially telling. Colonel Petiet of the Imperial Staff notes:

> However, we had no news of the Corps of Marshal Grouchy, while Bülow's troops arrived in front of our lines, extending into the right hand of Count Lobau, at the height of La Belle Alliance, the 6th Corps was immediately reinforced the division of the Young Guard, commanded by Duhesme, followed by Napoleon two batteries. Bülow attempted to destroy the French cavalry with his artillery because it had caused him such trouble. General Jacquinot displayed sang-froid and stoicism in the face of a situation that could have been so unfortunate for him. This general officer commanded two divisions of cavalry. A cannon ball came in from the flank of the 1st Lancers and took off the head of *Chef d'Escadron* Dumanoir, passed through the body of Colonel Jacquinot's [the general's brother] horse and cut off two legs of *Chef d'Escadron* Trentignant's horse. The three superior officers fell as one. Confusion spread through the ranks, Jacquinot, sword in hand, reordered the line himself with a firm voice and it was only after re-establishing order that he bent down to check if his brother was dead but who was happily unhurt. Taking the hamlet of La Haie stopped the movement of Bülow.[7]

We know very little about the operations of Domon in the battle, beyond the limited comments of the Prussians. However, General Domon prepared a review of his division on 6 July 1815, outlining the officers and men deserving of promotion or decoration. From this report, we learn a great deal about episodes of the battle on the French right flank.[8]

Squadron Commander Robert of the 4th Chasseurs was recommended to be made officer of the Legion of Honour for his acts of bravery in the battle. *Sous-Lieutenant* Mommot was recommended to be awarded the Legion of Honour for acts of bravery at Waterloo, as was *Sous-Lieutenant* Robinot. Adjutant-Sub-Officer Richard was also recommended for the Legion of Honour for his conduct and bravery in the battle. Domon noted that Sergeant Veyrems (a veteran who had returned from Moscow) was wounded in the battle and dismounted, but still fought bravely, for which he too was recommended for the Legion of Honour. Sergeant Philippe was also likewise recommended for the Legion of Honour, having been wounded in the action and returning to fight with his company on a captured horse in spite of his wounds. A similar recommendation was made for Sergeants Collin and Batty, so too was Sergeant-Major Bidault. Sergeant-Major Andre was also recommended for the Legion of Honour, as General Domon states that Bidault killed or wounded three Prussians in the space of four minutes.[9] Among the *4e régiment de chasseurs à cheval*, Lieutenant Hugues Pepin Claviere was shot with a musket ball to the right foot.[10] Sub-Lieutenant Jean Pierre Moutard took a gunshot wound to the left shoulder. He had served in the famed 7th Hussars from 30 October 1804, before entering the Lancers of Berg regiment on 1 September 1807.[11] Sub-Lieutenant Charles Benjamin Robinot had his horse killed under him and he was wounded at the same time.[12]

Among the 9th Chasseurs, Squadron Commander Petit was recommended for the decoration of officer of the Legion of Honour for the capture of 300 prisoners on 15 June. Also for his bravery on 15 June, Chasseur Parecellier of 6th Company was recommended for the Legion of Honour. Sergeant-Major Pierre Perrin General Domon records killing two Prussian hussars during the retreat, when he was searching for a line of retreat, which the Prussians endeavoured to block.[13] Were the hussars encountered by the 9th Chasseurs the same body as encountered by the 4th we wonder? Possibly.

In the 12th Chasseurs, Chasseurs Ferrant and Schneiblin were recommended for the Cross of the Legion of Honour for saving the life of Lieutenant-General Gérard and his chief of staff at the Battle of Ligny. Likewise, Sergeant-Majors Nicolas Rhis and Rhomer were recommended for the Cross of the Legion of Honour for capturing an enemy artillery piece at Ligny. At Waterloo, Adjutant-Sub-Officers Devina and Degennes, as well as Corporal Collard, were recommended for the Legion of Honour for their distinguished conduct.[14]

The table below gives the losses for the division as a whole.

3rd Cavalry Division						
Regiment	Killed	Died of Wounds	Wounded	POW	Missing	Total
4th Chasseurs[15]	5	-	2	14	24	45
9th Chasseurs[16]	9	-	11	3	22	45
12th Chasseurs	-	-	-	-	-	198[17]
TOTAL	14	-	13	17	46	140/298[18]

Despite our best efforts in accessing all the regimental muster lists for the *Armée du Nord*, that of the *12e regiment de chasseurs à cheval* is still considered too fragile to be viewed until it has undergone conservation work. We therefore have to rely on parade states to assess losses. On 10 June, the regiment mustered twenty-three officers with sixty-five horses, 273 men with 263 horses, along with six draught horses. In total, the regiment had twenty-nine officers and 289 other ranks. Sixteen men were lost and five officers.

Sub-Lieutenant Menzo and Corporal Bruguiere were killed. Captain Aubrey and Sub-Lieutenant Remy were wounded. In terms of losses of other ranks, the regiment lost 5 per cent of its strength at Ligny. In terms of horse losses for the other ranks, 9.6 per cent was lost, some twenty-five horses—a ratio of almost two horses lost for every other rank.

On the morning of 18 June, the regiment had 238 horses and 258 men. General Domon reports that 198 men were lost on and after 18 June along with 182 horses. The regiment had sixty men and fifty-six horses, with seven officers and fifteen horses in the field. At Waterloo, 76 per cent of the regiment's manpower was lost along with the same percentage of the regiment's horses. Of the twenty-three officers present at the start of the campaign, sixteen were dead or wounded.[19]

Martinien records that at Waterloo Lieutenant Richard was killed. Furthermore, he states Colonel Grouchy, Captain Joseph Laurent Constantin Huck, Captain Onesime Stanislas Dumont, Lieutenant Renard, Lieutenant Dolemans, and Sub-Lieutenant Lusignan were wounded.

Sub-Lieutenant Augustin Louis Pierre Perardel was born in Paris on 7 January 1788. He served in the *12e régiment de chasseurs à cheval* since 1807 and was promoted to sub-lieutenant on 8 January 1814.[20]

Sub-Lieutenant Antoine Faustin Renaud was born on 15 February 1791 at Cagliari in Sardinia. He was admitted to the 12th Chasseurs on 16 July 1814. He was wounded at Waterloo with a gunshot to the abdomen, and another to the right arm.[21]

Other ranks wounded included: Sergeant-Major Francois Hinout, born in 1793 at Rouen, was admitted to the *12e régiment de chasseurs à cheval* on 9 July 1811, with the matricule number 2762. He was promoted to corporal on 15 July 1812, fourier on 16 July 1812, sergeant on 9 July 1813, and sergeant-major on 21 September 1813. He had his horse killed under him at Waterloo. He was discharged on 21 December 1815 and died in 1881.[22]

Sergeant Valentin Lapp was born on 13 March 1787 at Gimbrett. Admitted to the 12th Chasseurs on 12 March 1807, he was promoted to corporal on 1 February 1813 and sergeant on 11 December 1813. He was wounded with a gunshot that passed through the right side of his chest at Waterloo.[23]

We can say nothing more, unless documentary sources await discovery in archives and private collections.

Subervie's Cavalry

D'Erlon tells us that Subervie's cavalry was sent to the French right wing. Jacquinot's command we know remained close to the field, with only the 7th Hussars heading off to look for Grouchy and *inter alia* the Prussians. So what of his operations? We know virtually nothing. The bulk of the operations that Subervie and Domon undertook are missing from French eyewitness testimonies of the battle. All we know is that Subervie headed off to Saint-Lambert, and no doubt became caught up in the Prussian advance, while Domon simultaneously found the Prussians heading from Moustier, both columns converging on Plancenoit. Subervie's Lancers had suffered heavy losses on the previous day, and counted just a few hundred men.

1st Regiment of Lancers

Dr Croyet of the *Musee emperi* reports the 1st Lancers lost thirty men at Ligny and fifteen at Genappe.[24] The source cannot be verified with the regiment's muster list. Losses of the regiment were as follows for Waterloo:[25]

1st Regiment of Light Horse Lancers					
Squadron	Killed	Died of Wounds	POW	Missing	Total
1	-	-	-	3	3
2	1	-	3	2	6
3	-	1	1	1	3
4	3	-	-	5	8
À la suite	-	-	-	2	2
TOTAL	4	1	4	13	22

In total, just twenty-two men were lost at Waterloo; when we add in the two men lost on 16 June and nine on 17 June, it makes the official loss as thirty-three. On 26 June 1815, the regiment fielded 299 men, suggesting the losses of the regiment overall were low—seventy-six men dead, wounded, POW, and unmounted since 10 June.

2nd Regiment of Lancers

According to Dr J. Croyet at Genappe on 17 June, the regiment lost 46 per cent of its effective strength—some 175 other ranks being killed or wounded. He reports that 28 per cent of the regiment's officers were wounded on 17 June.[26] However, this is not borne out by the regiment's muster list. If, however, the source found by Dr Croyet is correct, as we pointed out in *Waterloo Truth at Last,* the loss of horses on average seems to be a ratio of one man to every two horses wounded, which even at a ratio of 1 to 1.5 would give a loss of eighty-seven men, which reduces the regiment to 196 men at Waterloo, little more than a squadron strong. Given the possible high losses on 17 June, it is not impossible to imagine the regiment was badly shaken.

The regimental muster list records:[27]

2nd Regiment of Light Horse Lancers				
Squadron	Deserted	POW	Missing	Total
1	3	-	16	19
2	-	-	16	16
3	-	2	30	32
4	-	-	30	30
TOTAL	3	2	92	97

If we assume the losses for 17 and 18 June are listed under 18 June, then we can start to reconcile the archive sources and the statistics given by Dr Croyet. It is easily conceivable that 175 were lost at Genappe, if we assume the bulk of these men had their horses killed under them, but had much lower fatalities. Of the men, ninety-seven are listed missing on 18 June, and two men listed missing specifically at Waterloo. Are the men listed lost on 18 June the men at Genappe? Very likely. Indeed, this figure of ninety-five is close indeed to the hypothetical number of eighty-seven men lost based on the ratio of one man to two horses cited above. Of comment, the regiment further acknowledges the loss of twenty-five men as missing and two wounded in hospital. This makes a total loss of 124, or 128 if we included the loss of Ligny.

11th Regiment of Chasseurs

Brigaded with the two lancer regiments came the 11th *Chasseurs à Cheval*. In the fighting at Waterloo, Squadron Commander Brucelles was wounded. Lieutenant Anheiser was also wounded, as were Captain Larcohe, Captain Mathey, Sub-Lieutenants Billordeaux, Francois Lacombe, Grenier, Malval, Menu (who carried the regiment's eagle), and Periola. Also wounded were Captain-Adjutant Major Rosselange and Adjutant-Major Guichert. For such a high attrition rate of officers being wounded, we assume the regiment was involved in action to a greater degree than the Lancers.

Casualties recorded by the regiment were as follows:[28]

Squadron	Killed	Wounded	POW	Missing	Total
1	3	-	-	1	4
2	5	3	3	-	11
3	2	2	3	3	10
4	3	-	-	1	4
TOTAL	13	5	6	5	29

On 10 June, the regiment mustered 458 other ranks. At Waterloo, twenty-nine men were lost. In addition, five men were lost at Ligny, giving 543 men on the field on 18 June. A mere 6 per cent of effective strength was lost at Waterloo. We assume the officers leading their men from the front were 'easier targets' than the men who came behind.

Comment

Total losses were as follows for the division:

5th Cavalry Division	Killed & Died of wounds	Deserted	Wounded	POW	Missing	Total
1st Lancers	5	-	-	4	13	22
2nd Lancers	-	3	-	2	92	97
11th Chasseurs	13	-	5	6	5	29
Total	18	3	5	12	110	148

The losses are problemetic for the Lancers, as it seems casualties incurred on 17 and 18 June are combined, which hinders any firm conclusions, other than, assuming the heavy losses on 17 June, the division witnessed little action at Waterloo. This would fit with the division employed to reconnoitre, then fall back as the Prussians advanced. Cavalry without artillery and infantry support cannot hold terrain. The lack of 6th Corps being in its correct starting position to advance as ordered to Saint-Lambert must have been keenly felt, as well as the lack of manpower overall.

17

6th Corps is Sent to Stop the Prussians

The Prussians attacked the French hard: Napoleon was forced to commit more troops over the course of the afternoon. Henri Niemman of the Prussian 6th Hussars recalls:

> At two o'clock in the morning of 18 June we broke up and marched towards Wavre where Bluchers Corps concentrated itself. After a long and dreadfully hard march the whole day, in spite of the great battle of the 16th, and only one day rest and privation for men and horses, we arrived at last in full trot at the field of battle of Mont Saint Jean towards four o'clock. Our brigade of four regiments of cavalry was commanded by the brave Major-general von Folgersberg, Lutzow having been taken prisoner on the 16th. Hard work for the Prussian Army Again. Wellington was almost beaten when we arrived.... it was an evening no pen is able to picture: the surrounding villages yet in flames.[1]

After being in action for less than an hour, with Jacquinot's cavalry and Durutte's command from 1st Corps unable to stem the tide of Prussian troops, it was now that Lobau reinforced the faltering French lines. It is important to remember that despite arriving on the field of battle, the men were not fresh-faced. They had marched through thick mud and across arduous terrain since just after daybreak. These men were hungry, thirsty, and tired; with no rest, they were flung straight into action. The Young Guard and 6th Corps by comparison were fresh troops, who had to had to 'yomp' to battle to use Royal Marine Commando terminology. The Prussians may have arrived on the field of battle, but until field commanders had assessed the ground and state of play, given some of the men a much-needed rest, and more troops had arrived, the Prussians were initially not a major threat to the French. It must have become increasingly obvious to Napoleon that the threat now came from his right flank. His attention now fell on directing Lobau's troops, leaving Ney with a simple task: contain Wellington until the Prussian threat had been assessed, contained, and neutralised. Wellington and his redcoats now became a sideshow.

The thrust of the battle shifted away from the ridge and Wellington's 'thin red line'. The change in emphasis explains the change in tactics. The mass cavalry charges, often seen as a reckless gamble, are now seen in their true context.

Ney was left to direct the French left with minimal resources: Wellington was to be contained by 2nd Corps and the reserve cavalry. Ney had no reserve infantry, only Milhaud's 4th Cavalry Corps and elements of Kellerman's bruised 3rd Cavalry Corps. The 8th and 11th Cuirassiers had been so badly handled at Quatre Bras that they sat Waterloo out on 18 June at Quatre Bras along with Pire's lancer brigade. Ney's verbal orders must have been simple enough: keep Wellington on the ridge and, if possible, separate him from the Prussians. This explains perhaps why La Haie Sainte and breaking the centre became an obsession for Ney. D'Erlon relates:

> The troops having rallied in the squares of the 2nd and 4th divisions, order was re-stablished—these divisions did not take a single pace in retreat despite the heavy fire they were under; they were given the order to move to the main road, and the Emperor immediately sent the artillery of the guard to replace the guns that had lost their horses and the gunners could no longer serve. He came himself to the infantry that were close to farm of La Haye Sainte, and gave the orders to seize the place. Marshal Ney gave the orders for the attack himself; it was deadly; all of the exits were strongly barricaded, the gardens were surrounded by ditches and the hedges were full of infantrymen who defend themselves against our attacks. General Aulard was killed, and finally Comte d'Erlon having placed himself at the head of the 17th Line, had the door which leads to the road, broken down, and the farm was occupied by our troops. We endeavoured to establish ourselves in positions in advance, but the enemy forces were so considerable we were not able to do so. However, the 13th light remained on the edge of the steep slope that is found to the right of this farm and greatly assisted the troops which were occupying it, despite being attacked here several times. General Donzelot with the remains of his division and of the 1st was placed in front of the Bonne Alliance, on our right the troops of the 3rd and 4th divisions and the division of General Jacquinot, held the enemy columns in check that tried to debouche from Smohain and protected the artillery of the guard

which fired on the English masses and did the greatest harm to them. The division of Subervie which had been detached behind our extreme right wing, had since the appearance of the first Prussian [illegible], was taking orders from Comte Lobau. The Anglo-Belgian cavalry attempted several charges against our right but it was always driven back with losses by Jacquinot's division.[2]

As d'Erlon notres, the thrust of the battle now turned towards the *Bois de Paris*. An officer in the Prussian 18th Infantry regiment writes about the opening stages of the attack at Frichermont and pushing back French cavalry:

> When we reached Frischermont and found the farm buildings to the left of the village were occupied, we threw out sharpshooters under Captain von Pugwash and attacked the enemy positions. Their front line was taken by the first bayonet charge which was very determined. Captain von Pugwash's charge was a great contribution. Supported by the brigade artillery and the 2nd Silesian Hussar regiment under *Oberst* von Eicke, he forced the enemy to abandon their positions. The hussars drove back the enemy skirmish screen which was posted to the left of Frischermont and forced a chasseur regiment to retire. However, a second enemy cavalry regiment attacked them in the flank, throwing them back. The 3rd Silesian *Landwehr* cavalry under Rittmesiter von Altenstein and a horse artillery battery soon restored the situation.[3]

With the Prussians now arriving in numbers that Domon and Subervie's cavalry could contain, General Lobau with his 6th Corps were sent forward, along the road to the *Bois de Paris*, to take up positions at the eastern limit of the wood. If the Prussians were to be stopped, the village of Smohain, the châteaux of Frichermont, and the farms of Papelotte and La Haye became key strategic locations for the French and Prussians alike. Controlling this sector was vital to preventing a Prussian breakthrough. The fighting in the woods and sunken lanes was bitter and desperate and has sadly been largely omitted from the story of 18 June. Bülow's command mustered around 30,000 men against Lobau's 10,000 command. Since fighting on the Danube in 1809, Lobau had proved that he was a capable and resourceful general.

Lobau's command at Waterloo comprised the 19th and 20th Infantry Division. The 19th Infantry Brigade was commanded by *Général de Division* Baron Simmer, who was wounded at Waterloo, and the 20th by General Jeanin. Adjutant-Commandant Janin of 6th Corps narrates:

The 6th Army Corps moved forward to support the attack on the centre: as it arrived on the crest of the ravine that separated the two armies, General Durrieux and his staff, who had led the advance, turned back wounded and announced that enemy sharpshooters had penetrated our right flank.

The Comte de Lobau advanced with General Jacquinot and I to reconnoitre their positions, and soon we saw two columns on the march of about ten thousand men each: it was the Prussian Army Corps of Bülow. The destination of the 6th Army Corps was changed by this incident: it was no longer to continue the attack against the English, but instead was now to repel the Prussians.[4]

Assistant chief of staff to 6th Corps was Colonel Jean Isaac Suzanne Combes-Brassard. He was born on 11 February 1772 at Montauban, in Tarn-et-Garonne, the son of Pierre Thomas Combes-Brassard and Anne Presque d'Ollier. He writes about Waterloo as follows:

The 6th Corps formed the reserve, I was chief of Staff to the Corps, and it marched to support the attack of the right. The Corps was composed entirely of Infantry.

It was three hours and half [3.30 p.m.], when an infernal fire extended all along the line of the two armies. The 6th Corps completed its deployment in reserve on the right of the Army, when, returning to the extreme right, I recognized heads of columns emerging from the direction of Wavre, by Ohain and Saint-Lambert.

Still uncertain about the nature and the intentions of these troops, I approached them to reconnoitre their movements. I soon learned that this column was Prussian and manoeuvring to get on our flank and our rear, so as to cut the French Army from retreating to Genappe and the bridge on the Dyle.

I hastened to prevent this movement. There was still time, by taking the position where the Army had bivouacked the night before, to prevent the danger we were in. We had not a moment to lose. To lose, was to lose the Army. The fates had thus been cast. The Prussians manoeuvred towards our rear.

The Emperor, who had been obstinately trying to force the centre of the enemy, took no account of the movement which were made on the flanks. The Prussians had already joined the left of the English and deployed on our rear, so that the right of the wing of our Army and the 6th Corps were formed in an acute triangle where on two sides and the point where the English and Prussian Army.

A terrible fire of artillery and musketry welcomed us. The English, French and Prussian regiments disappeared like ghosts into the smoke.

The rear and flanks were engaged by the enemy. The 6th Corps opened a passage with their bayonets, we left the positions.[5]

When Did 6th Corps Attack?

When did the fighting start? Marshal Soult sent the following letter to Marshal Davout at 2.30 p.m. on 18 June:

> It is two hours and a half, the cannonade is joined all along the line. The English are in the centre, the Dutch and Belgians are on the right the Germans and the Prussians are on the left. The general battle has begun, 400 cannon have opened fire at this moment.[6]

Clearly, by 2.30 p.m., the Prussians had joined the line of battle. It was now that the battle for the French was irrecoverably lost. Soon after this letter was sent, I am pretty sure that Lobau moved off.

In the records of the 27th Line, corporal of the volitigeur company of the 2nd Battalion Charles Krause was killed at 3 p.m. with a gunshot to the head. Also killed at that time was voltigeur Jacques Mayer of the 1st Battalion with a gunshot to the chest.[7] This supposes that Simmer had headed off to confront the Prussians at about 2.30 p.m., and we suppose headed to Frichermont, with the voltigeur companies spread out in front to attack Bülow's head of column.

Judging by losses, the 20th Division began taking losses between 4 and 5 p.m. or thereabouts. Among the 10th Line, we find death certificates for Captain Roudilon of 1st Battalion, killed at 5 p.m.; Pascal Melav, fourrier, 2nd Company of 2nd Battalion; grenadier Boirraut of 1st Battalion; and grenadiers Barthe, Cubillier, Amien, and Paquet of 2nd Battalion, killed with gunshots.[8] This time of frame corrolates with the 5th Light Infantry's records. Simultaneously, Durutte's men went back into action. Battalion Commander Rulliers of the 95th Regiment of Line Infantry notes:

> Sometime between 3 for 4 o'clock we began to perceive movements of the Prussians on the right of our Army. Shortly after we received musket fire from their scouts. My battalion was ordered to stop them—we succeeded—a vigorous exchange of musketry began and reigned for a half hour.[9]

Lobau's Attack

At the head of the 5th Regiment of Line, heading the 1st Brigade of General Bélair, part of Simmer's 19th Division, was Colonel Jean Isaac Roussille. He was seriously wounded.[10] Also wounded was Battalion Commander Augustin Pierre Lefevre at the head of the regiment's 1st Battalion.[11] Serving with the Grenadier company was Lieutenant Jean Pierre Matter, who suffered a gunshot wound. Lieutenant Jean Antoine Ruffin of the 1st Fusilier company took a gunshot wound as did Sub-Lieutenant Jean Laurent. Wounded in the 2nd Fusilier Company was Lieutenant Jean Julien Vallette, who had been with the regiment since September 1813.[12] Marching at the head of the 3rd Fusilier Company, Captain Pierre Caillet took gunshot wounds to both legs, which crippled him, and he was picked off the field of battle by the allies and made a prisoner of war.[13]

In the firefight with the Prussians, the captain-adjutant-major of 2nd Battalion, Louis Bleut, was killed. Commanding the Grenadier company of 2nd Battalion was Captain Pierre Philibeaux, who took a gunshot wound. Also wounded from the same company was Sub-Lieutenant Leonard Giraud. The 1st Fusilier Company had its Sub-Lieutenant Jean Baptiste Gillet wounded, and the 2nd Fusilier Company had Sub-Lieutenant Jacques Griou killed. In the 3rd Fusilier Company, Lieutenant Pierre Paradis was wounded with a musket ball. At the head of the 4th Fusilier Company of the same battalion, Captain Nicolas Rimbault suffered a gunshot wound, as did Sub-Lieutenant Philippe Regnard. In the voltigeur company, Sub-Lieutenant Simon Andre was killed.[14] Other officers who were wounded attached to the regiment included Captain Descleves; Captain Honore Salomon Genibaud, who was also made a prisoner of war; and Captain Thebault, who was also captured, transported to England, and died upon his return to France on 11 January 1816. Sub-Lieutenant Delale was killed. Overall, according to Colonel Roussille, the regiment lost twenty-one officers dead or wounded and 1,200 men dead, wounded, or captured out of 1,600.[15]

In the accompanying 11th Line, Battalion Commander Jean Haulon, formerly of the Flanqueur-Grenadiers of the Imperial Guard, took a gunshot wound to the right knee.[16] Étienne Maxent, a career soldier with the 11th Line since volunteering to the regiment in 1800 as a private, and promoted to captain on 9 March 1815, had a musket ball pass through his left thigh.[17] Captain Guillaume Montegut, who served with the regiment since 1 December 1790, took a musket ball to the left arm.[18]

Hachin de Courbeville was a career soldier. Born on 2 April 1790, he joined the military school at Fontainebleau on 29 November 1806. Graduated as sub-lieutenant in the 11th Line on 28 April 1807, he was promoted to lieutenant on 20 June 1809, then captain on 11 June 1813. Placed on the non-active list on 26 July 1814, he was recalled to the 11th Line on 1 February 1815. Following Waterloo, he was named captain in the Legion of the Seine on 14 August 1816, then named battalion commander of the 20th Line in 1835, lieutenant colonel of the 8th Light Infantry 1842, colonel in the 25 Light Infantry in 1843, colonel in the 54th Line in 1848, and retired in 1850, leaving the army on 3 June 1852. He had been wounded at Znaime on 11 July 1809 and took a musket ball to the left arm at Waterloo.[19]

In the 2nd Battalion, Battalion Commander Antoine Bujon was wounded, having been wounded previously at Ligny. His aide, Captain-Adjutant-Major Jean Baptiste Delcombe, was also wounded. Commanding the Grenadier Company, Captain Etienne Marin was killed, and Lieutenant Servais Delbrouck was wounded. Captain Jean Joseph Regnault, commanding the 1st Fusilier Company, was wounded.

The 2nd Fusilier Company, at some stage, and perhaps the entire battalion, came under attack by presumably Prussian cavalry. In this attack, Lieutenant Dominique Ardussy was wounded with a sabre cut, as was Sub-Lieutenant Jean Laurent Martin Simon Litti. He suffered three sabre cuts to his head and a lance wound. Either before or after this attack, his company had come under the fire of an artillery battery, and a howitzer shell exploded close to him, which fractured the head of his tibia. He was left for dead on the battlefield and made prisoner of war, being returned to France on 2 January 1816. The 3rd Fusilier Company had Lieutenant Edouard Barthelemy wounded, and 4th Fusilier Company, Captain Louis Serravalle wounded.[20]

In the 3rd Battalion, at the head of the 3rd Fusilier Company, Captain Antoine Perrier was wounded. Also, wounded from the battalion were Lieutenants Clerc and Estelle, and Sub-Lieutenants Louis Masse and Francois Augustin Metzger, the latter serving in the voltigeur company.[21]

The leading regiment of the 2nd Brigade of the 19th Infantry under the orders of General Louis Marie Joseph Thevenet, who was mortally wounded at Waterloo, was the 27th Regiment of Line.

At the head of the Grenadier company of 1st Battalion, Captain Jean Verdier was wounded.[22] So too was Lieutenant Hartmann of the same company. Commanding the 1st Fusilier company was Francois Joseph Coliny, who suffered a gunshot to the right thigh.[23] In the 3rd Fusilier Company, Sub-Lieutenant Ambroise Sault was wounded.[24] Pierre Boudreaux of the voltigeur company was wounded. Commanding the 2nd Battalion was Antoine Bujon, who was wounded with a gunshot at Waterloo.[25] The battalion's captain-adjutant-major was Jean Baptiste Deloume. Killed at the head of Grenadier company was Captain Etienne Marin. Lieutenant Servais Delbrouck was also wounded according to

Martinien, but his service papers make no record of this.[26] Jean Joseph Regnault, commanding the 1st Fusilier Company, was wounded.

The 20th Infantry Division was commanded by General Jeanin. The division was under-strength, and only comprised three regiments. It comprised the 10th and 107th Line and the 5th Light Infantry. The 47th Line was still in the Vendée and had not joined the division by the time the Waterloo campaign began. Therefore, the 107th Line was broken up so a battalion was attached to the 10th Line, with the remainder to the 5th Light Infantry regiment. The *ad hoc* brigade was commanded by General Trommelin. Judging by the losses in the 5th Light, the regiment went into action between 3.30 and 4 p.m. and was in continuous action till 7.30 p.m. One of the first casualties was Captain Lacroix, who was killed at 5.30 p.m. at the head of the 4th Company of 1st Battalion. The heaviest losses in the 5th were 4.45 to 5.30 p.m., when fifteen men were killed, and between 6 and 6.30 p.m., when a further ten men were killed.[27] General Tromelin reports:

> At three o'clock in the afternoon, Jeanins Division followed by the 1st Division of Simmer, crossed the road 200 meters to the south of La Belle Alliance, moving behind Milhauds cuirassiers, and with Plancenoite [*sic*.] to their right, deployed to the rear of the 1st Division, on a ridge between two streams, a quarter of a league to the north of this village. The three regiments of the division were split into two groups, the 10th regiment of Line Infantry and a battalion commanded by Cuppe from the 107th regiment of Line Infantry were under my direct command, and were placed into a small wood. In front, were two horse artillery batteries from the cavalry division, which were already firing against the Prussians.
>
> To our left the squadrons of Milhaud quaked. The Prussian attack started towards 4 o'clock in the evening. Our cavalry sabred the enemy squadrons. Then we formed square by brigade and remained under the fire of forty Prussians guns which caused is great harm. We were unaware of what else was happening on the battlefield.
>
> About a half past 5 o'clock, the enemy were reinforced by infantry and cavalry, and the artillery fire became terrible. We kept a bold front, but suffering greatly from the fire of the guns, the four squares of the corps retired slowly in echelon formation towards Plancenoite where we finally established ourselves. We were outflanked by the Prussian cavalry, and we occupied the gardens and orchards of the village.
>
> It was then our right was extended by the Young Guard and then reinforced by my old commander General Morand at the head of a battalion of grenadiers. The fighting was terrible. This mix of units

repulsed several Prussian assaults, and even gained ground of several hundred trouises [*sic*.] beyond Plancenoit.

Towards eight o'clock decimated by the Prussian attacks which were constantly reinforced, our right was turned by Bluchers cavalry, whose squadrons our own cavalry could no longer contain, and on our left, the English cavalry launched a pursuit.[28]

An eyewitness to the role of the 107th Line at Waterloo, part of which served with Tromelin, was Sergeant-Major Marq, who served in the voltigeur company of 3rd Battalion. He writes about Waterloo and confirms the late departure from Genappe:

About ten o'clock in the morning (June 18, 1815), the regiment left its camp and headed to Waterloo, where the battle was already animated. The regiments that were part of our corps (the VI) were united. They marched in column to the battle. We were made to stand in this position until three o'clock in the afternoon, and having been exposed to a great number of cannonballs that were falling into our ranks, we marched in close column to the middle of the battlefield. Marching to this point, several men were killed in the ranks, and having arrived, we were made to form square because the British cavalry was near us and fought with the French cuirassiers. They came several times to press our square, but won no success. Bullets and shrapnel fell into our square like hail. We were there with orders not to fire a shot and having fixed bayonets. Many men were killed in this position. After a few hours in square at this position, the battalion commanders were ordered to send their voltigeurs out as sharpshooters.

I was sergeant major of the 3rd company and immediately gave the order. We were led by our officers. Having arrived near the enemy we were near a wood located on the road to Brussels. Being well emplaced and supported by columns of cavalry who were behind us, we forced the enemy to retreat, but soon our pursuit stopped, forty thousand enemies at once flushed us out of the woods and they opened fire on us.

The voltigeurs who were there were all killed and wounded. I was wounded by a bullet that went through my body through the left groin and came out after an incision, in the bulk of the right buttock. This dropped me to the ground and I was immediately picked up by two of my sergeants who were close to me. I was picked up and put on an artillery horse.

But hardly had I gone twenty paces on the horse that I was obliged to get off the said horse because I could not bear his movement. I stayed on the battlefield on 18, 19 and 20 June, when I was picked up by peasants and led away to Brussels. There my wound was dressed for the first time. I was part of a convoy of 1,500 wounded men.

The battle was terrible for the French. They had a complete rout, parks of artillery, ammunition wagons and food are left in enemy hands. The retreat was so hasty that there was hardly time to cut the traces of horses harnessed to pieces during the escape. Finally, I will not do the entire description of this unfortunate retirement, since I was taken prisoner. But having remained on the battlefield, I saw much of the enemy troops who marched in pursuit of the French.[29, 30]

In the action, Battalion Commander Jean Henri Cuppe, at the head of his 1st Battalion, 107th Line, took a gunshot to the stomach, which resulted in a hernia.[31] Colonel Druot, commanding the regiment, was wounded. Captain Vincent Frederick Delarue was grievously wounded to the left leg and was left for dead on the field of battle; he was made a prisoner of war.[32] Sub-Lieutenant Jean Antoine Azaret Scevola Anthouard was shot in the right thigh. He was unable to keep pace with his retiring regiment and was left on the battlefield to be captured by the allies. He was released from prison on 23 August 1815.[33]

In the closing stages of this firefight, Lieutenant Francois Xavier Dericq was wounded. He was aged twenty-four at Waterloo. During this exchange of musketry, he was shot in the right hand. Later in the day, with the Prussian cavalry flooding onto the battlefield, the rump of the 107th Line was attacked by Prussian cavalry. In this melee, Lt Dericq took a sabre cut to the right shoulder and three wounds from a lance. He, however, survived this ordeal and died in 1860.[34]

In the accompanying 10th Line, wounded at the head of the 1st Battalion was Battalion Commander Jean Francois Elie Decos. Captain Jacques Henri Gabriel Drouas was also wounded. Captain Jean Baptiste Auguste Rey de Morande was shot by a musket ball that passed through his left thigh in a firefight.[35] Captain Louis Auguste Lemaire was wounded, so too was Captain Bertrand Cazenave, who commanded one of the regiment's grenadier companies.[36] The eagle of the regiment during the campaign was carried by Lieutenant Edmee Bouchu. He was born on 15 January 1776 at Tonnerre. Between 1809 and 1814, he had served in the Royal Guard of Spain and thence the Imperial Guard. At Waterloo, in defence of the eagle, he took a gunshot wound to the left leg.[37] Lieutenant Germain Beaufrère was born on 26 December 1785, had joined the regiment on 31 April 1814, having served in the Imperial Guard since 26 September 1806, and had progressed through the ranks from private to sub-lieutenant. He too was wounded at Waterloo.[38]

Losses

With very limited eyewitness accounts of the fighting, we have to rely upon casualty reports to glimpse the fighting between Lobau and the Prussians.

5th Regiment of Line

Losses for 1st Battalion are as follows (with the tables representing the regiment's formation when in line in the field, with the grenadier company on the extreme right, but probably with the voltigeurs in open order):[39]

	Volt Coy	4e Coy	3e Coy	2e Coy	1er Coy	Gren. Coy
POW	5	3	7	8	12	7
Missing	-	1	1	1	-	-
Killed	-	-	1	3	-	-
Wounded	4	9	5	7	11	6
Total	9	13	14	19	23	13

Losses in the 2nd Battalion were as follows:

	Volt Coy	4e Coy	3e Coy	2e Coy	1er Coy	Gren. Coy
POW	13	15	12	19	10	9
Missing	-	-	-	-	4	-
Killed	2	2	5	1	2	-
Wounded	5	4	6	9	2	10
Total	20	21	23	29	18	19

The centre companies bore the brunt of the fighting. The POW and missing surely includes any wounded left behind as the regiment retreated. Losses with the 3rd Battalion were as follows:

	Volt Coy	4e Coy	3e Coy	2e Coy	1er Coy	Gren. Coy
POW	12	14	10	11	5	12
Missing	-	2	1	-	-	2
Killed	2	-	3	-	1	1
Wounded	9	8	5	7	12	9
Total	23	24	19	18	18	24

The chart shows the regiment deployed in line battle. The losses suggest the regiment was attacked on its flanks with a concentration to the left.

Total regimental losses at Waterloo are in the table below:

5th Line Losses, 18 June 1815				
	Wounded	POW	Killed	Missing
1st Battalion	42	45	4	3
2nd Battalion	36	78	12	4
3rd Battalion	50	56	7	5
Total	128	179	23	12

In terms of men killed, the heaviest losses fell on 2nd and 3rd Battalion, but all three were committed to the action. On 18 June, the regiment mustered 1,541 men in three battalions. The 3rd Battalion has so far never been listed in any order of battle for Waterloo despite an order issued 26 May 1815 ordering the battalion to join the *Armée du Nord*.[40] The regiment lost 342 men at Waterloo—22 per cent of effective strength.

11th Regiment of Line

The table below gives the losses for the 1st Battalion (with the regiment in line in the field, with the grenadier company on the extreme right, but probably with the voltigeurs detached in front):[41]

	Volt Coy	4e Coy	3e Coy	2e Coy	1er Coy	Gren. Coy
POW	2	1	5	11	2	1
Missing	-	1	-	-	-	-
Killed	5	2	5	5	6	3
Wounded	9	13	16	7	14	11
Total	16	17	26	23	22	15

The table below gives the losses for the 2nd Battalion:

	Volt Coy	4e Coy	3e Coy	2e Coy	1er Coy	Gren. Coy
POW	-	21	1	11	1	10
Missing	1	-	1	-	1	-
Killed	4	1	2	2	5	5

Wounded	14	13	13	10	10	5
Total	19	35	17	23	17	20

The table below gives the losses for the 4th Battalion, which had been amalgamated with the 2nd to bring it up to strength:

	Volt Coy	4e Coy	3e Coy	2e Coy	1er Coy	Gren. Coy
POW	-	1	-	5	4	-
Missing	-	-	1	-	-	-
Killed	-	-	-	1	-	-
Wounded	-	-	-	1	2	-
Total	0	1	1	7	6	0

The data says nothing of use. Total regimental losses at Waterloo are in the table below:

11th Regiment of Line Infantry				
	Wounded	POW	Killed	Missing
1st Battalion	70	11	26	1
2nd Battalion	65	44	19	3
3rd Battalion	Not at Waterloo			
4th Battalion	3	10	1	1
Total	138	65	46	4

In total, 22 per cent of the regiment's effective strength was lost at Waterloo.

27th Regiment of Line

The chart below shows the 1st Battalion deployed in line of battle:[42]

	Volt Coy	4e Coy	3e Coy	2e Coy	1er Coy	Gren. Coy
POW	2	10	11	5	2	7
Missing	-	6	8	3	1	1
Killed	-	1	2	1	2	6
Wounded	2	1	-	2	4	-
Total	4	18	21	11	9	14

The heaviest losses were to 4th Company, although the grenadiers sustained the most men killed. The chart below shows the 2nd Battalion deployed in line of battle:

	Volt Coy	4e Coy	3e Coy	2e Coy	1er Coy	Gren. Coy
POW	1	8	9	5	1	3
Missing	-	-	1	1	1	-
Killed	-	-	1	5	1	1
Wounded	2	3	3	3	6	3
Total	3	11	14	14	9	7

The concentration of men killed to the centre companies makes us think the battalion was attacked in front. The chart below shows the 3rd Battalion deployed in line of battle:

	Volt Coy	4e Coy	3e Coy	2e Coy	1er Coy	Gren. Coy
POW	-	4	2	1	-	3
Missing	-	-	-	2	1	-
Killed	-	-	-	1	2	1
Wounded	1	3	-	2	3	3
Total	1	7	2	6	6	7

The losses to the right-most companies suggests the Prussian attack was strongest against this flank. Total regimental losses at Waterloo are as below:

27th Regiment of Line Infantry				
	Wounded	POW	Killed	Missing
1st Battalion	17	43	4	21
2nd Battalion	20	28	8	3
3rd Battalion	11	10	3	4
Total	48	81	15	28

The regiment lost 171 men at Waterloo. Tentatively, the regiment mustered 1,161 men, thus losing 14 per cent of effective strength during the battle.

84th Regiment of Line
Regimental losses were as follows for the 1st Battalion:[43]

	Volt Coy	4e Coy	3e Coy	2e Coy	1er Coy	Gren. Coy
Wounded POW	-	-	1	2	-	2
Missing	8	1	1	-	-	1
Killed	6	2	-	3	1	-
Wounded	15	11	14	8	11	24
Total	29	14	16	13	12	27

The above chart represents the formation of the regiment when in the field, when in line. From the losses, the voltigeurs were strung out in front. The grenadiers also lost heavily, suggesting that whatever fighting they were involved in was of a different intensity to the centre companies. The losses in 2nd Battalion were as follows:

	Volt Coy	4e Coy	3e Coy	2e Coy	1er Coy	Gren. Coy
POW	-	-	10	-	-	-
Wounded POW	-	-	-	-	-	1
Missing	4	14	3	25	3	8
Killed	2	3	-	2	-	4
Wounded	2	4	12	5	1	4
Total	8	21	25	32	4	17

Unlike 1st Battalion, no discernible pattern can be made out of the losses. The heaviest losses fell in 3rd Company in terms of men wounded, but it is reasonable to assume the missing included men wounded and left behind on the battlefield.

The 3rd Battalion mustered 438 men and took to the field conjoined with the 4th, some 195 men:

	Volt Coy	4e Coy	3e Coy	2e Coy	1er Coy	Gren. Coy
POW	1	1	4	-	-	-
Wounded POW	-	-	-	1	-	-
Missing	4	6	11	-	4	8
Killed	1	-	-	-	-	2

Wounded	2	3	2	6	10	14
Total	8	10	17	7	14	24

The chart shows the battalion deployed in line of battle. The losses concentrate to the right-hand companies; it could be that the battalion was deployed in column of attack with the grenadiers at the front, thus more exposed to fire. Under this interpretation, we see the number of wounded tails off down the length of the column. Of course, the battalion may have been in line and the left flank sheltered from enemy fire by another unit or terrain.

Total regimental losses at Waterloo are as follows:

27th Regiment of Line Infantry					
	Wounded	Wounded & POW	POW	Killed	Missing
1st Battalion	83	5	-	14	11
2nd Battalion	28	1	10	11	57
3rd Battalion	37	1	6	3	33
Total	147	7	16	28	101

In total, the regiment lost 299 men at Waterloo out of 1,527 men, equating to 19 per cent of effective strength.

Comment

The losses for the 19th Division are in the table below:

19th Infantry Division						
	Wounded	Wounded & Pow	POW	Killed	Missing	Total
5th Line	128	-	179	23	12	342
11th Line	138	-	65	46	4	253
27th Line	48	-	81	15	28	171
84th Line	147	7	16	28	101	299
Total	461	7	341	112	145	1,065

The 5th Line bore the brunt of the fighting based on overall losses, followed by the 84th Line. However, the highest number of dead was the

11th Line, which we are told by eyewitnesses stood alongside the 84th Line. The 27th Line has the lowest number of losses from any regiment in the division. One wonders if the 27th were kept as a reserve, as the losses are significantly lower than the other regiments in the division.

20th Infantry Division

The losses for the 5th Light are minimal. The death certificate of Captain Jean Louis Leroy states he was killed at 6 p.m. In 1st Battalion we find:[44]

	Volt Coy	4e Coy	3e Coy	2e Coy	1er Coy	Carab. Coy
Killed	4	3	-	3	1	5

In the 2nd Battalion:

	Volt Coy	4e Coy	3e Coy	2e Coy	1er Coy	Carab. Coy
Killed	2	1	-	6	1	2

In total, twenty-eight men were listed killed. Interestingly, the first casualty is listed at 4 p.m., when seven men were killed. Twelve men were killed at 5 p.m. Three men were killed at 5.30 p.m., then another nine at 6 p.m. The Last man was recorded dead at 6.30 p.m. This shows the regiment, and the attendant division, were in action for two and a half hours before being pulled back. Regimental records report three wounded and three POWs.[45]

10th Regiment of Line

Losses in the 1st Battalion were as follows:[46]

	Volt Coy	4e Coy	3e Coy	2e Coy	1er Coy	Gren. Coy
POW	5	-	8	7	5	8
Killed	-	-	-	-	-	2
Total	5	0	8	7	5	10

The chart shows the battalion deployed in line of battle. The official records show thirty-four men lost, which is incredibly low. The POW may have been wounded. The records are almost meaningless, sadly. Below are the losses for 2nd Battalion:

	Volt Coy	4e Coy	3e Coy	2e Coy	1er Coy	Gren. Coy
POW	4	2	13	6	8	4
Killed	-	-	-	1	1	6
Wounded	-	-	-	1	1	-
Total	4	2	13	8	10	10

The bulk of the losses were the grenadiers and 1st Company. The regimental records report losses for the 3rd and 4th Battalions, which is seems were taken into the 1st and 2nd Battalions, but how or when we cannot say, as the 10 June parade shows only two battalions in the field. Losses for the 3rd Battalion were:

	Volt Coy	4e Coy	3e Coy	2e Coy	1er Coy	Gren. Coy
POW	7	1	9	8	7	11
Killed	-	-	-	-	-	1
Wounded	2	-	-	-	-	-
Total	9	1	9	8	7	12

The two flank companies suffered the greatest losses. Presumably, the voltigeurs were detached. From the 4th Battalion, we find:

	Volt Coy	4e Coy	3e Coy	2e Coy	1er Coy	Gren. Coy
POW	-	-	7	2	6	-
Killed	-	-	-	-	1	-
Total	0	0	7	2	7	0

Total regimental losses at Waterloo are in the table below:

10th Regiment of Line Infantry				
	Wounded	Wounded & POW	POW	Killed
1st Battalion	-	-	33	2
2nd Battalion	1	1	37	8
3rd Battalion	2	-	43	1
4th Battalion	-	-	15	1
Total	3	1	128	12

Compared to the 5th Regiment of Light Infantry, just five men were killed, which implies the light infantry were dispersed as sharpshooters rather than formed battalions. As Waterloo, the 10th Regiment of Line lost 137 men. The overwhelming majority were POWs. This number surely included wounded men. It had mustered 1,375 men on 10 June, suffering five men killed and a recorded four men wounded. The data suggests that the regiment was not in action for any great period of time, possibly held in reserve.

107th Regiment of Line

The table below shows the regiment as deployed in line of battle:[47]

	Volt Coy	4e Coy	3e Coy	2e Coy	1er Coy	Gren. Coy
POW	-	1	-	1	5	-
Killed	-	1	1	-	1	-
Missing	7	7	10	7	7	6
Wounded and POW	-	3	-	1	1	-
Wounded	11	7	3	4	5	4
Total	18	19	14	13	19	10

The data suggests that the voltigeurs and grenadiers were detached, leaving the four centre companies as a united body, which was attacked on the flanks. The 2nd Battalion losses were as follows:

	Volt Coy	4e Coy	3e Coy	2e Coy	1er Coy	Gren. Coy
Killed	4	1	2	-	-	1
Missing	2	9	12	13	11	12
Wounded and POW	-	-	-	1	-	-
Wounded	18	5	2	3	2	3
Total	24	15	16	17	13	16

The heaviest losses are with the voltigeur company, which, we assume, was detached as the losses are substantially above any other company. With eight men killed compared to the three of the 1st Battalion, the fighting was far deadlier for the battalion. The 3rd Battalion is as follows:

	Volt Coy	4e Coy	3e Coy	2e Coy	1er Coy	Gren. Coy
POW	-	1	-	1	4	-
Killed	-	-	-	1	-	1
Missing	2	4	4	2	8	-
Wounded	8	2	-	-	3	2
Total	10	7	4	4	15	3

Just two men were killed, with the majority going missing; presumably, wounded men were left behind. The high number of wounded in the voltigeur company suggests these men were detached, which corroborates Francis Marq's eyewitness commentary. Total regimental losses at Waterloo are at the table below:

107th Regiment of Line Infantry					
	Wounded	Wounded & POW	POW	Killed	Missing
1st Battalion	34	5	7	3	44
2nd Battalion	33	1	-	8	47
3rd Battalion	15	-	6	2	20
Total	82	6	13	13	111

The regiment lost 225 men on 18 June. The regiment began the campaign with 691 other ranks and forty-four officers, forming three battalions. Overall, 32 per cent of the regiment's effective strength was lost defending the French right flank.

Comment

Total losses for the 20th Division are in the table below:

20th Infantry Division						
	Wounded	Wounded & Pow	POW	Killed	Missing	Total
5th Light	-	-	-	28	6	34
10th Line	3	1	128	12	-	144
107th Line	82	6	13	13	67	168
Total	85	7	141	53	73	346

We have no data for the 5th Light, so we cannot offer any comment regarding divisional losses, but looking at the number of men recorded as killed, the regiment bore the brunt of the casualties in the division. The bulk of the 10th Regiment of Line were men, lost as prisoners of war, whereas the 107th had far more men killed and wounded, suggesting the 10th Regiment of Line Infantry listed all its losses as prisoners of war—*i.e.*, missing.

The fighting Lobau faced was intense as a young aide-de-camp reports:

Our right flank was attacked sharply in the evening by Blücher's army, and we were subjected to the most heavy fire. Every minute, men and horses fell. Roundshot was reaching us from all sides, even on our backsides. Eventually, the army was routed and despite its considerable casualties, the division held on perfectly and was not encircled.[48]

An eyewitness from d'Erlon's staff, Cheron, recalls:

The enemy was able to clear their centre to move to the flanks. The Emperor followed this movement. The flanks even tried to reach behind us and cut off our path.

Marshal Blache [Blücher] had arrived with his troops on our right. The enemy resumed firing on the centre, a fire which they had suspended only to strengthen our confidence, and we found ourselves surrounded, so to speak, with nothing left open other than the road.

18

Prussians and More Prussians

By early evening, Lobau was losing his grip on the right flank. Napoleon had no option but to turn to his reserve troops—the Young Guard, commanded by General Duhesme. The entire division was ordered up from its positions on the Brussels road and directed to the right flank.

Durutte, despite being bolstered by the 54th and 55th Regiment of Line, was unable to stem the flow of the Prussians which had come between his troopers at Papelotte and Frichermont. Without reinforcements, Durutte would have been forced to retreat. Simultaneously, Lobau with his two divisions filled the gap between Frichermont and Plancenoit was feeling under increasing pressure as more Prussians arrived. Sending forward the Young Guard was the last roll of the dice. It was too little, too late, but what other troops were available? The Old Guard was held in reserve: perhaps even now the emperor was perhaps planning a last desperate attack on the allied right. Even if it had succeeded, the French were too exhausted to exploit the situation. Sending the Old Guard to hold the Prussians in check and initiate a fighting retreat would have been the more sensible course of action, yet common sense had no place in the command decisions being made. Desperation at trying to save a lost battle—and the throne of France—gripped the emperor and other senior officers. They knew losing the battle was the end of the new regime and would very likely result in their execution or exile.

Lieutenant Jacqmin of the 85th Line recalls the retreat as follows:

> I was at Waterloo with the two first battalion of the regiment. At one hour after the commencement of the battle, following the wounding of Captain Chapuis and the death of Lieutenant Monsieur Legay, I took command of the company. At six o'clock in the evening, we perceived that we had been outflanked and part of the Army began to beat the

retreat. I was then reunited with the rest of the company and numerous other soldiers of the battalion, perhaps 150 men, who had marched forward as sharpshooters against the Scottish soldiers which we had pressed back.

A short time after this, our brave Colonel Masson who commanded the regiment saved our eagle, I assisted in taking hold of the shaft upon which was the eagle. This struggle lasted for ten minutes and was very heavy. The two battalions both suffered badly, and we retained perhaps a dozen officers.[1]

General Brue's brigade held the Papelotte–Frichermont line till the end of the battle, with 6th Corps holding the line between Frichermont and Plancenoit. Eventually, the brigade was overwhelmed by the Prussians, as Jacqmin notes. The collapse of the French defence here allowed the Prussians to sweep along the French right flank and threaten La Haie Sainte at the very moment the Old Guard attacked.

To bolster the right wing, the Young Guard were committed to the action, General Drouot notes:

Meantime the Prussian Corps which had joined the left of the English, placed itself *en potence* upon our right flank, and began to attack about half-past five in the afternoon. The 6th Corps, which had taken no part in the battle of the 16th, was placed to oppose them, and was supported by a division of the Young Guard and some batteries of the Guard. Towards seven o'clock we perceived in the distance towards our right, a fire of artillery and musketry.[2]

General Philibert-Guillaume Duhesme began his military career by joining the National Guard in 1789. Two years later, he was elected a captain in the 2nd Battalion of Volunteers of Saône-et-Loire, and in October 1793, Duhesme was promoted to *général de brigade* by the representatives of the people with the Army of the North. After Napoleon's abdication, Duhesme was made inspector general of infantry and a Knight of Saint Louis. When Napoleon returned to power in 1815, Duhesme rallied to him and was named a peer of France.

Deputy to Duhesme was General Barrois. Pierre Barrois first joined the French army in August 1793 when he enlisted in the battalion of Scouts of the Meuse, and in barely a month, he was made lieutenant. He served with distinction at Marengo. He was promoted to battalion commander in October 1800 and then was made colonel of the 96th Regiment of Line Infantry in 1803. He was promoted to *général de brigade* in 1811 and was given command of a division of the Young Guard for the campaigns in Germany of 1813. General Barrois's 1st Division was then ordered to assault the buildings at Smohain. The fighting was bitter and desperate, and Duhesme pushed back the Nassau troops. Advancing rapidly to the aid of Nassau troops came the Prussian 12th Infantry Regiment:

> General von Steinmetz ordered me to take two companies of schutzen to the village of sdmophain. Here I was to throw out the French ... four platoons of Schutzen moved on the lower paet of the illage and threw the enemy out there, while my fusilier battalion led by its skirmishers, alose moved through the village. Both the Schutzen and the fusilier battalion advanced against the enemy skirmishers who fought back ferociously. This struggle continued intil the enemy's general withdrawal began, whereupon our cavalry followed up.[3]

The arrival of the Prussian was vital as Ludwig von Reiche tells us:

> Before our eyes, the enemy attacked and captured the village of Smolhain, still occupied by the Nassau troops in front of their extreme left wing. The Nassauers, who left the village, came back en debandade to our newly arrived troops. They considered the Nassauers, who were dressed very much in the French style at the time, to be enemies and shot at them.... As long as the enemy remained in the village of Smolhain, the second and fourth army corps with their right wings were separated from the extreme left wings of the English army; it also stopped and endangered a sustained intervention of our army corps in the battle.
>
> The two batteries of the vanguard, along with the two firing companies and the fusilier battalions of the 12th and 24th regiments, supported by the reserve cavalry, were preferred. With the greatest speed they formed themselves into an attack on Smolhain, which the enemy did not wait, but left the village.[4]

As more Prussian troops arrived on the battlefield, Napoleon was faced with either withdrawing or committing his last reserves—the Old Guard and what remained of the cavalry—to try and snatch victory. Most of 2nd Corps was committed to the attack of Hougoumont and 6th Corps under Lobau was deployed against the Prussians at Papelotte and La Haye. The hedges, sunken lanes, and back gardens of scattered farms and isolated houses became the scenes of bitter fighting as the French fell back.

The Prussian assault on the La Haye–Frichermont line was the vital turning point to the battle, as Adjutant-Commandant Janin of 6th Corps narrates:

Despite of the inferiority of our artillery, we stopped the march of the leading Prussian Corps. However, they began extend beyond our right flank, necessitated the intervention of the guard.

The commander in chief of the Young Guard was Lieutenant-General Duhesme, his chief of staff being Adjutant-Commandant Mellinet. The 1st Brigade comprising the 1st regiments of Tirailleur and voltigeur was led by Jean Hyacinthe Sébastien Chartrand, and the 2nd Brigade comprising the 3rd regiments of Tirailleur and voltigeur by General Nicolas Philippe Guye, Marquis de Rios-Molanos.[5]

The Young Guard held their position for an hour or more against an ever-increasing tide of Prussians. General Barrois related:

The 18 June at Waterloo, was charged to defend the right of the line, at the village of Smohain where a Prussian Corps attacked. He maintained this position till seven o'clock in the evening, and only retired when he was wounded.[6]

From the initial deployment beyond the woods of Frichermont, Lobau had been pushed back over the course of two hours or more due to ever mounting pressure from the Prussians to a defensive line between Frichermont and Plancenoit. The Young Guard's actions here is recalled by Major Ludwig Wirths, a former captain (*Hauptmann*) in the 2nd Battalion, 2nd Nassau Regiment, concerning the part played by the battalion during the battle:

The 2nd Battalion of the 2nd Nassau Regiment was ordered to take its position behind the farm of La Haie, fronting this farm on the small height leading gently down towards it; forming from there the extreme left wing of the Army, in close columns. Just a little in rear of this position an English light dragoon regiment arrived. The 3rd Battalion was sent forward towards the farm of Papelotte. In this position, obliquely opposite to the enemy's right wing battery, the 2nd Battalion received, after the battle had begun, an assault from several 8 pounders from the same battery, which injured and killed some of the men. Just at the beginning of the affair, the 2nd Flanqueur Company, which was under the command of 1st Lieutenant Fuchs, was sent forward to the farm of La Haie to operate against the artillery on the enemy's right wing and to prevent it from moving on to our left wing. After several hours, around 3 o'clock in the afternoon, Sergeant Lind from this company let us know that all 3 of the lieutenants [Captain Joseph Müller had already been injured on the 16th], 1st Lieutenant Fuchs and 2nd Lieutenant Cramer were wounded and unable to continue in the battle and that the junior 2nd Lieutenant von Trott was dead; so, I was ordered by the commander of the battalion, von Normann, to go and to support the Flanker Company with my own, the 8th. I met the rest of that company, which had suffered a great deal, in the farm of La Haie, with some of the men in the gardens surrounding the farm, they being occupied in combating the enemy artillery. As a result of the reinforcement from my company, our combined and stronger fire made the enemy retire towards its right wing and I subsequently passed the farm with my company and moved down the grass valley leading to Smohain, and having passed this deep but narrow valley, I arrived on the open field, and at one side of the enemy's Army, by turning a little to the right, I was faced by a line of artillery, which was covered by 2 batteries ready to open fire and a battalion of the *Moyenne Garde*. I operated here, half advancing, half driven back again, until I could place myself into a hollow way which protected my front and from where I advanced to drive the enemy back with a heavy fire, and I did not have to leave this position until the end. During this combat the company lost many men, although I cannot state the exact number. Leiter and Wagner, two of the 2nd Lieutenants were wounded, the first on his leg, the second by a shot in his head, and I myself was also slightly wounded, being heavily bruised by a shot in the lower leg which, however, did not force me to leave my position. Towards 6 o'clock in the evening, the Prussians arrived in rear of my position, coming from Smohain with their artillery, and so it happened that they fired upon my company for a short time, thinking that we were French; however, this error was soon discovered.[7]

The comment regarding the *Moyenne Garde* may of course be perfectly true, but rather it was the Young Guard. The Young Guard was deployed in this sector, but we have no evidence of it being deployed at Papelotte; however, it seems that Wirths was engaging the Young Guard closer to Plancenoit than to Papelotte. Flanqueur Pinstock, 1st Battalion, 28th Orange-Nassau Regiment, writes to his parents, brothers, and sisters in Eisemroth on 22 July 1815 recalling the events of Waterloo:

At 6 o'clock the Prussians came to our assistance, and then the French had to run for 5 days and nights until they had reached Paris. We followed them to Paris, and there we had to lie in our camp for 10 days, but on the 17th July, we were billeted in the city. From the 15th to the 17th June we had to lie in the fields at night, drenched in water and covered in mud, my knapsack was the pillow under my head, my coat was my blanket and the sky my hat.[8]

These Prussian troop were Zieten's men. From now on, the battle only had one outcome.

Zieten Arrives

Captain Carl Rettburg, commanding the light company of the 2nd Battalion, 3rd Nassau Regiment, notes:

> Between 3 and 4 o'clock in the afternoon the reinforced enemy artillery line moved forward again, and it was supported by a significant formation of infantry. I was forced to leave my position and withdrew to Papelotte, which I had prepared in this very short time as well as possible to serve as a point of retreat.
>
> I requested reinforcements and Captain Frensdorf sent the 10th, 11th and 12th Companies, accompanied by the Flanqueur Company from the 2nd Battalion of our regiment, with orders to obey my command. The enemy formation was stopped by the fire from Papelotte and from the detachment in the small houses, where the units bravely resisted, and was thrown back and pursued to the previously mentioned furthest hedge. Here we were welcomed by an enemy battery and their muskets, only 500 paces away. Our loss was great, the 3rd Flanqueur Company lost 2 officers in its position and was reduced to half of its number by the end of the battle, but the enemy did not attempt another serious attack and contented itself by shooting heavily from a hedge beyond the grass valley at the foot of its position. This attack was delivered by a part of the division commanded by Durutte; I cannot tell exactly the force of this formation, but it was composed of many more men than I had at my disposal.
>
> Towards 6 o'clock in the evening the enemy appeared on my left wing. I had lost contact with the 1st Battalion Orange-Nassau. The enemy had taken Smohain and La Haie and moved the line of artillery forward to Papelotte. Even though this attack was very lively it was not supported by the infantry columns, so it was not very difficult as were in an advantageous position to push the enemy back. After 7 o'clock in the evening, the enemy retired without being forced to do so. This event was as inexplicable to me as the heavy canon and musket fire, which seemed to be coming from Smohain and Plancenoit; shortly afterwards my line, which I had pushed forward towards La Haie was forced back to the road which separated La Haie from Papelotte, and was forced back by artillery fire followed by a great many infantry units, which were also in my rear. Having driven these back I realised that we were engaged with the Prussians. They also realised the error, which had lasted for

no more than 10 minutes, but had cost both of us several killed and wounded.

I left Papelotte, which I had defended the whole time, but it was now that it was set on fire and this made it too difficult to defend any longer, and I joined the Prussians advancing towards Plancenoit.[9]

The attacking force in this second attack mentioned by Rettburg was undoubtedly the 95th and 85th Line. Around 7 p.m., a voltigeur company and two fusilier companies of the 95th Line were detached, under the orders of Battalion Commander Rulliers, to attack the enemy troops that were firing against the French artillery to the left of General Brue's brigade and held off the enemy for an hour and a half.[10]

Captain Pontecoulant of the Imperial Guard Horse Artillery notes from his position close to La Belle Alliance:

> Blücher, whose column heads we had seen for an hour in the village of Ohain, whose infantry had finally managed to reach defiles of Saint-Lambert. He then brought the head of two brigades, to the hamlet of La Haie and farm of Papelotte to get in communication with the left wing of the English Army. These points were occupied by two battalions of the Young Guard, which Napoleon had sent to relieve the troops of the Count d'Erlon, who had gloriously stood, but were worn out with fatigue ... Seeing themselves assailed by fresh troops, and very superior numbers at the end of a day so deadly, the two battalions were taken with a panic, and, without attempting a useless resistance, they retired in the greatest disorder. It is even asserted that in this hasty retreat, we heard the cry of every man for himself! ... our men became demoralised.[11]

General Baron August von Kruse writes as follows about the 2nd Nassau Regiment based at Papelotte and La Haye about the arrival of the Prussians:

> Shortly after 7 o'clock the enemy suddenly retired and numerous skirmishers from the Royal Prussian Army, followed by columns, appeared. They advanced from Smohain and Plancenoit and fired on the Nassau troops, who returned the fire at the beginning as they had not been informed of the arrival of the Prussians. The fire lasted for about ten minutes. There were dead and wounded on either side. However, the mistake was soon realised and the firing was stopped. Now Papelotte was left and the Prussians and Nassau advanced together. This movement was followed by the 2nd Battalion, which had maintained its position throughout the battle, but had been under artillery fire the whole time.

This movement is marked on the map in yellow. The losses of the 2nd Regiment on the 18th June 1815: 4 officers and 69 non-commissioned officers and soldiers killed; 20 officers and 153 non-commissioned officers and soldiers wounded. It should also be noted that two officers serving on my Staff were wounded. With the expression of my most perfect esteem, I have the honour to remain your most obedient Kruse.[12]

Against Lobau and Duhesme, Bülow had been making little headway as he advanced out of the *Bois de Paris*. A war of attrition had worn down both parties: the Prussians had fresh troops to commit, the French had none. Milhaud and Kellerman's cavalry had been frittered away by Ney, 1st Corps had been in constant action now for seven hours, and Lobau had been in the thick of the fighting with 6th Corps for five hours. Yet so far, the Prussians had been held in check, as the French had been slowly and surely pushed back. Lobau and Duhesme's firefight had started to 'chip away' at the Prussian steamroller. By the time Zieten's command began to reach Waterloo, the fighting at Papelotte and Frichermont had reached another crisis point. So serious was the situation that when General Zieten approached the battlefield, he was so concerned at the sight of stragglers and casualties coming from Wellington's left that he stopped his advance. No doubt, from Zieten's point of view, these troops heading to the rear appeared to be withdrawing. Fearing that his own troops could be caught up in a general panic, after assessing the situation, Zieten started to head away from Wellington's left flank.

It was crucial that immediate and decisive action be taken to prevent a French breakout. About the same time, General Thielmann was in desperate need of reinforcements to fend off Grouchy. At long last, the French 4th Corps was now in action, and if Grouchy (finally with troop superiority to the Prussians) was to be held in check, Thielmann needed more men. To that end, he sent a desperate dispatch calling Zieten back to Wavre. Zieten hesitated and then began the journey. A crisis point had been reached.

The Prussian army liaison officer to Wellington, General Muffling, seeing Zieten's command and its subsequent about-face, galloped over to find the general and persuaded him to support Wellington's left flank.[12] The outcome of the battle, thanks to Muffling, was now in the favour of the allies. If Zieten had headed back to aid Thielmann at Wavre, then the outcome of the day may have been different. Grouchy's action at Wavre—traditionally 'written off' as unimportant—was clearly a major cause of concern for Prussian High Command, and far from being ineffective, it seems Grouchy was pushing hard at the Prussians. Keeping Zieten at Waterloo turned the day for the allies and sacrificed Thielmann to keep Grouchy's forces at bay long enough to cement victory at Waterloo.

If Grouchy had not been at Wavre, then the entire Prussian III Corps would have swept into the field and totally annihilated the *Armée du Nord*. Grouchy saved the defeat from being totally catastrophic, and Muffling's action was the harbinger of victory for the allies.

With Zieten's men now arriving on the battlefield, by 8 p.m., Lobau and Duhesme's position was increasingly untenable. He had to pull back. At Plancenoit, the Prussians were making their first tentative moves. This left the 6th Corps and the Young Guard deployed in front of the Bois du Paris in a very vulnerable position. That Lobau and Duhesme had clung tenaciously to this position for perhaps four hours is of great credit to these generals, but Lobau and Duhesme had no choice but to fall back to Plancenoit to stop their command being surrounded on both flanks. Senior aide-de-camp to Marshal Ney, Colonel Pierre Heymès, admits:

> Between seven and eight o'clock, the right of the Prussian Corps together with the left of the English, forced our extreme right and drove back toward the centre in the same time threatening the rear of 6th Corps.[14]

Due to this threat, Lobau retreated. Marshal Ney writes, 'the Prussians continued their offensive movements, and our right sensibly retired, the English advanced in their turn.'[15] The French headed back to Plancenoit. General Trommelin recounts this final episode of the battle as follows:

> At about eight o'clock in the evening, decimated by the Prussian attacks, which had been constantly reinforced, turned our right wing and the cavalry of Blücher pushed to the left with the English cavalry and began the pursuit of the Army which fell into disorder, I had to order my battalions to abandon Plancenoit which was in flames and return to the main road.
>
> At that moment when the last brigade of the 1st Division passed mine I started my own retreat, my square was pressed from all directions, and broke in disorder. Remaining alone, I had a great trouble to remount, and went to rally my men in a wood to the rear of my position. I found it occupied by the Prussians, who forced me onto the main road, with those men that remained to me. I rallied some men to the left of the square of Grenadiers of the Imperial Guard, but noticing that they were unsteady, I decided to reach the main road where I found the divisional command.[16]

This retrenchment to Plancenoit now left Napoleon's right flank dangerously exposed. Lieutenant Pontecoulant of the guard artillery summarises the situation on the French right:

Count Lobau, fearing being cut off, carried out his retreat towards our centre. The consequences of this movement were to allow the Prussian batteries, who had been substantially reinforced, and which counted more than 60 guns, to gain ground so that their balls and even their case shot, fell as far as the Charleroi road, which served as the main line of communications for our army, around the farm of la Belle Alliance, and even the high ground around Rossome where the emperor was in the middle of his Guard. The trees lining the road were riddled, and often men, horses or caissons, moving from the reserve to the line of battle, were struck.[17]

Lobau and Duhesme combined lacked the men to be able to halt the Prussian advance—some 14,000 against 30,000 Prussians. That these two commanders held out as long as they did is admirable. The French forces were strung out from Frichermont to Plancenoit, the left being held by Durutte. Durutte's men were, however, ordered to move towards the Brussels road, thinning out the French defensive line even more. This fatally weakened the French resistance. From 1st Corps, only Donzelot's division, with what remained of Quiot's and Marcognet's division, now held the line between the Brussels road and Frichermont. Lieutenant Domonique Fleuret of the 55th Regiment of Line notes:[18]

> The regiment was reduced to about 400 men, and they were formed into a single battalion. We were used as sharpshooters along with the Young Guard. We marched against the Prussians, who moved against our right wing to cut off the Army's line of retreat.[19]

Despite being initially checked by the French, Bülow therefore did what all competent generals do—extend the line and search for a way to outflank the position. He found what he was looking for at Plancenoit. The village was the largest population centre in the area, with the impressive church rising from its northern side.

As Bülow advanced, he immediately sent part of the 15th Brigade out on his right to secure Frichermont and its neighbouring wood, to prevent any flank attack from Durutte's troops. This was achieved with relative ease, and the Prussians linked up with Saxe Weimar's Nassau troops, but not without a number of 'friendly fire' incidents. The rest of the 15th Brigade then moved on to engage Lobau's main force on the ridge north of Plancenoit, while the 13th Brigade followed them in reserve. The 16th Brigade marched forward with their artillery and the cavalry protecting their flanks, determined to take the village of Plancenoit. Possession of the village would leave Napoleon's rear completely unprotected, making his army very vulnerable; for the French, it was vital that the village was held.

Bülow therefore directed his precious reserves to Plancenoit and forced Lobau to retire or risk being outflanked. The French redeployed quickly and in good order, moving into position behind Plancenoit and placing a strong garrison in the village. The depleted elements of Durutte's division continued to engage the hamlets around Smohain, having more or less gained supremacy at Frichermont, supported by Domon and Subervie. Hiller's 16th Brigade formed line and the six battalions marched directly on Plancenoit, determined to oust the French defenders, with the 14th Brigade moving up in their rear to form a reserve. The Prussian assault was initially successful, pushing the French defenders back as far as the open space around the church, which sat on a small hillock and was surrounded by a defensive wall. Here they met a furious resistance and the advance was halted.

Bloody hand-to-hand fighting seesawed through the village without either side truly gaining the upper hand, although the Prussians did capture some cannon and a few hundred prisoners. Fighting in built-up areas was always some of the bloodiest in the Napoleonic wars, and Plancenoit would be no exception. It was hard to keep any kind of cohesion—units broke down into small groups of men either assaulting or defending, while individual buildings became fortresses. Given the amount of hatred between the French and the Prussians, quarter was neither asked for nor given.

Two battalions of 15th '3rd Reserve' Infantry Regiment pushed into the village and then on to the high walls of the cemetery and church. The Prussians found themselves under fire from French snipers stationed in the houses. A murderous exchange of shots erupted from a distance of no more than twenty paces.

By this point, information had been passed back to Napoleon and the headquarters staff about what was happening on the right flank. The news was dire, and there was no doubt a great deal of unease in the staff. The high morale of the French at the start of the battle was wavering. The Prussian intervention was having a telling and damaging effect on the French, the battle against the allies on Mont-Saint-Jean was also not yielding morale-boosting results, and now the Prussians were threatening to overwhelm the rear.

In order to assess the battlefield performance of the 6th Corps at Waterloo, we turn to the total losses sustained. Total losses for 6th Corps were 142 cavalry, 1,065 in the 19th Division, and 716 in the 20th Division—a total of 1,923 men lost. The 1st Young Guard Brigade lost 1,115 men and the 2nd Brigade 986 men—a total loss of 4,024 men.

The 19th and 20th Infantry Division was involved in action against the Prussian 13th and 15th Brigade. The 13th Brigade comprised the

1st Silesian, 2nd Neumark *Landwehr*, and 3rd Neumark *Landwehr*, the 15th Brigade the 18th Regiment, 3rd Silesian *Landwehr*, and 4th Silesian *Landwehr*. Hiller's 16th Brigade, comprising the 15th Regiment, 1st and 2nd Silesian *Landwehr*, seem to have been kept as a reserve. The Prussian losses compared to the French were huge. The 13th Brigade lost 716, 15th Prussian brigade lost 1,631 men, and the 16th some 1,645 men—a total of 3,992 men. The Prussians, if the French data is correct, lost few men less than the French, suggesting that Lobau was no easy pushover. Standing in prepared positions with artillery support, fighting on terrain of the French's choosing, Lobau in effect dictated the terms of the conflict with the Prussians. Defending troops clearly had the advantage here. So we must ask what caused the left wing of Lobau's 6th Corps—arguably, the 107th Regiment of Line with the 10th Regiment of Line—to fall back.

After making a stand in front of the *Bois de Paris*, between 7.30 and 8 p.m., Lobau's men had withdrawn back to Plancenoit, leaving the defence of the French right flank dangerously thin, as all that stood in the gaping void in the French right flank were the battered rumps of Donzelot and Marcognet's and Durutte's single brigade under the orders of General Brue. Such a gap in the French right wing seems to have been brutally exploited by the Prussian cavalry, which we are told were at La Haie Sainte at the climax of the battle when the Old Guard attacked.

Weight of numbers and the fear of being outflanked had caused Lobau to withdraw. The choices he faced as field commander was to stand and fight an ever-increasing flood of Prussians or to withdraw back to the main body of the *Armée du Nord* and get as many men as possible off the field of battle, seeing the battle was irrecoverably lost. Lobau, it seems, acted with caution and withdrew.

19

Plancenoit

Plancenoit was in flames. The Prussians had captured the village and forced the French back towards the Brussels road. Pockets of French troops remained, barricaded in the cemetery and houses. Almost no French troops filled the line between Smohain and the larger village. This gap would be brutally exploited by the Prussians. Buoyed by the sight of fresh troops of their own, with the arrival of Pirch's 5th Brigade commanded by Tipplskirch, Bülow was able to rally his men for another assault. The Prussians were now able to launch over 40,000 men against less than 15,000 French. On paper, the eventual outcome of an allied victory here was almost guaranteed. Despite holding on against overwhelming odds, sheer weight of numbers finally overcame the French and they were slowly forced back.

Despite the efforts of their officers, many men of the Young Guard fled in disarray. The situation on Napoleon's right flank was now critical. Prussian cannon balls were now landing on the Brussels road. It was vital that the French right wing was propped up. By 8 p.m., Lobau and Duhesme had withdrawn to Plancenoit, using the village as a defensive bastion to hold off the Prussians. The village was to remain in French hands for the next hour, during which Napoleon launched the remainder of his Imperial Guard against Wellington's army in an attempt to break the allied lines in the centre. Prussian General Gneisenau narrates:

> Towards six o'clock in the evening, we received the news that General Thelma, with the third Corps, was attacked near Wavre by a very considerable Corps of the enemy, and that they were already disputing the possession of the town. The Field-marshal, however, did not suffer himself to be disturbed by this news: it was on the spot where he was, and nowhere else, that the affair was to be decided. A conflict, continually

supported by the same obstinacy, and kept up by fresh troops, could alone ensure the victory, and if it were obtained here, any reverse sustained near Wavre was of little consequence. The columns, therefore, continued their movements. It was half an hour past seven, and the issue of the battle was still uncertain. The whole of the fourth Corps, and a part of the second, under General Pvich [Pirch] had successively come up. The French troops fought with desperate fury: however, some uncertainty was perceived in their movements, and it was observed that some pieces of cannon were retreating. At this moment, the first columns of the Corps of General Zieten arrived on the points of attack, near the village of Smouhen [*sic*.], on the enemy's right flank, and instantly charged. This moment decided the defeat of the enemy. His right wing was broken in three places; he abandoned his positions. Our troops rushed forward at the pas de charge, and attacked him on all sides, while, at the same time, the whole English line advanced.

Circumstances were extremely favourable to the attack formed by the Prussian Army; the ground rose in an amphitheatre, so that our artillery could freely open its fire from the summit of a great many heights which rose gradually above each other, and, in the intervals of which the troops descended into the plain, formed into brigades, and in the greatest order; while fresh Corps continually unfolded themselves, issuing from the forest on the height behind us. The enemy, however, still preserved means to retreat, till the village of Plancenoit, which he had on his rear, and which was defended by the guard, was, after several sanguinary attacks, carried by storm.[1]

As Prussians once more headed into the streets and alleys of Plancenoit, bitter street fighting broke out. The skull of a combatant here that has recently been rediscovered shows blunt force trauma to the left eye: a bayonet wound had penetrated the skull and the eye socket had been destroyed, presumably by a musket butt. The fighting was viscious, with no quarter given. We hope the villagers had fled. Homes were ransacked and destroyed, and the church burned out in an orgy of destruction reminscent of the bitter street-fighting at Saint-Armand and Ligny that many of the guardsmen had participated in. The Young Guard had managed to fall back into the village and use the churchyard as a defensive bastion, much as the Prussians had done at the church of St Armand at Ligny only two days before. General Hiller himself recalls receiving support from the 1st Battalions of the 1st and 2nd Pomeranian *Landwehr*:

> Overcoming all difficulties and with heavy losses from canister and musketry, the troops of the 15th Infantry and 1st Silesian *Landwehr*

penetrated to the high wall around the church yard held by the French Young Guard. These two columns succeeded in capturing a howitzer, two cannon, several ammunition wagons, two staff officers and several hundred men. The open square around the churchyard was surrounded by houses, from which the enemy could not be dislodged in spite of our brave attempt. A firefight continued at fifteen to thirty paces which ultimately decimated the Prussian battalions. Had I at this moment, the support of only one fresh battalion at hand, this attack would have indeed been successful.[2]

The Old Guard Attacks

Plancenoit had to be held at all costs to stop the Prussians encircling the *Armée du Nord*. No other troops were to hand other than the Old Guard, so three battalions of the Old Guard were ordered to march to the village. Colonel Auguste Louis Petiet of the Imperial Staff noted that 'About eight o'clock the Prussians forced our right and threaten the rear of the 6th Corps, four battalions of the guard were sent by the Emperor.'[3]

In reality, just two battalions made their way to the village. The 1st Battalion of the 1st Grenadiers (and we assume the 2nd Battalion) were established *en potence* on the road leading to the village, but were not committed to the attack. General Pelet, commanding the 2nd Chasseurs à Pied, continues:

> We were always in square, the grenadiers behind me, the 3rd and 4th Chasseurs were in front. I remember there was confusion about the order of the squares, and I do not know if the Grenadiers were not then passing on the other side of the road. Finally, the General Morand said go with your 1st battalion to Plancenoit for the Young Guard is all but beaten. Support them. Support this point because it will only leave your 2nd Battalion, and the 1st Chasseurs for the last reserve.[4]

General Christiani, commanding the 2nd Grenadiers à Pied, notes:

> At five or six o'clock, maybe later I received the order to send a battalion of the regiment into the village that was to right, behind the position I occupied, to drive out the Prussians, they said that they were about to capture It. It was Mr. Golzio, head of the 1st battalion of the regiment, that went on this mission, I saw him that evening during the retreat. I do not remember if he has lost many men but only that he told me he had done much harm to the enemy.[5]

With their towering bearskins, blue greatcoats, and white crossbelts, the grenadiers and chasseurs made a conspicuous target. Many in the Prussian lines would have fresh memories of the attack by the Old Guard two days earlier at Ligny: were they filled with panic at the sight of the Old Guard moving or filled with a desire to avenge dead comrades? Perhaps both. Needless to say, the two battalions of the Old Guard were noted by the Prussians:

> Since Napoleon saw, that the Prussians penetrated by force, the second regiments of Grenadiers and Chasseurs of the old guard were ordered to send a battalion each to Plancenoit, and these two battalions, which led the General Morand, took back the village, and pursued the Prussians up to their position behind the village. Their skirmishers came up to the Prussian batteries, but were chased away from them by the 2nd squadron of the 1st Silesian Hussars Regiment. The French cavalry made a move to advance, and a regiment of lancers were repulsed by Major von Colomb with the 2nd hussar regiment; they however then came under the fire of a French infantry battalion, formed in line of and had to retreat back to their starting place, however, a French hussars regiment was repulsed by the Prussian Infantry.
>
> Meanwhile, a battalion from the French 1st Grenadier Guard Regiment on the right of the road was placed at a height which dominates the road that leads from the highway to Plancenoit, the 2nd Battalion of this regiment stood together with six guns left the road.[6]

The Hussars mentioned were surely Marbot's 7th. This clearly indicates the regiment had been pulled back from its advanced posts to towards Saint-Lambert and was operating on the field of battle. This made sense as Subervie's cavalry and elements of the 13th Light Infantry had taken their place. Victor Dupuy, squadron commander of the French 7th Hussars under Colonel Marbot, recalls:

> Until about 4 o'clock, we remained quiet spectators of the battle. In one moment, General Domon came to me when the fire of English was almost stopped, and he told me that the battle was won, the enemy was retreating, we were there to make junction with the troops of Grouchy and that we would be that evening in Brussels, he departed. A few moments later, instead of joining with the troops of Marshal Grouchy as we expected, we received an attack from a regiment of Prussian Lancers. We repulsed him vigorously and gave chase, but we were forced to retreat by the fire of canister from six pieces of cannon, behind which the lancers retreated. Colonel Marbot was wounded by a lance thrust in the chest in the attack

of the Prussians. They were attacked then by the infantry, we redeployed in the centre, slowly retreating. In our retrograde movement, we met the Marshal Soult, General Staff, which made us take post near a battery and give it support, the enemy's cannon made us no harm.[7]

Second-in-command of the 1st Brigade of the Prussian I Army Corps under Zieten was General Hoffmann. In this capacity, he witnessed much of the fighting firsthand:

> The brave Colonel Hiller, had at about half past six, with 3 columns, each of 2 battalions, stormed the two flanks and the centre of Plancenoit. The wing-columns took the outlying part and the cemetery, but had to yield to superior force, a second attack, supported by two battalions of the 15th Brigade had the same success, and both were followed by the French cavalry to the other side of the height. We had to wait for reinforcements.
>
> Napoleon had sent in just before this attack the two 2nd Battalions of the old guard of General Morand, and soon after that upon perceiving in the distance preparations of Blücher two other battalions, under General Pelet, one of which to the right of Plancenoit was in nearby forest of Chantelet.[8]

Hoffmann counted four French battalions—two were clearly those that fought in the village; the one at Chantelet is surely that commanded by Battalion Commander Duuring; and the enigmatic fourth battalion could well be that of the 1st Grenadiers, which was established at the junction of the Brussels road and the Plancenoit road acting as a reserve. Hoffmann also comments that, in addition, Prussian Horse Battery No. 6 was posted on the high ground upon the right of the wood of Virere and was principally occupied in diverting the fire from a battery of the Imperial Guard Horse Artillery, which had one half of its guns above the hollow way formed by the road leading down into Plancenoit from La Maison du Roi, and the other half detached to an elevated spot in the south part of the village, whence it had a commanding view of a considerable portion of the advancing columns. The cavalry was clearly that of Domon or Subervie, but due to a lack of source material from the French and Prussians, we are not able to elaborate on what occurred.

General Petit, commanding the 1st *Grenadier à Pied*, narrates:

> The enemy, however, had made much progress on our right which was singularly overwhelmed. The Young Guard, who had been sent at 2 hours, and having been forced into a retrograde movement from the village

of Plancenoit, the 2nd Regiment of Chasseurs and the 2nd Regiment of grenadiers were ordered to detach a battalion and enter the village. The enemy was immediately chased out with great loss. We pursued them with bayonets up on the hill. The Chasseurs and Grenadiers marched right up to the Prussian batteries, which were for a time abandoned.

The movement was effected at 6 pm.

During this movement the 1st Grenadier Regiment was formed in two squares, one per battalion. The first was to the right of the roadway [facing the enemy] on an elevated position overlooking the small path that opens out into a highway and that leads to Plancenoit. We sent some men with an Adjutant-Major to the far right of the village to observe the enemy, that was there in force.[9]

The adjutant major sent with the 150 grenadiers was Charles Fare, who recounts:

It was half past six. The troops on being extended to the right of the Army were close to the woods whereby we expected Grouchy to arrive. Their appearance raised a cry of joy in the Old Guard, but soon the Prussian bullets hit their square and destroyed this brief illusion ... Blücher's full attention was focused on Plancenoit, which was occupied by the 6th Corps and the Young Guard, and were in charge of opposing the march of the Corps of Bülow. If they captured this village, the French Army would be turned on his right and this movement would cause the enemy to fall on our flank and into the rear of our troops.

Pursuant to the Orders of Blücher, Colonel Hiller soon formed three columns of attack, two battalions of the 15th regiment, commanded by Major Wittich, right, two battalions of the 1st Silesian *Landwehr*, under the command of Major Fischer centre, and Lieutenant-Colonel Blandowski, with two battalions of the 2nd Silesian *Landwehr*, left. The 14th brigade, following in reserve, were detached the first battalions of the 14th line and 1st Pomeranian *Landwehr* to support the attacks.

The columns on the right and left, entered the village through a pit of fire and captured a howitzer and two pieces and moved to the cemetery, but they cannot push back the Young Guard and the detachments of the 6th Corps from the houses and orchards where they are maintained during the first attack. At thirty yards began a most deadly fusillade which ended with the retreat of six Prussian battalions when their rear was threatened by a column of cavalry of General Domon. This cavalry wanted to engage, but was stopped by the fire of a battery that it charged. The Prussian battalions rallied, the second battalion of the 11th line and the 1st Pomeranian *Landwehr*, of the 14th Brigade, joined them and they all moved forward, followed by the 15th regiment. This second attack made with resolution by fourteen battalions succeeded. The Young Guard was forced to evacuate the village.

The Prussians strongly pushing forward, two battalions of the old guard are sent to their aid, the first battalion of the 2nd Chasseurs and the 1st Battalion of the 2nd Grenadiers, strong between them of about 1,100 men and commanded by General Count Morand, Colonel of Chasseurs, and under his command by General Pelet of the same arm. The Emperor concerned with the movements of Bülow, he entered the square of the second grenadiers, and gave orders for the attack: Do not fire a single shot, come on them with the bayonet. The battalion immediately dispersed its square, moved to the right and came opposite to a hedge that separated them from the Prussians.

The charge was beaten, and in an instant the hedge was crossed by 530 grenadiers. A Prussian battalion was unmasked. He had no time to execute a volley. It was pushed back by the bayonet. In a fight lasting no more than few minutes the battalion was annihilated. After having destroyed them, the grenadiers rushed to the Prussian masses who already crowd the ravines, orchards and streets of Plancenoit. Again, in this place a dreadful slaughter was made. The enemy sought to escape the furious blows of the grenadiers with difficulty, and were desperate to win back the village. Nothing could stop them. They had promptly done the task that was asked of them by the Emperor himself.[10]

The few men from the 1st Grenadiers arrived before the two battalions arrived. Perhaps moving at *pas redouble* (double pace of 120 paces a minute), the grenadiers arrived sooner. Yet what could 150 men conceivably achieve? The Young Guard with Duhesme mortally wounded was a spent force, so Lobau's men and those from the 54th and 55th were 'on their knees' rhetorically speaking. More men were needed, and quickly, if the village was to be held. General Pelet continues:

It was about six o'clock, perhaps seven. I do not know how long I remained here, but it seemed to me a long time. I called Lieutenant Gourahel[11] to me and, finding Lepage[12] in the first houses of the village, I told him to move to the last houses of the village and to occupy them strongly.

Entering, I met poor General Duhesme, who was being carried dead or dying on his horse, then the voltigeurs running away, Chartran[13] who told me that he could do nothing, Colonel Hurel[14] was not lacking men but they were all retiring. I promised them I would stop the enemy, and urged them to rally behind me. Indeed, I moved to the centre of the village and there, seeing Lieutenant Lepage's men approaching and the Prussians that pursued them, I ordered Captain Peschot[15] to advance with the 1st Company and attack the enemy who were coming down the road opposite the one we were on, with the bayonet. His sergeant, Cranges, who was very keen, gave the order to the first platoon, and marched with it. He executed my order, but hardly had the enemy turned his back than the men began to skirmish and he lost control of them.

The enemy sent new forces; Peschot was not able to concentrate his platoon and he was pushed back.

I advanced another, it wanted to skirmish. I led it myself and the enemy fled. But this platoon dispersed and, with each charge made the same thing happened. The men of my last company shouted '*en avant*!', started firing and also dispersed.

I had the church occupied by some men that I led there and I found myself face to face with the Prussians who fired at me from point blank range, but missed. Then, seeing what a strong resistance we put up, they launched a shower of shells into the village and attempted to turn it by the valley of the Lasne and the woods there.

I sent an officer there, I think it was Captain Angnis.[16]

In all these attacks, we took many prisoners; our soldiers were furious and cut their throats. I rushed to them to prevent it and, as I for there, I saw them perish under my own eyes (they faced having their throats cut with '*sang froid* [sic.]' and hung onto my men). I was revolted, overcome with fury, I took several under my protection, including an officer who prostrated himself, telling me of his French friends and those of his family.

I put him behind my horse and then handed him over to my sapeurs, saying they would answer to me for his safety. I sent Captain Heuillette[17] to the left, to occupy and defend the church; he went well ahead and next to the wood opposite the enemy; from the rear came some men of the Young Guard who charged into the village.

However, the combat, having gone on for a long time, had dispersed all my men as skirmishers. I could not rally a single platoon, the enemy did not enter the village, but he deployed on all sides and, in each interval between the gardens, I saw muskets aiming at me from forty paces. I do not know why I was not struck down twenty times.

I went to and from on Isabelle [his horse]; I had taken off my riding coat and yet out men did not seem to recognise me as a general officer. Certainly, I still held the village; I came, I went, I had the charge beaten, the rally, then the drum roll; nothing brought together even a platoon. Finally, at the moment I was most embarrassed, most pressed and at the same time totally exposed, a platoon of Grenadiers[18] arrived, sent by whom I do not know but then I was content. I stopped it and use it to rally some chasseurs, then I had it charge with the bayonet, without firing a shot. They went forward like a wall and overthrew everything they encountered.

I remained there in the middle of this hail of shells, lit up by the fire that had started to burn in a number of houses, in a terrible and continuous fusillade; the Prussians surrounded us with numerous skirmishers. I didn't care, we held like demons; I could not form up my men, but they were all hidden away and laid down a murderous fire on the enemy that contained him; they were stopped despite the numbers that should have overwhelmed us.

Whilst I came and went continually between the entry and the exit [of the village], animating and holding in place all those in the middle of this skirmishing, I encountered Colomban[19] who appeared to me a little pale and I noticed this with regret, for perhaps he was thinking the same of me, although I certainly felt as calm and tranquil as I had only a few times in my life, even in the middle of these enemies that I believed bore me a particular grudge.[20]

The fighting surged from house to house. Flames burst through the roof of the church and neighbouring houses. Children's cherished toys were smashed underfoot and heirlooms destroyed as the fighting carried on from room to room at the point of the bayonet. Despite the close confines of the village streets, some Prussians found the chance to use their muskets as intended rather than as clubs and fired into the mass of French soldiers. Captain Louis Crete of the 1st Battalion, 2nd Grenadiers, was shot in the heart by a Prussian sergeant, then cut down with a sabre cut to his right shoulder.[21] He was the only officer of the regiment to be killed. Captain Heuillette of the 2nd Chasseurs remembers:

> The regiment, commanded by General Pelet and to which I belonged, was ordered to the village of Plancenoit which the Prussians had just taken possession, the village was taken with the points of our bayonets. Count Lobau, with the 6th Corps and the Young Guard, were there with us.
>
> We drove back the 30,000 men a half-mile from the village. The battle was in our favour again, but an hour later, Blücher arrived with 30,000 men to reinforce the Corps of Bülow, which brought the figure to 60,000. Our soldiers exhausted by a long combat then had to retreat in face of this number, we were cut off from the left flank.[22]

The two battalions of the Old Guard, the battered rump of the Young Guard, and Lobau's corps had recaptured Plancenoit. However, the counterattack came at a cost—the French had taken major losses in the attack, and without any reserves to bolster their depleted troops, the victory was a hollow one as it could neither be exploited or maintained. As the Prussians fled from Plancenoit, they were pursued by the cavalry of Jacquinot and Subervie. Prussian sources tell us that Subervie's two lancer regiments charged the flanks of the fleeing Prussians, inflicting more casualties. Buoyed by this success, the French advanced beyond the confines of the village, and in doing so came under a heavy artillery barrage fire from the Prussian artillery, which forced the French to withdraw back to the confines of the village. To cover the retreat, lancers from either Jacquinot or Subervie went into action, forcing the Prussian artillery to withdraw and abandon several batteries.[23]

Yet what could the French do? Help was not on its way. The remainder of the Old Guard and whatever men from Reille's 2nd Corps and Milhaud's cavalry were ordered to attack Wellington's positions to the left of La Haye Sainte, rather than head to Plancenoit. As more Prussians arrived, it was only a matter of time before Plancenoit fell and the Prussians got behind the French Army and blocked the Brussels road. The final act in the great tragedy was unfolding. The allies' trap had been sprung and was now closing extricably around the battered and exhausted French. In order to expel General Pelet from the bastion that was the churchyard, Prussian reinforcements were moved into the churchyard. Like Massena in the granary at Essling, General Pelet tenaciously clung on to the bastion. The churchyard was almost impossible to attack: from the east, it was defended by a steep slope, and if the Prussians attempted to outflank the churchyard by advancing along the low open space on its south, they would become exposed to musket fire from its walls, as well as from the from the houses opposite the churchyard, which were also occupied by the French.[24]

Prussian High Command decided to pound the French into submission. To do so, they deployed No. 10 Foot Battery, No. 6 Horse Artillery Battery, to open fire as close as possible to the churchyard. Under the cover of the barrage, the Prussians sent forward the Fusilier Battalion of the 25th Regiment and the 2nd Battalion of the 2nd Infantry Regiment from the 5th Brigade to capture the churchyard. At the same time, two Westphalian *Landwehr* Battalions were ordered to attack the right side of the village. In support was the 1st Battalion, 2nd Regiment. Every inch of ground, house, garden wall, and hedge was bitterly contested. Withdrawn to comparative safety in the Bois du Paris, the 11th Line and Pomeranian *Landwehr* regiment with the 1st Silesian *Landwehr* were able to be rallied, and in consequence were sent back to the attack.[25]

The Prussians boldly attacked the churchyard and sent detachments to outflank the village. With the village now almost totally surrounded, the churchyard position was no longer tenable, and the French had no option but to retreat. Wellington was now able move troops from his left flank to protect his battered centre thanks to the arrival of Zieten and Pirch. These troops were virtually unopposed by the French, as we shall see, and so they were able to sweep down onto the exposed and vulnerable French right wing and centre. The French were now surrounded. In a letter addressed to General Pelet dated 27 April 1835, General Guyot, commanding the heavy cavalry of the Imperial Guard, notes:

> During the first part of battle I learned that a Prussian corps of 30,000 men commanded by Bülow after being spotted at four o'clock in the afternoon had eventually deployed into the village of Plancenoit and was close to getting their hands on the General Headquarters. This news placed our army's rear area into great alarm.[26]

20
D'Erlon's Last Offensive

The time was fast approaching 9 p.m. Since 4 p.m., Ney had launched wave after wave of cavalry against the allied right wing, supported by 2nd Corps—'if at first you don't succeed, try and try again' must have been his mantra that day. He, like the emperor and other senior officers, knew that if they lost the battle, it was all over. They had one throw of the dice to win; loss meant exile or execution. Maybe this desperation to win at any cost is what drove Ney forward. Be that as it may, the French right was crumbling.

The Old Guard were ordered to attack to break the allied right. A French eyewitness writing in 1815 notes:

> He formed, for this purpose, a fourth column, almost entirely composed of the guards, and directed it at the pas de charge on Mount Saint Jean, after having dispatched instructions to every point, that the movement, on which he thought victory to depend, might be seconded. The veterans marched up the hill with the intrepidity which might be expected of them.[1]

To bolster the moral of the French, the news that Grouchy had arrived was spread. This was a deeply cynical move which had disastrous results when the reality of the situation became known. This lie at the heart of the battle was a major contributing factor to what happened next. Not everyone was convinced that the attack was sensible: General Haxo narrates the events as he witnessed them in a letter of 23 June 1815 held in the author's collection:

> The army corps of General Bulow advanced on the right flank of the army, and we began to feel its fire. In the position where the emperor was, already Prussians cannon balls crossed with those of the English. Then he

persuaded himself that the body of General [*sic.*] Grouchy, whom he had ordered to make a great movement, had arrived in the rear of the Prussians. He sent for Haxo to go and recognize the efforts Grouchy made, but he discovered nothing, and remained convinced that it was a fable invented by the Emperor to encourage his troops.... General Haxo, returning from his reconnaissance, found that the emperor, without waiting for the result of his mission, had committed his Guard. This attack could only have been planned so-that Grouchy would come in effect to stop the General Bulow, otherwise, even though the French would have broken the British line which was opposed to them, then they would have been taken from behind by Bulow, and the consequence of their success would have been the same to make us all prisoners. Instead, the guard was shaken by a huge loss and it was thrown back, and immediately putting into disorder the Army Corps that were further back.[2]

The attack, as Haxo says, was foolhardy. The French were caught in a trap. Wellington's red coats had been an 'anvil' against which 2nd Corps and the cavalry had been hurled with no success. On the right the Prussian juggernaut mercilessly advanced. A fighting retreat rather than one last gamble would have been a much more common sense approach to the situation; but common sense was sorely lacking, and desperation dictated the events. By now it was 9.30 p.m. The French army was fleeing for its lives.

About the climax of the battle, d'Erlon recalls:

The troops that were holding La Haye Sainte and its environs could not maintain themselves and had great difficulty in retreating back to the squares of General Donzelot had formed to receive the [enemy? Missing word] but did not hold for any length of time; the troops on the right withdrew in good order and were marching in square. General Jacquinot repulsed several cavalry charges. It was going from one square to another that General Durutte had his right wrist struck and received numerous severe injuries.

During the course of the day the 1st Corps suffered large losses; they were not able to be determined in any exact way; despite this, through the efforts of the Come d'Erlon, he united his troops as much as possible at Charleroi, and Beaumont, Maubeuge and Avesnes. It was only in Laon that he was able to rally 17,500 infantry and nearly 2,000 cavalry of those he had available on the 18th June. In the morning he had retained with him 500 [illegible] and 1000 horses. The 1st Corps had in the battle of the 18th General Aulard killed; Generals Durutte, Bourgeois, Noguès, Gobrecht wounded; Colonels Rignon of the 47th [*sic.*] and Carre of the 21st Killed.[3]

D'Erlon failed to stem the flood of cavalry. Durutte recalled the same scene:

> Around seven o'clock, we realized that our two wings faltered. That's when the Emperor decided to make an effort on the centre, with part of the Guard which until then he had held in reserve.
> He observed advancing along the main road heading to the left onto the heights, where the enemy had numerous artillery batteries, the head of a column of grenadiers. The sinuosity of the land did not permit General Durutte to see what was happening on this point. He was busy watching over a column of cavalry approaching on his right flank.
> He sent several officers from his staff to notify the Emperor. He then made his dispositions to cope with this approaching column, that seemed to be very strong. All of a sudden, he saw on the road, a lot of French soldiers who were retreating. Part approached the four twelve-pounders that General d'Erlon had at its disposal: they communicated this terror to drivers and gunners of this battery.
> He saw the battery flee at full gallop the despite the efforts of the officers of his staff who could not stop it. He then marched with the brigade Brue, towards the main road to try to stop the fugitives, and to try and make them rally behind this brigade which was in perfect order and fairly calm. Their efforts were fruitless. He could see the corps on the left to fall back quickly. As General Durutte was about the most advanced, he foresaw that he would soon be surrounded by the enemy, if he did not begin a retrograde movement. He executed this movement with the intention of endeavouring to cross the road to try to rally with the brigade of General Pégot who was on the other side, and which had, on arrival of the Emperor, been prescribed to follow the movements of the guard.
> He met at this time General d'Erlon, who was alone with some officers of his staff and General Garbe. General d'Erlon promised to stay with the General Durutte, and march with the brigade, which probably was the only company of his army corps which was in order at this moment: everything retreated in confusion.[4]

The body of cavalry that General Durutte observed was Prussian. In Plancenoit, all was lost as a Prussian account graphically narrates:

> Despite their great courage and stamina, the French Guards fighting in the village were beginning to show signs of wavering. The church was already on fire with columns of red flame coming out of the windows, aisles and doors. In the village, itself was a scene of bitter hand to hand fighting, everything was burning, adding to the confusion.

However once Major von Winztleben's manoeuvre was accomplished the French Guards saw their flank and rear threatened, they began to withdraw. The Guard Chasseurs under General Pelet formed the rearguard. The remnants of the Guard left in a great rush, leaving large numbers of artillery, equipment and ammunition waggons in the wake of their retreat. These spoils of war went to the victor. The evacuation of Plancenoit led to the loss of the position that was to be used to cover the withdrawal of the French Army to Charleroi. The Guard fell back from Plancenoit in the direction of Maison du Roi and La Caillou.[5]

The position was somewhere close to Rossomme. Another Prussian eyewitness notes:

> The French defended this position until the very end. The Generals Duhesme and Barrois were wounded, General Pelet struck into the village, but all these efforts merely delayed the utter defeat of the French. They were all thrown out of the village, and the allied cavalry flooded the field. At the outputs of the village were taken by Fusilier Battalion of the 2nd Regiment.[6]

With Plancenoit lost, the Prussians flooded onto the battlefield, cutting off any chance Napoleon had of covering his retreat and fighting a rearguard action. As Napoleon watched the Old Guard assail the allied right, the Prussians broke through what remained of Lobau's lines and flooded the battlefield, reaching La Haye Sainte. The French army broke and fled in a sea of fugitives. Napoleon's last great gamble had failed. With no field commander for the French right wing to co-ordinate the defence against the Prussian onslaught, Lobau and Pelet were left, in essence, abandoned to their fate while Napoleon concentrated his efforts on the French left. Colonel Gourgaud, attached to Imperial Headquarters, realising that all was lost, comments:

> The attack of the Guard having failed, I judge the case to be lost, I try to get myself killed, I met officer ordinance Amillet, and he stopped me from throwing myself in the midst of enemies.[7]
>
> The disorder was around me in our ranks, cries of 'Save us we are cut off' can be heard. The attack of the Prussians, on our right was again renewed with new fury during our general movement on the center of the English. Mouton, and Duhesme were crushed by their number and finally the army of Blücher fires their cannon on the road along which we were fleeing.[8]

The Prussian Fusilier Battalion of the 15th Regiment, that of the 1st Silesian *Landwehr* (under Major Keller), and the men of the 25th Regiment (under Major Witzleben) pursued the defeated Imperial Guard in the direction of Maison du Roi and come into contact with the 1st Battalion, 1st Chasseurs, which had advanced from La Caillou.[9]

The breakthrough of the Prussians broke the will and remaining resolve of the French army. Total chaos spread through the French ranks. Within minutes, most of the French units were completely destroyed. Bellina Kupieski, a colonel attached to the Imperial Headquarters, notes in a dispatch to Marshal Davout dated 23 June 1815 that the prince was originally at Beaumont and then moved to Avesnes:

> The Prince Jérôme rallied at Beaumont bit by bit some 8,000 men, comprising infantry and cavalry and around 12 pieces of artillery. The Major-General, had rallied bit by bit around 3,000 men at Philippeville, which left this place for Rocroi, where they arrived on the 20th where there already was 800 men of the Old Guard with two or three canons. The same day, Prince Jérôme and his party at Beaumont moved to Avesnes, where he united a great number of soldiers of all arms and marched them to Vervins, where they arrived on the 21st. I estimate he had 10,000 men, the major part being cavalry.[10]

By now it was about 10 p.m., the sun would have totally set in an hour. The arrival of the Prussians on the battlefield, which had bled Napoleon's right flank dry from around 3 p.m., had robbed the French Army of at least half its manpower, with what remained of 1st Corps, 6th Corps, the entire Young Guard, and two battalions of the Old Guard being pinned down in a vicious attritional struggle between Papalotte and Rossome.

The Prussian attack on the French right was the vital tipping point of the battle. The collapse of the French right wing sealed the fate of Napoleon's army and secured victory. The defeat of the Imperial Guard was now a forgone conclusion. As the story of Waterloo is primarily anglophonic, the defeat of the Imperial Guard by the 'plucky band of redcoats' is seen as the great deciding moment of the day, thanks to Wellington's guiding genius. The truth is that the victory owed everything to Blücher, Zeiten, and Bülow. The defeat of the guard made the defeat far more total and hastened the end of the *Armée du Nord*. The battle was already lost for the French by the time the Guard moved off. One French eyewitness writing on 24 July 1815 summed up the situation in a document in the author's collection:

> It appears from the reports, that a part of Marshal Bluchers army, which from the 16th concentrated itself in the environs of Wavres, had

eluded the vigilance of Marshal Grouchy, and being joined by the 4th Prussian corps, under General Bulow, had rapidly joined the English line, to co-operate with Lord Wellington. Marshal Grouchy had, in reality, briskly pursued the Prussians during their retreat to Wavre, and attacked in that place the portion of the Enemy which remained there. He was, therefore, engaged at the same moment we were, against a small division, which he mistook for the whole of the Prussian army, and over which he continued to obtain signal advantages: but, favoured as they were by the difficulties of a hilly country, intersected with woods and ravines, these corps made a sufficiently obstinate resistance, if not to stop his march, at least to impede it very considerably. Thus, they succeeded in holding him in play at a distance from the principal seat of action.

He could not, therefore, be of any assistance to us; and hence it was that the English received a considerable reinforcement, whose concerted intervention put them in a situation no longer to fear our most vigorous attacks; but, on the other hand, to resume the offensive, and presently to overpower us. Confidence was restored amongst them, and, calculating their manoeuvres by the favourable circumstances that occurred, they resisted our efforts with all their force, and with an ard or that seemed to redouble itself.

It is evident that this operation had been preconcerted by the two Generals in Chief, and that the English defended their positions with such invincible tenacity, only to give the Prussians time to affect that combined movement, on which the success of the battle depended, and the signal of which was waited for from one moment to the other.

Our witness is perfectly correct: the French Army had 'walked into a trap' of the allies' making. All was lost save honour, and there was precious little of that in the route to Genappe. A staff officer with d'Erlon recalled:

Our troops fell back one after another and finally ended up in a state of disorder that is impossible to describe.

Our army marched day and night without halting and we arrived here in a frightful state. It was a retreat absolutely similar to that from Moscow; as then, the soldiers threw away their weapons, abandoned their cannons.

21

Rout and Retreat

The scattered remains of the French army that had fought at Waterloo was fleeing along the various roads from Charleroi, moving towards Avesnes, Laon, and Philippeville. Grouchy conducted his retreat so as to join the remnants of the army. An unknown French general, probably Baron Albert Louis Emmanuel Fouler Count de Relinque (grand equerry to the emperor), wrote the following report to Marshal Davout dated Avesnes, 20 June 1815:

> On the 18th, the Emperor attacked with the 2nd, 1st and 6th corps without success. In the evening a Prussian corps presented its self on our right and eventually seized the village of Plancenoit, while the Emperor, instead of evacuating the battlefield and take position by withdrawing his right, threw all his guard recklessly on the centre of the enemy in an operation which was unsuccessful and resulted in the rout being more complete because there were no troops that had not been in action. The rout continued until Laon and some of the soldiers returned to their homes.
>
> The loss of our army in these four days is between 30 to 40,000 men and 200 guns. All the 2nd, 1st and 6th Corps, as well as the guard, cannot present no more than 6,000 men and 20 cannons, and the cavalry, has barely 2,000 horses. There yet remains the 3rd and 4th Corps but they have suffered greatly at Fleurus. We cannot say as usual, that the consequences of this defeat are incalculable, but on the contrary, they must lead to the loss of the emperor's throne and the annihilation of France.[1]

The emperor and the bulk of the army arrived at Philippeville sometime on 19 June. On that day, Marshal Soult wrote to Marshal Davout, the minister of war in Paris:

Monsieur the Marshal,

I have the honour to write to you for the first time since I wrote to you on the field of battle of Waterloo at half past two o'clock when the battle was begun and we had experienced great success, however at 7 o'clock a false movement was carried out with the orders of the Emperor, all was changed. The combat continued until night fell, and a retreat was affected, but it was in disorder.

The Emperor rallied the army at Philippeville and Avesnes and began to organise the corps and to tend to their needs. You can well imagine that the disaster is immense.[2]

D'Erlon recalls:

The 19th June at 6 o'clock in the morning the Comte d'Erlon arrived at Charleroi [illegible] where a great part of the army had passed through [illegible] and formed the [illegible] and rested at Charelroi until 9 o'clock in the morning when he departed for Beaumont were [sic.] he expected to join with other troops, and he arrived there at midday. From here a great number of troops and General Officers had gone in the direction of Avesnes, whilst many of the others had marched with the Army Corps and headed to Maubeauge.... He left Beaumont at 9 o'clock at night because the scouts of the Prussian army had started to arrive in the town.[3]

He adds some more detail in 1844:

The Emperor repassed the Sambre and retired to Philippeville I retired to Charleroi, where I was still at noon the next day. I left this city to go to Beaumont, where. I found soldiers of all arms and many wounded. I took care of having them transported to the interior, and formed several battalions composed of men of various corps of the army. Towards evening, some cavalry parties presented themselves before Beaumont, whom I left at eleven o'clock, after having distributed to the troops the provisions which were there, to carry me to Maubeuge; there I learned that the Emperor had left Philippeville and had gone to Laon. I found my cavalry at Maubeuge, where I spent all day visiting the place, passing the reviews of the garrison, which I engaged with all my strength to make a vigorous resistance. The next morning, I left that town with the infantry and cavalry I had assembled, to conduct myself to Avesnes, where I arrived at ten o'clock in the morning. The commandant of this place informed me that General Reille had departed at two o'clock in the morning, and that a considerable party of Prussian cavalry had summoned him, in the name of Louis XVIII, to open the gates, which was answered by a refusal, this cavalry had departed. I left Avesnes at one o'clock and went to Vervins, where I met a portion of the Imperial Guard, with whom I set out for Laon the next day. The Emperor went to Paris and the command of the army was entrusted to Marshal Soult, who ordered the following day the retreat on Soissons.[4]

Fighting for the battered wreck of 1st Corps was not yet over. Soult had not heard from d'Erlon on 20 or 21 June. It was not till the 23rd that Soult had information from d'Erlon and was able to transmit orders: d'Erlon was ordered to march to Soissons along the Mons to Laon road via Clacy, leaving at midday.[5] On the night of 23 June, the army entered Soissons.

Here at Soissons, Soult began a process of endeavouring to regenerate the army. Soult noted that 1st Corps mustered 4,132 men, 2nd Corps 7,418 men, and 3,008 men with 6th Corps, which was to be disbanded into the 1st and 2nd Corps, headed by d'Erlon.[6] In order to make up heavy losses in 1st Corps, Soult ordered the depots of the 21st, 25th, 45th, and 46th Regiments of Line be emptied and the men dispatched to the army.[7]

If the Prussian juggernaut that was steamrolling to Paris was to be stopped, important bridges at La Fere and Compiegne had to be held. Late on 25 June, Soult outlined his plans to defend Compiegne:

> I am preparing a flanking movement in order to stop the enemy's march, who appears to have the intention of heading to Compiegne, and I will propose to M. *Maréchal* Grouchy to support the left of the army at Compiegne where he will have a little less than half the army, and his right at Soissons, the line being covered by the Aisne and the light cavalry as far possible on the right bank of the Oise, however the movement will take four days to complete, and I do not know if we have enough time, as the Prussian officers at the advanced posts at Laon, have repeated that they have been ordered not to open fire unless we do so. However, it appears their troops are marching on the right bank of the Oise.[8]

It must have been obvious to Soult that the Prussians were heading to Paris and that the wreck of the army from Waterloo was unable to act offensively, though France may yet be saved. Only Grouchy with 3rd and 4th Corps retained troops capable of defending Paris. The defence of the capital had to be organised, yet he was not yet totally despairing that the situation was completely hopeless. He outlined his plans to Davout again the following morning at 5 a.m.:

> On the subject of this measure, I think it would be premature and that it appears to be better to wait until the movements of the enemy are

clearer, and it appears to me that their movements should be stopped, at least for a moment, if the army takes a position at Compiegne, where it will be covered by the rivers Aisne and Oise, supporting their right on Soissons, and having behind the forest of Compiegne, which offers a very defensible position.[9]

As the morning of 26 June wore on, it must have become obvious to Soult from the dispatches that arrived with him that there was very little he could do. Reille was nominal commander of the men that had rallied, and moreover, if Paris was to be attacked, he reasoned that he was needed more in Paris, so he handed command to Grouchy and left for Paris. Marshal Grouchy, who had skilfully retreated with his victorious army from Wavre, now turned his considerable skills to blocking the Prussian advance. He seems to have thought that the best way to halt the advance of the allies was to attack them in their flank, somewhere between Creil and Pontoise. Yet he correctly judged that any such action would be of little importance as the action was too late to make any lasting impression on the tide of advancing allied troops.[10] Despite his concerns about the combat effectiveness of d'Erlon, Grouchy dispatched orders to d'Erlon at 7 a.m.:

> The government did not know that you were here when it amalgamated your Corps with that of General Reille and general Comte de Lobau Since this provision is quite contrary to the good of the service, I think I have to suspend its execution, I will report this to the minister.
>
> Please, my dear general, take the 1st Corps to Compiègne, where you will take a position: I want you to be established their tomorrow. I put under your command the 3rd and 4th Corps of cavalry, commanded by General Kellerman and Milhaud. They are, both on the road from Soissons to Compiègne, the 1st in Ambleny, and the 2nd in the village of Châtellet. You will send them orders and dispose of them to illuminate the roads of Noyon, Mondidier and others, culminating in Compiègne.
>
> You will restore the defensive work that had been done last year, for the defence of this city, you will order that preparations are undertaken to blow up the bridge of Compiègne and you will make a reconnaissance along the right bank of the Oise, taking a position at the intersection of Paths from Compiègne to Clermont, and from Pont-St-Maxence to Roye. By keeping this point continually monitored, we will be assured if the enemy is on the Oise, and manoeuvres on our left flank, as various reports announce.
>
> I wish, my dear general, that you destroy all the boats that can be found on the Aisne, from Soissons, to Compiègne. Please also ensure that bridge over the River, at the of the village of Attigny is destroyed.

Finally, my dear general, I defer to your judgement, as to movement of the left wing of the army, and urge you to keep me well informed of everything you learn about the movements of the enemy,

Receive, etc., etc.[11]

Simultaneously, the cavalry of Domon, Kellerman, and Milhaud were to march to Compiegne in support of d'Erlon and 1st Corps, which had been dispatched to undertake this flank attack.[11] Prussian troops headed to Compiegne on 26 June. This was a large-scale operation, which if it had succeeded would have delayed the Prussian army and given Vandamme with more time to get to Paris, along with Reille with the remains of 2nd and 6th Corps. The daring plan, however, did not bank on the fact that 1st Corps would not fight.

Early on the 27th, d'Erlon's corps observed elements of the Prussian 1st Army Corps around 3.30 a.m., and d'Erlon duly occupied the bridges of Verbie and Pont-Saint-Maxence. D'Erlon attacked around 6 a.m. but had not prevented the Prussians occupying Compiègne in force and began to withdraw to Gilicourt. The bridges were to be occupied and then destroyed to secure Vandamme's flank. The Prussians were in position by 5 a.m., by which time d'Erlon's columns had already been observed. Prussian artillery reportedly opened fire, checking the advance around 6 a.m.[12] How could 1st Corps and two corps of cavalry have been so easily pushed back by just four artillery pieces? Simply put, the morale of 1st Corps was so shattered that a few salvos of artillery fire sent the corps running for cover in the Bois de Compiègne. A force of just seventy Prussian cavalry cleared the wood. The men of Waterloo no longer had any desire to fight: d'Erlon faced 3,000 Prussians with 4,500 infantry and 4,000 cavalry, but were so 'shellshocked' at the first Prussian shots being fired that they panicked and routed.[13]

The only troops capable of fighting was Vandamme's 3rd and 4th Corps, supported by Pajol and Exelmans, and from 27 June, Vandamme regained Vallin's and Domon's cavalry. An eyewitness to these events was General Kellerman, who felt it was a huge mistake not to send troops on 26 June:

Marshal Soult on first hearing the news of the enemy's approach had retreated to Soissons, Marshal Grouchy replaced him, and arrived there at 4 o'clock in the morning of the 27th. The danger was pressing there was no time to be lost for gain the bridges over the Aisne or Oise, and why did he not on the 26th or at least early on the 27th occupy Compiegne which the enemy occupied at 7 o'clock in the evening of the same day.

The Comte d'Erlon was sent on the following, day, the 28th, was sent but could not make an entry and had to retire into the forest; the Comte de Valmy and the Comte Milhaud also went to this place, but the place had already been occupied.[14]

D'Erlon had fought and lost his last battle for Napoleonic France—indeed, it can hardly be called a battle at all, more a tragic skirmish that ended in humiliation and defeat for d'Erlon. He arrived with his battered and demoralised men in Paris at the end of the month. On 29 June, Grouchy sent word to Davout:

> General D'Erlon is with the debris of his Corps at Bondi. This Corps consists of only 1500 men, both infantry and cavalry.
>
> The troops I have with me, and those of D'Erlon are in such a state of demoralization, that at the first gunshot they hear, they run away. Twelve artillery pieces have been captured from us on the march and six in engagements. It results from this state of affairs, that the Government can count for the defence of Paris, only on a very weak army, which has no desire to fight, and one that is completely disorganized.
>
> I believe it is my duty to educate you in haste about this sad situation, so that the government will not be deluded by the means it has to defend Paris, which I will lead.
>
> I will be in Paris at midnight having the enemy on my flank at Tremblay.[15]

Over 2,500 men had dropped out of 1st Corps since leaving Soissons. Once in Paris, from his cantonments at Belleville, d'Erlon conducted a root-and-branch shakedown of 1st Corps.[16] His command took no part in the fighting to defend the city. After three days of fighting under the walls of Paris, the city surrendered to the Prussians on 3 July. The First Empire was over, and the Bourbons were secure on the throne of France until 1848, when the second Napoleon came to power. The outcome of the campaign had perhaps always been inevitable.

Napoleon's top table of officers at Waterloo were hardly a dream team. D'Erlon at the head of 1st Corps was hardly a great soldier, nor were his subordinates any better. Donzelot had no field command experience whatsoever, and Durutte was out of his depth commanding a division, let alone a brigade. Charles Esdaile remarks that the *Armée du Nord* was nothing like the *Grande Armée* and was less likely to win battles or to be able to sustain defeat—how right he was.[17]

22

Conclusions

Following Waterloo, General d'Erlon was exiled from France for over a decade, and yet he would be elevated to the title of marshal of France in 1843. D'Erlon was a staff officer of some merit, yet as corps commander, he was out of his depth.

It is undeniable that his bungling on 16 June lost the campaign, yet Ney and the emperor share equal culpability. At Waterloo, he handled his corps well enough, and indeed, he may at a stroke have won Waterloo, yet fate decided otherwise. Napoleon always asked if a general was lucky—d'Erlon was a man whose luck was only bad it seems. His journal offers an insight into the campaign as it happened and how he consciously edited and sifted the events in his mind before committing it to paper. The lack of testimony for the events on 16 June is telling: did he write something and then dispose of it, or has it been stolen for money? We cannot tell. I suspect as d'Erlon did eventualy put pen to paper to write about the events of the 16th, that he did write somthing down at the time, and then, we guess, conveniently lost the papers once his published version events had 'hit the bookshops' as it were.

Many have sought to find reasons for why Napoleon lost, as if to shift the blame from the emperor to other factors. Marshals Ney, Grouchy, and Soult have all been blamed for the defeat. The answers seem to be more prosaic. Since 8 a.m. at least, Napoleon knew the Prussians were a threat and sought to contain or neutralise that threat. He had not planned for Lobau being out of position. Indeed, as 18 June dawned, 2nd Corps had arrived only sometime after midnight; the heavy cavalry of the *Garde Impériale* was at Maransart. Why was this? Writing on 25 June 1815, in a letter presented in the author's collection, General Haxo commanding the engineers of the *Garde Impériale* succinctly commented in third person:

The overriding error in his eyes had been arriving from one direction, making it a long deployment as well as making the withdrawal much more difficult, because the troops withdrawing would naturally be on the same road by which they arrived. This way, behind the army, was congested by all the vehicles that made that defeat so fatal.

General Haxo's comments ring true: the 'logjam' on the Brussels road had serious implications for the operational capability of the French Army, a fact often overlooked by historians.

If a strong force had been sent toward Lasne, Chapelle de Saint Lambert to head off the Prussians from swinging south to the field of Waterloo, maybe the outcome of the day could have been altered. For this to be successful, it assumed one thing: that at 9 a.m., Lobau was close to hand and able to march with due celerity as needed. As we have seen, marching the 1st and 2nd Corps, the *Garde Impériale*, cavalry and artillery on the Brussels road meant that a 'tail back' of huge proportions ensued, meaning Durutte's division only arrived shortly after midday, and Lobau further behind only arrived some two hours later. With the artillery, baggage, and munitions marching on a single road, with cavalry and infantry trying to cut cross-country across saturated boggy ground fatally delayed the concentration of the *Armée du Nord* to confront Wellington and Blücher. The campaign had been compromised by the moving of focus of operations from Mons to Charleroi, meaning the initiative had been lost. The 'congestion' on the Brussels road cost the day.

Waterloo can be considered a typical Peninsular battle: no daring, innovative French tactics, merely a slogging match of attacking columns against a static British line. Ney of Elchingen, the emperor at Marengo, or Soult at Austerlitz would not have acted in this way, yet they did. Part of this failure was a lack of competent field commanders. Very few of the senior officers at Waterloo had experienced anything other than defeat: d'Erlon had a proven track record of failure. Every time the French had faced Wellington, they had been defeated. The psychological impact of this must surely have played a part in the outcome of the day.

The emperor's presence was estimated to be worth an additional 10,000 men in terms of morale, but what of the nagging doubts of the officer corps in facing Wellington? As it was, the emperor's overconfidence in his own abilities and the competency of his army lost the day—arguably, the campaign was lost a week earlier in the colossal administrative breakdown concerning the shift from Mons to Charleroi as the main objective. That shift in operations placed d'Erlon's 1st Corps out of position; it meant he failed to achieve his objectives on day one, which meant on day two of the campaign, his troops were not to hand when needed by Ney or for that matter by the emperor, costing a decisive victory at Ligny. The change in focus of the theatre of operations was the emperor's greatest mistake, and only he was to blame. In summing up, d'Erlon was not a great commander, lacking the ability to lead a corps and the personality to stand up to his subordinates, and his failings coupled with those of the commander in chief contributed to the inevitable defeat.

The Butcher's Bill

So what was the human cost of the battle? The table below presents the facts we know from regimental muster lists:

	Wounded	Evacuated Wounded	Wounded POW	POW	Killed	Missing	Total
Grenadiers à Pied	165	-	-	615	23	469	1,272
Chasseurs à Pied	71	-	-	1,653	18	189	2,736
Young Guard	229	-	-	559	96	1,362	2,225
I Corps	518	-	854	3,896	215	3,140	8,623
II Corps	639	1,174	65	1,411	387	1,090	4,766
VI Corps	546	-	14	482	140	256	1,913
III Cavalry Corps	33	-	58	75	87	389	642
IV Cavalry Corps	65	-	-	187	54	364	660
1st Cavalry Division	-	-	-	3	2	36	41
2nd Cavalry Division	14	-	-	-	5	61	88
3rd Cavalry Division	13	-	-	17	14	46	90
5th Cavalry Division	18	-	-	27	32	65	142
Guard Cavalry	167	-	-	13	71	354	605
TOTAL	2,478	1,174	991	8,938	1,144	7,821	22,546

The army mustered perhaps 72,000 men. Of these, 22,546 men were casualties—30 per cent of the army. The British, Belgians, Dutch, and Germans lost 15,000 casualties, or 1 in 4 engaged. The Prussians lost 7,000 men killed and wounded. The allied losses totalled approximately 22,000 men; the French, on paper, were about equal with 23,000 losses when we add in artillery, engineer, and regiments with no muster lists to consult.

The wounded came to 4,643 men. We know of over 2,600 in Netherlands hospitals; many of these are likely to be the wounded men recorded as prisoners of war or missing but we cannot say how many. A ballpark figure for the wounded could be 6,500 men by adding the wounded recorded by the French and allies. This equates to roughly 10 per cent of the men present as wounded. The 1er Corps had the highest losses of any body of troops at Waterloo as we suppose. The French army managed to evacuate from the field 1,175 wounded men with a further 2,478 men wounded who did not pass through a field hospital. What we are not seeing are the men recorded as missing who were left behind on the field of battle as wounded.

Of the recorded prisoners of war, we find the following were transported to prisons in England and then returned to France:[1]

	POW registered at Dartmoor	POW registered at Fleet Prison, Plymouth	POW returned to France
Guard Infantry	598	24	581
Guard Cavalry	19	4	25
Guard Artillery & C	7	0	26
Line Cavalry	260	15	188
Line Artillery & C	319	21	184
1st Corps	2,423	139	1,955
2nd Corps	1,092	108	868
3rd Corps	121	8	48
4th Corps	49	8	49
6th Corps	348	38	329
Armée du Nord ?	75	6	
TOTAL POW	5,310	371	3,385

Some 5,681 POWs made it to Dartmoor, and it seems many lay buried in English soil. The disparity between the recorded prisoners of war and the total who made it into captivity is a combination of factors. We are seeing incomplete records in England and France, and we are also seeing a lot of men recorded as prisoners of war who were either in reality dead, AWOL, or wounded and died later of wounds. What is fascinating is that men from Grouchy's command were picked up as prisoners of war. We assume Grouchy's field hospital had been overrun.

Further, what we are seeing in the regimental muster roles is what the company adjutants were told and thought had happened when the company roll was called. No doubt many men had gone home, AWOL, after the battle and were listed as prisoners of war. We are, moreover, not seeing the French wounded who were evacuated to Charleroi, Soissons, Philippeville, and Laon, who were no doubt made prisoners of war by the allied armies and were never heard of again by their parent regiment, so were listed as POWs, but had in all probability been sent home. We are dealing with a very fragmentary data set, but despite these major issues, as with the regimental muster lists, it provides objective data from which we can start to interpret the true events of the day of 18 June 1815 by being able to compare casualty dates from all armed forces present. We have no way of reconciling the missing 'Factor Y' into the lists. No doubt a good number, not known, of men listed as prisoners were in fact dead or had deserted. Further, we do not have the data of 'Factor Z', the men who died as prisoners before embarking in the Netherlands and those who died in England. Discounting these two unknown factors, we still have the details of over 5,500 men from the *Armée du Nord* as prisoners of war in England.

The missing men are no doubt AWOL, dead, and wounded. We have no way of analysing the missing data as we have no idea about percentages of dead, wounded, and genuine AWOL and perhaps also prisoners of war in the mix of missing. Indeed, our very superficial analysis of the prisoners of war and wounded data is just that. We have basic figures—we have definite figures of total prisoners of war and wounded, but nothing more to be able to break down the figures even more.

Waterloo Losses in Context

In percentage terms, the butcher's bill at Waterloo was similar to Ligny two days earlier. On 10 June 1815, III Corps mustered 15,114 other ranks. A total of 2,964 men were killed, wounded, or missing where the recorded data exists; III Corps lost 19.6 per cent of effective strength at Ligny:

Battle of Ligny: II, III, and IV Corps				
	Wounded	Killed	Missing	Total
7th Division	206	40	4	250
8th Division [4]	914	81	641	1,636
10th Division	640	99	9	748
11th Division [5]	493	39	46	578
12th Division	291	43	60	394

13th Division	139	40	56	235
14th Division	656	103		759
Total	3,339	445	816	4,500

Looking in detail at Ligny, Habert's 10th Infantry Division of 3rd Corps has a series of remarkable documents that adds much detail to this. Death certificates from the 22nd Regiment of Line, at the head of the 2nd Brigade, show that between 2 and 8 p.m., twenty-four men were killed, the majority between 3 and 5 p.m. A further seven men were lost between 4 and 6 p.m. on 18 June.[4]

The 34th Regiment of Line formed the head of 1st Brigade and sustained thirty-two killed between 3 and 6 p.m., with nine killed at 4 p.m. and ten killed at 5 p.m. At Wavre, eight men were lost.[5]

We do not have all the returns for IV Corps, but in basic figures, IV Corps lost 4,690 men from the 12th, 13th, and 14th Divisions on 16 June—a loss of 40 per cent of effective strength.[6] For the 96th Regiment of Line, we have records of twenty-seven men killed.[7] We do not have the full returns for the 7th Division, but what is notable is that in the street-fighting at Ligny and Saint Armand, where it is assumed 'the carnage was appalling', the number of men killed outright was low: 2 per cent of the 1,384 men present in the 34th Line were killed, 1.7 per cent in the 22nd Line. In terms of immediate mortality, it was incredibly low, which is important when we consider Waterloo and the overall low numbers of men recorded as killed in action. Napoleonic warfare was not as deadly as we suppose it to have been. Of the 1,214 men present on morning 16 June in the 63rd Line, just fifteen were killed in action, or 1.2 per cent.[8] Fatalities were below 2 per cent.

We can compre these figures to fighting at Waterloo. The 3rd Regiment of Line attacked Hougoumont: we assume from most histories of the battle that this was a 'bloodbath'. Yet when we look at the death certificates issued, we record nine deaths, all recorded at 4 p.m., which gives us a fixed point in time for when this regiment was committed to the action. Much later than nearly every history of the battle would allow for.[9] In comparison, the losses at La Haie Sainte suffered by the 51st Regiment of Line records seventeen fatalities of officers and men. The certificates report two men killed at 2 p.m., one man at 3 p.m., seven men killed at 4 p.m., and four men at 5 p.m.; thereafter no deaths were officially recorded. This gives us fixed points in time for the attack on La Haie Sainte by Donzelot's command, with eleven men killed in an attack lasting perhaps two hours.[10] Therefore, the losses at Hougoumont were far less than Ligny; the action at La Haie Sainte was again not as deadly, but the fighting of the 5th Light Infantry around Plancenoit was on par with Ligny.

The recorded French wounded for Ligny were presented in a report made on the morning of 17 June by *Maréchal de Camp* Antoine Joseph Claude Le Bel, who was assistant chief-of-staff serving under Lieutenant-General François Gedeon Bailly de Monthion. Le Bel writes:

> There exists in the town of Fleurus five ambulances, of which one is for the Imperial Guard.
> Ambulance of the Imperial Guard: Officers: 2, NCOs and solders 112
> In the four other ambulances:
> Officers: 78, NCOs and soldiers 1,666
> Evacuated to Charleroi:
> Officers: 33, NCOs and soldiers 807
> Total wounded listed at this time 2,076
> All the wounded listed here are those that have been taken in, more may be received during the morning.
> The ambulances of the headquarters are missing doctors and infirmiers.
> The marshal-du-camp [*sic*.]
> Commandant headquarters staff
> Le Bel.[11]

In a letter from Comte Daure, dated 17 June 1815, concerning the wounded, he noted that around 1,600 had been taken to the five ambulance posts, 800 wounded holders of the Legion of Honour had been sent to Charleroi, and a further 800 wounded at the time the letter was written to Soult were being taken to the ambulances.[12] This inflates the number of recovered wounded from Ligny to 3,676 men, which makes approximately 10 per cent of the men present on the field as wounded. This is roughly 200 men higher than the regimental lists account for. Presumably some of the missing were wounded.

We turn to Quatre Bras and Ney's losses here to compare to Ligny and Waterloo. Losses at Quatre Bras were as follows for II Corps:

II Corps						
	Wounded	Wounded & Pow	POW	Killed	Missing [presumed POW]	Total
5th Division	370	-	75	46	19	510
6th Division	291	17	12	48	102	470
9th Division	524	-	45	54	83	706
Total	1,185	17	132	148	204	1,686

In total, II Corps lost 1,686 men at Quatre Bras. However, it seems two brigades, for whatever reason, were not in action. Only the 2nd Brigade of 5th Division was in any serious fighting and sustained the heaviest losses overall. The corps had mustered another 13,131 ranks on 10 June. This represents a loss of 12 per cent of effective strength, giving the corps 11,538 men under arms on the morning of 18 June 1815. Much lower than Ligny, but again, the wounded percentage was the same 10 per cent, the same also as Waterloo when one factors in the wounded men in Netherlands hospitals. One can see why Napoleon abandoned the army at Ligny and took the force in better shape to defeat Wellington: 1st Corps had lost virtually no men and was, in theory, a crack combat force come 18 June.

The broader context of the losses at Waterloo shows us that the recorded casualties are highly comparable to those of Ligny. The Ligny figures were prepared in detail immediately after the battle, and therefore are highly reliable and accurate, providing a comparison to Waterloo. Of the total casualties recorded at Ligny, immediate fatalities was 10 per cent of all casualties. At Waterloo, it was 5 per cent, but at Ligny, total casualties were 20 per cent of those at Waterloo. The huge number of men AWOL/missing at Waterloo compared to Ligny makes direct comparison more difficult. Comparing wounded to dead, for Ligny, reveals a mortality—killed by or died soon after being wounded—rate of 19 per cent of the 4,155 men wounded; at Waterloo, 5,787 men were wounded, of those wounded, 19 per cent were killed or died very soon after of their wound, which shows Waterloo was no different to the 'bloodbath' of Saint Armand. The recorded losses can therefore be judged to be reliable. The great unknown are the men who died of wounds long after the battle and what 'missing' actually means.

Without more research, we will not be able to assess the total French loss in the battle, but based on the recorded losses, the *Armée du Nord* lost around 30 per cent effective strength. Conspicuous among the dead and wounded was the high number of officers. Lack of command and control due to dead or wounded officers and NCOs, as well as demoralised men, was to have a major contributing factor in the battlefield performance of the III and IV Corps over the days to come, and overall lost 20 per cent effective strength. Compared to Waterloo, Ligny was a bloodbath, which was not unexpected given the vicious street-fighting that took place. It also has major implications on the strength and competencies of the troops under Grouchy's command: the impact of the heavy losses at Ligny on the infantry under Grouchy's command has been overlooked. We are told in many accounts that Grouchy had over 30,000 men doing nothing: the truth is, when we look at the facts, he had distinctly under 30,000 men at his disposal and was missing key personal. Yet Grouchy, through strength of character, aided by Vandamme, managed to shape the wreck of the army at Ligny into something like a combat force to follow the Prussians.

We must also remember that contrary to eyewitnesses writing after the fact, the Prussians were expected at Waterloo since 8 a.m. Soult's aide-de-camp writes:

> Major General [Soult], still haunted by the anxiety that the Prussians might arrive on our right during the affair, observed this point with very particular attention. I saw him, towards one o'clock in the afternoon, approach Napoleon, and warn him that he very distinctly saw a numerous corps whose arms were in bundles. A few moments later, a quartermaster of the Prussian cavalry, who had just been captured, had been searched, was brought to Napoleon, and on whom was found a note written in pencil, addressed by General Bülow to the English general [Wellington], to announce to him that he was in a position to support him. It was only then that the Emperor determined to send an officer to Marshal Grouchy to order him to march, by Saint-Lambert, against the corps of General Bülow, but it was too late, and we see from the report of this marshal that this officer could not reach him until seven o'clock in the evening. It required nothing less than this discovery, made by the Major-General, to convince the Emperor that he ran the risk of seeing part of the Prussian army arrive on his right flank; until then he had refused to believe in the possibility of this unfortunate incident.[13]

The Prussians were very much expected: hence when we use memories written very much after the fact, we must use them with caution. The documents written within days of the battle offer a very different story of the battle. We must use the archive documents and other sources written as close to the battle as possible to reduce the effects of false memory, which makes much of the Siborne material unreliable, especially as the writers were prompted to write about certain events by Siborne.

In returning to the events of 18 June, we must not forget that over 50,000 men walked off the battlefield of Waterloo. Hard as you look at the data, there was no massacre at Waterloo. All three armies were as equally affected and traumatised by the battle. What destroyed the French army was a collapse of morale. In simple terms, Napoleon lost the campaign as his army was outperformed by the allies as they made fewer tactical errors when it mattered.

Endnotes

Introduction

1. Fussell, P., *The Great War and Modern Memory* (Oxford University Press, Oxford, 1975), p. 311.
2. Coates, J., *The Hour Between Dog and Wolf* (Fourth Estate, London, 2012).
3. Guverich, A., 'The French Historical Revolution: The Annales School' in Hodder *et al.*, *Interpreting Archaeology* (Routledge, London and New York, 1995), pp. 158–161. This short paper offers a good introduction to the notion and concept of the Annales school for those unfamiliar with the theory of history.
4. Fussell, *op. cit.*, p. 311.
5. Green A. and Troup K., *The Houses of History* (Manchester University Press, Manchester, 1999), p. 231.
6. Anon, 'Operations of the Fifth or Thomas Piston's Division in the Campaign of Waterloo' in *United Services Magazine*, Part 2, June 1841, p. 180.

Chapter 1

1. *Journal Militaire 2e semester 1814*, p. 28.
2. Noel, *Souvenirs Militaires d'un officer du Premier* (Empire Librerie des Deux Empires, 1999), p. 216.
3. *Journal des débats politiques et littéraires 3e Juin 1815*, p. 3
4. *Ibid.*
5. *Journal des débats politiques et littéraires 2e Juin 1815* p. 3
6. *Ibid.*
7. Steigler, *Le Maréchal Oudinot* (Paris, 1894), p. 371.
8. *Service Historique du Armee de Terre* (hereafter SHDDT): C15 35. Situation reports *Armée du Nord 10e Juin* dated 13 June.
9. *Archives Nationales* (hereafter AN) 400 AP 109. Bertrand to Soult, 10 June 1815.
10. SHDDT: C15 11. Soult to Gerard, 12 June 1815.
11. SHDDT: C15 5. Soult to Grouchy, 12 June forwarding orders dated 10 June. Copy made in 1865 by Comte du Casse.
12. Lettow-Vorbeck, *Napoléons Untergang 1815* (Berlin, 1906), p. 514.

Endnotes

13 SHDDT: C15 5. *Correspondence Armée du Nord 11 Juin au 21 Juin 1815, dossier du 16 Juin.*
14 SHDDT: C15 35. *Situation rapports Armée du Nord. Dossier 15 Juin 3e Corps de Cavalerie.*
15 SHDDT: C15 5. Dossier 15 June 1815. Grouchy to Soult, 16 June timed at 5 a.m.
16 SHDDT: C15 5. Dossier 15 June 1815. Grouchy to Soult, 16 June timed at 5 a.m.
17 Esdaile, C., *Napoléon, France and Waterloo: The Eagle Rejected* (Pen & Sword, Barnsley, 2016) p. 70.

Chapter 2

1 AN: 28AP *Registre* d'Erlon.
2 SHDDT: C15. *Registre d'ordre et de correspondance du major-general à partir du 13 Juin jusqu'au 26 Juin au Maréchal* Grouchy, p. 12.
3 *Ibid.*, p. 13.
4 *Ibid.*
5 *Archives Diplomatique* 53MD 1875.
6 SHDDT: C15 5. Dossier 16 June 1815, d'Erlon to Soult timed at 4.30 p.m.
7 *Ibid.*, d'Erlon to Soult, timed at 8 p.m.
8 *Ibid.*, Soult to d'Erlon, timed at 9 p.m.
9 SHDDT: C15 5. Dossier 15 June 1815, Ney to Soult at 11 p.m. Copy of the now lost original document made on 20 February 1890.
10 Martin, J. F., *op. cit.*

Chapter 3

1 AN: AFIV 1939 *Registre d'Ordres du Major-General 13 Juin au 26 Juin 1815*, p. 31.
2 *Ibid.*, p. 32.
3 *Ibid.*, pp. 37–40. See also: Grouchy, E., *Relation succincte de la campagne de 1815 en Belgique* (Delanchy, Paris, 1843), pp. 13–14. Grouchy states this is a verbal order, but it is written into Soult's order book, so clearly Grouchy is mistaken on this point, unless Soult recorded verbal orders.
4 SHDDT: C15 5. Dossier 16 June. Copy of the now lost original order made by Ney's son in 1837. See also: Grouchy, E., *op. cit.*
5 John Franklin, personal communication, 7 October 2013.
6 SHDDT: GR 1M 717.
7 SHDDT: C15 5. Dossier 16 June. *Ordre Maréchal Ney 16 Juin 1815 à 11.00*. The document cited is a copy of the now lost original sent to the son of Marshal Ney by General Reille in 1829. This order is not found in the pages of General Reille's correspondence book preserved at the French Army Archives at Vincennes.
8 SHDDT: C 15 5. Dossier 16 June 1815, Lobau to Napoleon.
9 AN: AFIV 1939 *Registre d'Ordres du Major-General 13 Juin au 26 Juin 1815*, pp. 41–42.

Chapter 4

1 SHDDT: C15 5. Dossier 16 June, de la Salle. Copy of original order dated 1896.

2   AN: AFIV 1939 *Registre d'Ordres du Major-General 13 Juin au 26 Juin 1815*, pp. 42–43.
3   SHDDT: GR 1M 717.
4   de Chéron, A., *Mémoires inédits sur la compagne de Russie—Présentés par Robert de Vaucorbeil* (Teissèdre, 2001), p. 2.
5   SHDDT: C15 5. Dossier 16 June 1815, d'Erlon to Duc d'Elchingen in 1829.
6   Drouet, J. B., *Le Maréchal Drouet, Comte d'Erlon: Vie militaire écrit par lui même* (Guvatve, Paris, 1844), pp. 95–96.
7   SHDDT: C15 5. Dossier 16 June 1815, d'Erlon to Duc d'Elchingen on 9 February 1829.
8   Baudus, vol. 1, p. 213.
9   Baudus, vol. 1, pp. 212–3.
10 Col. Heymès, *Relation de la campagne de 1815, dite de Waterloo* (Gaultier-Laguionie, Paris, 1829), p. 11.
11 SHDDT: C15 5. Dossier 16 June 1815, Ney to Soult timed at 10 p.m. Copy of the now lost original document made on 7 April 1906.
12 AN: AFIV 1939, *Registre d'Ordres du Major-General 13 Juin au 26 Juin 1815*, pp. 43–45.

Chapter 5

1   *La Sentinelle de l'Armée*, fourth year, no. 134, 8 March 1838.
2   Chapuis, 'Waterloo' in *La Sentinelle de l'Armée*, 24 February 1838.
3   SHDDT: GD 2 1135.
4   Chapuis, *La Sentinelle de l'Armée*, 24 February 1838.
5   Ibid.
6   Ibid.
7   A letter dated 3 November 1837 published in *La Sentinelle de l'Armée*, 24 February 1838.
8   Letter of General Brue dated Tarbes 13 March 1838, published in *La Sentinelle de l'Armée*, 24 March 1838.
9   SHDDT: C16 23. Robert de Gordon *à sa Femme*, 4 July 1815.
10 SHDDT: GR 7 Yd 389.

Chapter 6

1   SHDDT: C15 5. Dossier 16 June 1815, d'Erlon to Duc d'Elchingen on 9 February 1829.
2   SHDDT: C15 35. Rapport Roussel d'Hurbal Mellet, 17 June 1815.
3   Grouchy, Vol. 4, pp. 146–151.
4   SHDDT: C15 5. Dossier 17 June 1815, Soult to Grouchy. This is the original handwritten order from 17 June 1815.
5   *Revue Etudes Napoléoniennes* (1932), pp. 360–365.
6   Siborne, *Waterloo Letters*, No. 75.
7   Ferrari's map identifies Wais as Wais Le Hupte, due east of Genappe.
8   AN: 28AP Registre d'Erlon.
9   D'Erlon, p. 96.
10 Chapuis, 'Waterloo', in *Sentinalle de l'armée*, 24 February 1838.
11 Bassford, C., Moran, D., and Pedlow, G. W., *The Campaign of 1815*, Chapters 30–39, 'On Waterloo', available at clausewitz.com/readings/1815/five30-39.htm [accessed 10 February 2013].

12 Cuthbertson, A., personal communication, 17 June 2012.
13 SHDDT: C15 5. Dossier 18 June 1815. Grouchy to Napoleon timed at 11 a.m. Copy made by Comte du Casse in June 1865. See also Lettow-Vorbeck (1904), *Napoléons Untergang 1815*, Vol. 8. p. 390, who states the letter was sent at 10 a.m. In Grouchy's register, the letter has no time (Grouchy Vol. IV, p. 28).
14 SHDDT: C15 5. Dossier 17 June 1815. Grouchy to Napoleon 10 p.m.
15 SHDDT: C15 5. Dossier 17 June 1815. Bertrand to Grouchy. Copy of the now lost original order made by Comte du Casse in June 1865. We cannot corroborate this order since no other versions of the order exist. We have to trust that it is a direct copy of the original.
16 Berton, J. B., *Précis historique, militaire et critique des batailles de Fleurus et de Waterloo, dans la campagne de Flandres, en juin 1815*, Wallez, J. S., La Haye, 1818, pp. 49–50.
17 SHDDT: C15 5. Dossier 16 June, Domon to Soult.
18 SHDDT: GR 24 YC 274.
19 SHDDT: C15 5. Dossier 17 June.
20 SHDDT: GR 24 YC 299.

Chapter 7

1 *Journal de l'Empire*, 27 June 1815, pp. 1–2.
2 *Journal de Rouen*, 19 June 1815.
3 Ali, M., *Souvenirs sur l'Empereur Napoléon. Présentés et annotés par Christophe Bourachot* Arléa (2000).
4 Houssaye, H., *1815: Waterloo* (Flamairon, Paris, 1903), p. 311.
5 *Ibid.*, pp. 311–312.
6 No original copy of this order can be found in the boxes of documents at Vincennes nor at the *Archives Nationales* in Paris, in the order book of Marshal Soult. The first order on 18 June is timed at 10 a.m. to Marshal Grouchy. However, the transcript we present was published in 1826 by Vaudoncourt. Vaudoncourt clearly had access to material now lost.
7 Pflugk Harttung, J. von, *Vorgeschichte der Schlacht bei Belle-Alliance*, p. 420.
8 *Ibid.*, p. 422.
9 *Ibid.*, pp. 620–621.
10 Tondeur, J. P., Courcelle, P., Megnak, P., and Patyn, J. J., *Le Caillou: Les Combats de Genappe: Waterloo 1815: Les Carnets de la Campagne No. 10* (Editions de la Belle Alliance, 2007), p. 88.
11 SHDDT: C15 5. Dossier 18 June 1815. Grouchy to Napoleon Copy of original order made June 1863. See also Lettow-Vorbeck, *Napoléons Untergang 1815* Vol. 8. (1904), p. 390.
12 AN: AFIV 1939 *Registre d'Ordres du Major General 13 Juin au 26 Juin 1815*, pp. 49–50.
13 Ollech, *Geschichte des Feldzuges von 1815 nach archivalischen quellen* Berlin (1876).
14 *Ibid.*, p. 193.
15 *Ibid.*, pp. 190–191.
16 AN: 28AP *Registre* d'Erlon.
17 *Ibid.*
18 Aywiers Abbey is towards Couture. The abbey stands north east of Plancenoit by roughly 4 miles, or an hour's march distant from the field of battle.
19 russborough.com/omnium_g/manuscripts/ney-waterloo-dispatch.html accessed 1/04/2023.

Chapter 8

1. Bruno, 'Le 3e Chasseurs à Cheval a Waterloo' in *Sentinalle de l'armée*, 1 March 1838.
2. *Nouvelle Revue Retrospective* (Paris, January 1897), p. 374.
3. Captain Eloy, appointed 7th Company, 3rd Squadron, 15 December 1814. SHDDT: Xc 249 7e Hussard. Dossier 1815.
4. Lieutenant of Elite company. SHDDT: Xc 249 7e Hussard. Dossier 1815.
5. Grouchy, *Relation succincte de la campagne de 1815*, Vol. 4, pp. 141–5.
6. SHDDT: C15 5. Dossier 18 June. Excelmans to Gerard, 1 February 1830.
7. AH: LH 2782/98. Edmond François Blocqueville de Coulliboeuf was born on 15 February 1789 at Falaise. He was awarded the Legion of Honour while a captain on Grouchy's staff on 31 January 1814 while serving in the 16th Chasseurs. He was then made an officer of the Legion of Honour on 16 August 1823 while serving as squadron commander in the 5th Chasseurs. He was promoted to *general de brigade* on 30 April 1849 and died in 1861, aged seventy-two.
8. AH: LH 169/57. AN: LH 169/57. Didier Louis Ferdinand Bellanger Desboullets was born in Paris on 26 July 1784 and admitted to the 3rd Hussars in 1803. He was promoted to corporal and sergeant in the following year and to sub-lieutenant on 26 November 1806, before being listed as lieutenant aide-de-camp to Duc de Plaisance on 10 May 1807. He was promoted to captain on 28 December 1809, then squadron commander aide-de-camp to General Dupont on 23 August 1814, and dismissed on 25 March 1815. He joined Grouchy's staff on 22 April 1815 and was discharged from the army on 6 June 1817.
9. Grouchy, Vol. 4, pp. 141–5.
10. SHDDT: C15 5. Dossier 18 June 1815. Handwritten statement from Blocqueville to Grouchy, no date.
11. SHDDT: C15 5. Dossier 18 June 1815. Statement by Sénécal dated 1829 and copied by Comte du Casse in 1865.
12. Grouchy, *Relation succincte de la campagne de 1815*, Vol. 4, pp. 141-5.
13. Berton, p. 64.
14. Gérard, *Quelques documents*, pp. 41-2.
15. SHDDT: C15 *Registre d'Ordres et de correspondance du major-general a partir du 13 Juin jusqu'au 26 Juin au Maréchal* Grouchy, p. 30. SHDDT: C15 5. Dossier 18 June 1815. Soult to Grouchy 1 p.m. copy of original order made by Comte du Casse in June 1863. Du Casse either copied Grouchy's version of the letter or had access to a duplicate set of material. This order is missing from the correspondence register of Marshal Soult.
16. clausewitz.com/readings/1815/five40-49.htm#Ch45 accessed 10 February 2013.
17. SHDDT: 29 Yc 422 Contrôle Nominatif Troupe 7e Hussards 9 September 1814–12 August 1815.
18. Louvat, E. C. C., Historique du 7e Hussards (Pirault, Paris, 1889).
19. SHDDT: GR 24 YC 422.
20. Smith, I., pers. comm., 1 February 2018.
21. National Archives, Kew. Prisoners of war records 1715-1945. ADM 103/102 Dartmoor. French prisoners of war, 1815 See Also: ADM 103/513 Alphabetical List of POWs, Dartmoor, 1755-1831; ADM 103/99 Dartmoor. French prisoners of war, 1815; ADM 103/311 Plymouth. French prisoners

Endnotes

of war, 1815; ADM 103/595 Register of French POWs Released on Parole, Okehampton and Oswestry, 1815.
22 SHDDT: GR 24 YC 422.
23 Smith, I., pers. comm., 1 February 2018.

Chapter 9

1 *La Sentinelle de l'Armée, 4e année*, No. 134, 8 March 1838.
2 SHDDT: C15 5. Dossier 16 June 1815. This copy is dated September 1859, signed by General Rogniat as an exact copy of the original. For another exact copy but annotated by Ney see also SHDDT: C15 5. Dossier 16 June Documents Inedit XIX, pp. 53–54. The document is signed 'Order dictated by the Emperor on the field of battle of Mont-Saint-Jean 18th, at 11:00, written by Marshal Soult, Duke of Dalmatia, Major General. Paris 21st June 1829'. It was also published in 1826 by Vaudoncourt. It is not impossible Rogniat and Ney Junior copied this text. The original is lost, but clearly as it existed in 1826, it is unlikely to be a fake.
3 SHDDT: C15 5. Dossier 16 June. Documens Inedit XIX, pp. 53–54. Copy made in 1829. It was also published in 1826 by Vaudoncourt. It is not impossible Rogniat and Ney Junior copied this text.
4 Levavasseur, O., *Souvenirs militaires, 1800–1815* (Librerie des Deux Empires, 2001), pp. 303–305.
5 SHDDT: GR Xz 63.
6 SHDDT: GR 2Ye 1980.
7 SHDDT: GR 2Ye 3658.
8 Houssaye (1815) cites Reille as saying that Wellington 'was well posted, as Wellington knows how to post it and attacked from the front, I consider English infantry to be impregnable, owing to its calm tenacity, and its superior aim in firing. Before attacking it with the bayonet, one may expect half the assailants to be brought to the ground. But the English Army is less agile, less supple, and less expert at manoeuvring as our own. If we cannot defeat it by a direct attack, we may do so through manoeuvring'. The story may be apocryphal, but Reille had fought Wellington and may well have indeed have had misgivings about his master's plans. However, Reille was too good a soldier to disobey orders. Reille may have been cautious in his attack, but attack he would have done if ordered to do so, and when the opportunity arose. Perhaps Reille did not think until d'Erlon had reached the allied lines that he needed to move off. Wellington's cavalry was well hidden, and no French officer could conceive of the massive and sudden cavalry attack that descended on d'Erlon with the rapidity that it did.
9 'Des extraits des Souvenirs du général Dessales, ou de Salle' in de *la Revue de Paris*, 15 January 1896.
10 General Bro, *Memoirs, 1796–1844* (Librerie des deux Empires, 2001), p. 148.
11 AN: 82 AP 5 Fonds Bro de Commerce, Dossier 2. 1814–1819.
12 Franklin, J., pers. comm., 19 October 2012.
13 Levavasseur, O., *Souvenirs militaires, 1800–1815* (Librerie des Deux Empires, 2001), pp. 303–305.
14 Lot, H., *Les deux généraux Ordener. Préf. de Félix Rocquain* (Paris, R. Roger et F. Chernoviz, 1910).
15 Franklin, J., *Waterloo Hanoverian Correspondence Volume 1* (1815 Ltd, 2010), pp. 26–27.
16 Deleveot, 'Cowards at Waterloo?' in *Napoléon* No. 16, Summer 2000, p. 31.
17 Lancaster, M., pers. comm.

18   AN: 28AP *Registre* d'Erlon.

Chapter 10

1. Deleveot, 'Cowards at Waterloo?' in *Napoléon* No. 16, Summer 2000, p. 31.
2. *Ibid.*, p. 33.
3. The National Army Museum: 1981-12-53-557. Transcript provided by John Franklin.
4. AN: 28AP *Registre* d'Erlon.
5. *Leeds Mercury*, 1 July 1815.
6. Fleuret, F., *Description des Passages de Dominique Fleuret* (Firmin Diderot, Paris, 1929), pp. 148–157.
7. Canler, p. 21.
8. *Revue Etudes Napoléoniennes* (1932), pp. 360–365.
9. SHDDT GR 8 Yd 1707 letter, 21 May 1838.
10. *Mémoires du général Noguès sur les guerres de l'Empire, publiés par le baron André de Maricourt* (Paris, Lemerre, 1922), pp. 273–276.
11. Martin, J. F., *Souvenirs d'un ex-officer 1812–1815* (Paris, 1867), pp. 275–276.
12. SHDDT: GR 21 YC 456 *50e régiment d'infanterie de ligne* (ex-54e *régiment d'infanterie de ligne*), 21 July 1814–10 May 1815 (*matricules* 1 à 1,660).
13. SHDDT: GR 21 YC 463 *51e régiment d'infanterie de ligne* (ex-55e *régiment d'infanterie de ligne*), 1 August 1814–3 August 1815 (*matricules* 1 à 2,049).
14. SHDDT: GR 21 YC 264 *28e régiment d'infanterie de ligne*, 6 July 1808–23 June 1815 (*matricules* 1 à 1,762).
15. SHDDT: GR 21 YC 771 *86e régiment d'infanterie de ligne* (ex-105e *régiment d'infanterie de ligne*), 13 August 1814–21 Februray 1815 (*matricules* 1 à 1,800). See also SHDDT: GR 21 YC 772 *86e régiment d'infanterie de ligne* (ex-105e *régiment d'infanterie de ligne*), 24 February 1815–10 August 1815 (*matricules* 1,801 à 1,881).
16. SHDDT: GR 21 YC 197 *21e régiment d'infanterie de ligne*, 18–20 May 1815 (*matricules* 1 à 1,800). See also SHDDT: GR 21 YC 198 *21e régiment d'infanterie de ligne*, 29 April 1815–16 June 1815 (*matricules* 1,801 à 1,817).
17. SHDDT: GR 21 YC 238 *25e régiment d'infanterie de ligne*, 1 August 1814–20 January 1815 (*matricules* 1 à 1,800).
18. SHDDT: GR 21 YC 391 *42e régiment d'infanterie de ligne* (ex-45e *régiment d'infanterie de ligne*), 1 August 1814–4 June 1815 (*matricules* 1 à 1,800).
19. SHDDT: GR 21 YC 400 *43e régiment d'infanterie de ligne* (ex-46e *régiment d'infanterie de ligne*), 1 August 1814–31 May 1815 (*matricules* 1 à 1,800). See also SHDDT: GR 21 YC 401 *43e régiment d'infanterie de ligne* (ex-46e *régiment d'infanterie de ligne*), 31 May 1815–30 July 1815 (*matricules* 1,801 à 2,075).
20. SHDDT: GR 25 YC21 *2e Artillerie à Pied* 1814–1815.
21. AN: LH 2670/44.
22. SHDDT: GR 25 YC 21 *2e Artillerie à Pied* 1814–1815.
23. SHDDT: GR 25YC 14.

Chapter 11

1. de Mauduit, H., 'Vieille Militaire. Charleroi, Fleurus et Waterloo' in *La Sentinalle de l'armée*, 24 June 1836.
2. SHDDT: GD 2 1135.
3. *La Sentinelle de l'Armée, 4e année*, No. 134, 8 March 1838.

Endnotes

4   Dalton, C., *The Waterloo Roll Call* (Eyre and Spottiswood, London, 1904), p. 254.
5   *Nottinghamshire Guardian*, 30 May 1873, p. 3.
6   *La Sentinelle de l'Armée*, 4e année, No. 134, 8 March 1838.
7   de Mauduit, H., 'Vieille Militaire. Charleroi, Fleurus et Waterloo' in *La Sentinalle de l'armée*, 24 June 1836.
8   AN: LH 864/38.
9   AN: LH 268/41.
10 AN: LH 1445/40.
11 *La Souvenir Napoléonien* No. 337, September 1984.
12 SHDDT: GD 2 1135.
13 Chapuis, 'Waterloo' in *Sentinalle de l'armée*, 24 February 1838.
14 *Ibid*.
15 Author's collection.
16 SHDDT: Xd 360 *Artillerie Armée du Nord*. Situation Report, 1 June 1815.
17 'Des extraits des Souvenirs du général Dessales, ou de Salle' in de *la Revue de Paris*, 15 January 1896.

Chapter 12

1   SHDDT: GR 7 Yd 603 *lettre*, 27 February 1834.
2   SHDDT: GR 7 Yd 603 *lettre*, 16 February 1834.
3   The Scots Greys. Their bearskin caps being reminiscent of those of the Elite Gendarmes of the Imperial Guard.
4   1st Dragoons we assume.
5   SHDDT: GR 7Yd 1074 *lettre*, 10 August 1839.
6   'Correspondence: To the Editor of the *Hereford Times*. Death of General Ponsonby at Waterloo', *Hereford Times* (23 August 1845), p. 7.
7   Sub-Lieutenant Jeanne Marie Verrand, appointed 21 May 1813, received the regiment's eagle on 1 June 1815. SHDDT: Xc 182 3e *et* 4e Lanciers. Dossier 4e Lanciers. Folio 1815.
8   MAT No. 6 Francois Orban, sergeant, 1st Company, 1st Squadron, 4th Lancers. Born in St-Denis in the department of Ain, 12 January 1778. Admitted to the regiment on 17 December 1798, he was promoted to corporal on 1 October 1813, then sergeant on 1 March 1815. He stood 1.72 m tall, had nut-brown hair and blue eyes. Discharged from the regiment on 16 September 1815, he died on 8 April 1848. His discharge papers make no mention at all of him killing Ponsonby. AN: LH 2020/22. Given in other regiments, officers and men recorded their deeds of valour and glory in the immediate aftermath (for instance, Isaac Palaa of the 9th Cuirassiers taking a colour at Waterloo), it seems unlikely that Orban would not have commented upon this. Orban, I have no doubt, was involved in a melee with the Scots Greys, but I doubt he killed Ponsonby as neither he nor his commanding officer could have recognised Sir William Ponsonby on the field of battle.
9   How did Bro know this? I have no doubt that the 4th Lancers were involved in a melee with the Scots Greys, but Bro could only have known after the fact that General Sir William Ponsonby was killed by Lancers. Given Ponsonby was shot dead while with the Royal Dragoons at the moment Corporal Styles of that regiment took the eagle of the 105th Line, Orban cannot have killed Ponsonby. It is highly likely that Bro was claiming the credit for the death of Ponsonby for his regiment, and to provide some degree of authenticity, added a name of a member of the regiment, claiming he killed three officers from the Scots Greys. This

seems very unlikely that of the eleven recorded officer casualties, Bro killed three. Beyond Colonel Bro, there is no historical evidence that Orban killed Ponsonby.

10   Major Perrot joined the regiment 12 June 1815. SHDDT: Xc 182 3e *et* 4e Lanciers. Dossier 4e Lanciers.
11   Assistant Surgeon Motet joined the regiment on 10 June 1815. SHDDT: Xc 182 3e *et* 4e Lanciers. Dossier 4e Lanciers.
12   General Bro, *Memoirs, 1796–1844* (Librerie des deux Empires, 2001).
13   SHDDT: C15 5. Dossier 21 June 1815. Letter Major 21e Line to Soult.
14   Smith, I., pers. comm. 24 June 2012.
15   De Mauduit, Vol. 2, p. 300.
16   SHDDT: C15 5. Dossier 21 June 1815. Letter Major 21st Regiment of Line Infantry to Soult.
17   Dulaure, J-A., *1814–1830. Histoire des Cent-Jours* (Paris, 1834), p. 205, citing Armand Jean Flotard of the 4th Lancers.
18   British Library Newspaper collection, *Middleton Albion*, Saturday 15 February 1868, p. 4.
19   Smith, I., pers. comm. 2 June 2015.
20   AN: LH 1206/63.
21   AN: LH 1593-39.
22   AN: LH 64/3.
23   AN: LH 829/70.
24   AN: LH 758/71.
25   *Carnet de la Sabretache* (1909).
26   Joseph Pozac was born on 31 July 1781. He volunteered to the 12th Hussars on 25 May 1798. Promoted to corporal 20 April 1799, by which time the Hussars had become the 30th Dragoons, he was made fourrier on 22 March 1800, sergeant-major on 26 February 1801, sub-lieutenant on 28 June 1803, and lieutenant on 18 September 1806. Named aide-de-camp to General Fournier on 12 November 1807, he was then named aide-de-camp to General Dalton on 9 July 1809. Made captain in the newly formed 12th Hussars on 8 November 1809, Pozac was promoted to squadron commander on 21 March 1813 in the 23rd Chasseurs. He was then passed as squadron commander to the 3rd Chasseurs on 16 August 1814. AN: LH/2218/13.
27   Bruno, 'Le 3e Chasseurs à Cheval a Waterloo', in *Sentinalle de l'armée*, 1 March 1838.
28   Brue, J. L., '*Lettre Addresse au* Colonel Chapuis' in *La Sentinalle de l'armée*, 1 March 1838.
29   SHDDT: C 15 5. *Rapport 2e Corps sous les ordres du General en Chef* Reille.
30   SHDDT: Gr 24 YC 107 3e Lanciers.
31   SHDDT: Yj 11. See also SHDDT Yj 12; SHDDT Yj 13. See also National Archives, Kew. Prisoners of war records 1715–1945. ADM 103/102 Dartmoor. French prisoners of war, 1815. See also: ADM 103/513 Alphabetical List of POWs, Dartmoor, 1755–1831; ADM 103/99 Dartmoor. French prisoners of war, 1815; ADM 103/311 Plymouth. French prisoners of war, 1815; ADM 103/595 Register of French POWs Released on Parole, Okehampton and Oswestry, 1815.
32   SHDDT: Gr 24 YC 107 3e Lanciers.
33   *Ibid.*
34   SHDDT: C 15 5. *Rapport 2e Corps sous les ordres du General en Chef* Reille. See also SHDDT, Xc 182 3e et 4e Lanciers 1811–1814. Dossier 4e Lanciers 1815.
35   AN: LH 1930/45.

36   SHDDT: GR 24 YC 114 Lanciers de Monsieur.
37   GR 24 YC264.

Chapter 13

1   AN: 28AP *Registre* d'Erlon.
2   SHDDT: 8Yd 1510 *lettre*, dated 9 March 1831.
3   *Nouvelle Revue Retrospective* (Paris, January 1897), p. 374.
4   SHDDT: GR 8Yd 1510 *lettre*, 21 January 1833.
5   *Ibid.*, *lettre*, 16 February 1833.
6   *Nottinghamshire Guardian*, 3 August 1854 p. 4.
7   Low, E. B., *With Napoléon at Waterloo* (London: 1911), pp. 144–5.
8   Delort, '*Notice sur les batailles de Fleurus et de Mont Saint Jean*' in *Revue Hebdomadaire*, June 1896, pp. 379–380.
9   SHDDT: 24YC 36 *5e* Cuirassier.
10 AN: LH 376/26.
11 AN: LH 1245/18.
12 AN: LH 1034/42.
13 AN: LH 2476/74.
14 de Juzancourt, G. G., *Historique de 10e regiment de Cuirassiers (1643–1891)* (Paris, Librerie Militaire, Berger-Levrault, 1893), p. 88.
15 SHDDT: GR 24 Yc 60 *Contrôle Nominatif Troupe* 10e Cuirassiers 15 April 1815–27 July 1815, organisation 1814.
16 *Ibid.*
17 *Nouvelle Revue Retrospective* (Paris, January 1897), p. 374.
18 Lot, *Les deux généraux Ordener.*
19 AN: LH 1666/5.
20 AN: LH 1263/65.
21 Jacques Desmot was born in Meuville, in the department of Calvados on 2 April 1770. He was admitted into the 12th Chasseurs on 27 January 1789. He was promoted to corporal on 1 July 1793, then to sergeant later the same year, then to sergeant-major in 1799, and sub-lieutenant later the same year. Admitted into the *chasseurs à cheval* of the Consular Guard in 1800, he passed to the *Grenadiers à Cheval* in 1803 and was promoted to second lieutenant, being promoted to first lieutenant in the following year. Following the Battle of Eylau, he was appointed captain on 18 February 1807. Transferred as major of the recently activated 13th Cuirassier regiment, he then served in Spain on 16 October 1811. Passed to major of the 4th Cuirassiers on 16 November 1812 and thence major of the 7th Cuirassiers on 16 January 1815, he was awarded the Legion of Honour in 1804 and was made a Knight of the Legion on 14 May 1806. He was discharged from 7th Cuirassiers on 27 November 1815.
22 SHDDT: GR 24 YC 46 *Contrôle Nominatif Troupe* 7e Cuirassiers, 9 August 1814–6 August 1815.
23 *Ibid.*
24 *Ibid.*
25 Ruby and De Labeau, *Historique du 12me Régiment de Cuirassiers.*
26 SHDDT: 24YC 69 *12e* Cuirassier
27 National Archives, Kew. Prisoners of war records 1715–1945. ADM 103/102 Dartmoor. French prisoners of war, 1815. See Also: ADM 103/513 Alphabetical List of POWs, Dartmoor, 1755–1831; ADM 103/99 Dartmoor. French prisoners of war, 1815; ADM 103/311 Plymouth. French prisoners

of war, 1815; ADM 103/595 Register of French POWs Released on Parole, Okehampton and Oswestry, 1815; SHDDT: Yj 11; SHDDT: Yj 12; SHDDT: Yj13.
28   Lot, H., *Les deux généraux Ordener*. Préf. de Félix Rocquain (Paris, R. Roger et F. Chernoviz, 1910)
29   de Rochefort, M., *Histoire de 4e regiment de Cuirassiers* (Paris, A. Lahure, 1897), p. 346.
30   SHDDT: GR 24 YC 46 *Contrôle Nominatif Troupe* 7e Cuirassiers, 9 August 1814–6 August 1815.
31   SHDDT: 24YC 69 12e Cuirassier.
32   SHDDT: GR 25 YC 14 1er Artillerie à Cheval.
33   SHDDT: Xc 103 *5e regiment de* Cuirassiers. Dossier 1814.
34   SHDDT: GR 24 Yc 60 *Contrôle Nominatif Troupe* 10e Cuirassiers, 15 April 1815–27 July 1815, organisation 1814.
35   SHDDT: GR 24 YC 41.
36   SHDDT: GR 24 YC55.
37   SHDDT: GR 25 YC 40 3e *Artillerie à Cheval*.

Chapter 14

1   SHDDT: C15 *Registre d'Ordres et de correspondance du major-general a partir du 13 Juin jusqu'au 26 Juin au Maréchal Grouchy*, p. 30. See also: SHDDT: C15 5. Dossier 18 June 1815. Soult to Grouchy, timed at 1 p.m. Copy of the original order made by Comte du Casse in June 1863. Du Casse either copied Grouchy's version of the letter, or had access to a duplicate set of material. This order is missing from the correspondence register of Marshal Soult.
2   von Pflug-Harttung, J., *Vorgeschichte der Schlact bei Belle-Alliance—Wellington* (Berlin, 1903), p. 206.
3   Franklin, J., pers. comm. citing *Niedersachishes Hauptstaatarchive* (Hannover: Hann 41XX1 156).
4   Franklin, J., pers. comm. 7 September 2016, citing *Hessisches Hauptstaatsarchiv* (Wiesbaden: Abt.1041, Nr.1). Letter, dated 14 July 1815.
5   Franklin, J., *Waterloo Hanoverian Correspondence* Vol. 1 (1815 Ltd, 2010), pp. 164–167.
6   *La Sentinelle de l'Armée, 4e année*, No. 134, 8 March 1838.
7   de Witt, P., pers. comm.
8   *Historiche Beilage* Vol. 56 No. 11 (Herbon, 1988).
9   Franklin, J., pers. comm.
10 Franklin, J., pers. comm. 7 September 2016, citing *Das Leben des Herzog's Bernhard von Sachsen-Weimar: königlich niederländischer General der Infanterie* (Gotha, 1865).
11 Franklin, J., pers. comm. 7 September 2016, citing *Hessisches Hauptstaatsarchiv* (Wiesbaden: Abt.202, Nr.1163).
12 Franklin, J., pers. comm. 7 September 2016.
13 *Ibid*.
14 de Witt, P., pers. comm.
15 von Pflug-Harttung, J., *Vorgeschichte der Schlact bei Belle-Alliance—Wellington* (Berlin, 1903), p. 206.
16 de Witt, P., pers. comm.
17 WL No. 82.
18 Franklin, J., pers. comm. 7 September 2016, citing *Hessisches Hauptstaatsarchiv* (Wiesbaden: Abt.202, Nr.1372).

Endnotes

19 von Pflug-Harttung, J., *Vorgeschichte der Schlact bei Belle-Alliance—Wellington* (Berlin, 1903), p. 76.
20 *Ibid.*
21 Tissot, P. F., *Histoire de Napoléon, rédigée d'après les papiers d'état, les documents officiels, les mémoires et les notes secrètes de ses contemporains, suivie d'un précis sur la famille Bonaparte. L'ouvrage, orné de portraits et plans, est précédé de réflexions générales sur Napoléon*, Vol. 2 (Delange-Taffin, Paris, 1833), pp. 277–278.
22 Franklin, J., pers. comm. 7 September 2016.
23 Franklin, J., pers. comm. 7 September 2016, citing *Hessisches Hauptstaatsarchiv* (Wiesbaden: Abt.202, Nr.1372).
24 SHDDT: GR 21 YC 74 8e *régiment d'infanterie de Ligne dit régiment de Condé*, 30 August 1814–11 May 1815 (*matricules* 1 *à* 1,800). See also SHDDT: GR 21 YC 75 8e *régiment d'infanterie de ligne dit régiment de Condé*, 14 May 1815–10 July 1815 (*matricules* 1,801 *à* 2,379).
25 SHDDT: GR 21 YC 271 29e *régiment d'infanterie de ligne*, 21 July 1814–24 December 1814 (*matricules* 1 *à* 1,800). See also SHDDT: GR 21 YC 272 29e *régiment d'infanterie de ligne*, 24 December 1814–21 July 1815 (*matricules* 1,801 *à* 2,226).
26 SHDDT: GR 21 YC 665 73e *régiment d'infanterie de ligne* (ex-85e *régiment d'infanterie de ligne*), 16 September 1814–29 July 1815 (*matricules* 1 *à* 1,285).
27 SHDDT: GR 21 YC 717 79e *régiment d'infanterie de ligne* (ex-95e *régiment d'infanterie de ligne*), 26 August 1814–25 May 1815 (*matricules* 1 *à* 1,800).
28 Wedell, p. 166.

Chapter 15

1 SHDDT: C15 *Registre d'Ordres et de correspondance du major-general à partir du 13 Juin jusqu'au 26 Juin au Maréchal Grouchy*, p. 30.
2 de Bas, F., and de T'Serclaes de Wommersom, J., *La Compagne de 1815 aux Pays-Bas d'Après les Rapports Officiels Néerlandais* Vol. 2(Brussels: Libraire Albert Dewt, 1908), pp. 524–528.
3 Karl-Weiß, H., pers. comm., 1 April 2023.
4 Author's collection.
5 Combes-Brassard, *Notice sur la bataille de Mont-Saint-Jean, dans Souvenirs et Correspondance sur la bataille de Waterloo* (Librerie Historique Teissèdre, Paris, 2000).
6 Author's collection.
7 Karl-Weiß, H., pers. comm., 1 April 2023.
8 de Bas, *op. cit.*, p. 507.
9 SHDDT /GR 21 YC 116 *13er régiment d'infanterie Legere 1806 à 1815*.

Chapter 16

1 Tissot, P. F., *Histoire de Napoléon, rédigée d'après les papiers d'état, les documents officiels, les mémoires et les notes secrètes de ses contemporains, suivie d'un précis sur la famille Bonaparte. L'ouvrage, orné de portraits et plans, est précédé de réflexions générales sur Napoléon* Vol. 2 (Delange-Taffin, Paris, 1833), pp. 272–273.
2 Bruno, 'Le 3e Chasseurs à Cheval a Waterloo' in *Sentinalle de l'armée*, 1 March 1838.
3 AN: 28AP *Registre* d'Erlon.

4   *Nouvelle Revue Retrospective* (Paris, January 1897), p. 374.
5   Gourgaud (1820), p. 94.
6   de Mauduit, H., '*Veillee Militaire Charleroi, Fleurus et Waterloo*' in *Sentinale de l'armée*, 16 June 1836.
7   Petiet, pp. 445–446.
8   SHDDT: Xc 192 *4e regiment Chasseurs à Cheval*. Dossier 1815. *Rapport 6 July 1815*.
9   *Ibid*.
10 AN: LH 547/37.
11 AN: LH 1958/37.
12 AN: LH 2356/28.
13 SHDDT: Xc 192 *4e regiment Chasseurs à Cheval*. Dossier 1815. *Rapport 6 July 1815*.
14 *Ibid*.
15 SHDDT: GR 24 YC 274.
16 SHDDT: GR 24 YC299.
17 For the period 18 June–23 June, and therefore lists losses of men after Waterloo. It is likely the losses are, as with the other regiments in the division of under fifty.
18 *Ibid*.
19 SHDDT: C15 6. *Correspondence Armée du Nord 23 Juin au 3 Juillet*. Dossier 23 Juin. Domon to Soult.
20 AN: LH 2094/42.
21 AN: LH 2296/12.
22 MSH 148375.
23 AN: LH 1480/20.
24 Croyet, J., '*Le 1er Chevau-Leger-Lancier*' in *Traditions Magazine*, Vol. 3, 3 August 2015, pp 26–32.
25 SHDDT GR24 YC96.
26 Croyet, J., *op. cit.*, p. 37.
27 SHDDT: GR 24 YC 102 2e Lanciers.
28 SHDDT: GR 24 YC 309.

Chapter 17

1   'The Journal of Henri Niemann of the Sixth Prussian Black Hussars' in *The English Historical Review*, Vol. 3, July 1888, pp. 539–45.
2   AN: 28AP *Registre* d'Erlon.
3   Karl-Weiß, H., pers. comm., 1 April 2023.
4   Janin, pp. 35–36.
5   Combes-Brassard, *Notice sur la bataille de Mont-Saint-Jean, dans Souvenirs et Correspondance sur la bataille de Waterloo* (Librerie Historique Teissèdre, Paris, 2000).
6   AN: AFIV 1939 *Registre d'Ordres du Major General 13 Juin au 26 Juin 1815*, pp. 50–51.
7   SHDDT: GR Xz 30.
8   SHDDT: GR Xz 25.
9   SHDDT: GD 2 1135.
10 AN: LH 2407/25.
11 AN: LH 1548/79.
12 Boisnard, J. M., pers. comm. 3 June 2012.

13 AN: LH 407/2.
14 Boisnard, J. M., pers. comm. 3 June 2012.
15 *Carnet de la Sabretache* (1902), p. 691.
16 AN: LH/1271/67.
17 AN: LH/1806/47.
18 AN: LH/1919/71.
19 AN: LH/1256/59.
20 Boisnard, J. M., pers. comm. 3 June 2012.
21 *Ibid.*
22 AN: LH/2688/27.
23 AN: LH/565/14.
24 AN: LH/2464/38.
25 AN: LH/392/54.
26 AN: LH/707/79.
27 SHDDT: GR Xz 51 *Liste de Soldats, sous-officiers et officiers tues du 5e regiment d'infanterie legere, tues a la bataille du* Mont St Jean.
28 Lachouque, H., *Le Général Tromelin* (Bloud & Gay, 1968), pp. 227–229.
29 SHDDT: GR 21 YC 781 88e *régiment d'infanterie de ligne* (ex-107e *régiment d'infanterie de ligne*), 21 July 1814–6 July 1815 (*matricules* 1 à 1,396). No. 131 Francois Marq was born on 13 December 1792, son of Louis Marq and Mary Thérèse Briodar in Eclaron, in the canton of Staint Dizier in the department of Haute-Marne. By trade he was a shop assistant. He stood 1.73 meters tall, had an oval face, grey eyes, with chestnut brown hair and eyebrows. He was admitted to the 56th Cohort of the National Guard on 17 April 1812. Promoted to corporal 26 April 1812, he was transferred to the 153rd Line on 22 February 1813 and was quickly promoted to corporal 22 February 1813 and sergeant-major 26 March 1814. With the disbandment of the 153rd Line, he was passed to the 88th Line, which had been the 107th Line on 21 July 1814. The 88th Line became the 107th Line again on 1 April 1815. He was wounded on 18 June.
30 *Revue Napoléonienne* (1901).
31 AN: LH 640/78.
32 AN: LH 703/88.
33 AN: LH 819/72.
34 AN: LH 738/25.
35 AN: LH 2309/35.
36 AN: LH 458/41.
37 AN: LH 307/70.
38 Boisnard, J. M., pers. comm.
39 SHDDT: GR 21 YC 49 5e *régiment d'infanterie de ligne dit régiment d'Angoulême*, 6 September 1814–23 December 1814 (*matricules* 1 à 1,800). See also SHDDT: GR 21 YC 50 5e *régiment d'infanterie de ligne dit régiment d'Angoulême*, 23 December 1814–25 August 1815 (*matricules* 1,800 à 2,208).
40 *Les inédits napoléoniens de A. Chuquet-Tome*, No. 3,302, p. 478.
41 SHDDT: GR 21 YC 100 11e *régiment d'infanterie de ligne*, 9 September 1814–4 February 1815 (*matricules* 1 à 1,800). See also SHDDT: GR 21 YC 101 11e *régiment d'infanterie de ligne*, 4 February 1815–23 August 1815 (*matricules* 1,801 à 2,690).
42 SHDDT: GR 21 YC 255 27e *régiment d'infanterie de ligne*, 1 August 1814 (*matricules* 1 à 1,800). See also SHDDT: GR 21 YC 256 27e *régiment d'infanterie de ligne*, 1 July 1814–19 July 1815 (*matricules* 1,801 à 2,778).

43 SHDDT: GR 21 YC 653 72e *régiment d'infanterie de ligne* (ex-84e *régiment d'infanterie de ligne*), 1 August 1814–4 February 1815 (*matricules* 1 à 1,800). See also SHDDT: GR 21 YC 655 72e *régiment d'infanterie de ligne* (ex-84e *régiment d'infanterie de ligne*), 20 January 1815–24 July 1815 (*matricules* 1,801 à 2,756).

44 SHDDT: GR Xz 51 *Liste de Soldats, sous-officiers et officiers tues du 5e regiment d'infanterie legere, tues a la bataille du* Mont St Jean.

45 SHDDT: GR 22 YC 48. See also SHDDT: GR 22 YC47.

46 SHDDT: GR 21 YC 92 10e *régiment d'infanterie de ligne dit régiment Colonel-Général*, 1 September 1814–6 May 1815 (*matricules* 1 à 1,800). See also SHDDT: GR 21 YC 93 10e *régiment d'infanterie de ligne dit régiment Colonel-Général*, 6 May 1815–22 July 1815 (*matricules* 1,801 à 1,943).

47 SHDDT: GR 21 YC 781 88e *régiment d'infanterie de ligne* (ex-107e *régiment d'infanterie de ligne*), 21 July 1814–6 July 1815 (*matricules* 1 à 1,396).

48 Chéron, p. 74.

Chapter 18

1 Largeaud, J-M., pers. comm. 10 August 2012.
2 Author's collection.
3 Smith, I., pers. comm.
4 Karl-Weiß, H., pers. comm.
5 Janin, E. F., *Campagne de Waterloo* (1820), pp. 35–36.
6 *Revue de l'Empire, fondée en 1842 par Ch.-Ed. Temblaire, directeur-rédacteur* (Paris, 1845), pp. 260–261.
7 Franklin, J., pers. comm. 7 September 2016, citing *Hessisches Hauptstaatsarchiv* (Wiesbaden: Abt.1049).
8 Franklin, J., pers. comm. 7 September 2016.
9 von Pflug-Harttung, J., *Vorgeschichte der Schlact bei Belle-Alliance—Wellington* (Berlin, 1903), p. 206.
10 de Mauduit, H., 'Vieille Militaire. Charleroi, Fleurus et Waterloo' in *La Sentinalle de l'armée*, 24 June 1836.
11 Pontecoulant, pp. 327–328.
12 Franklin, J., pers. comm. 7 September 2016, citing *Hessisches Hauptstaatsarchiv* (Wiesbaden: Abt.202, Nr.1372).
13 Franklin, J., pers. comm.
14 Colonel Heymès, *Relation de la campagne de 1815, dit de Waterloo: pour servir à l'histoire du Maréchal Ney* (Gaultier-Laguionie, Paris, 1829), pp. 26–27.
15 *The Times*, 13 July 1815.
16 Tromelin, pp. 227-228.
17 Pontecoulant, pp. 323-327.
18 MAT No. 231 Dominique Fleuret was born on 30 April 1787 at Bouthenville in the department of the Meuse, the son of Domonique Fleuret and Ann Folly. He stood 1 m 64. Conscripted 55th Line on 12 May 1807, he was promoted to corporal on 9 March 1809, then adjutant on 1 July 1813. He was discharged on 1 September 1815. SHDDT: GR 21 YC 463 51e *régiment d'infanterie de ligne* (ex-55e *régiment d'infanterie de ligne*), 1 August 1814–3 August 1815 (*matricules* 1 à 2,049).
19 Fleuret, F., *Description des Passages de Dominique Fleuret* (Firmin Diderot, Paris, 1929), pp. 149–154.

Chapter 19

1. Franklin, J., pers. comm.
2. Ollech, *Geschichte des Feldzuges von 1815 nach archivalischen quellen Berlin* (1876), pp. 248–249.
3. Petiet, A., *Souvenirs Militaires* (Paris, 1844), pp. 221–222.
4. D'Avout. *'L'infanterie de la garde à Waterloo'* in *Carnet de la Sabretache* (1905), Vol. 13, pp. 37–39.
5. *Ibid.*, pp. 111–113.
6. Wagner, p. 90.
7. Dupuy, V., *Memoires Militaire, 1794-1816* (Librerie des deux Empires, 2001).
8. Hoffmann, *Zur Geschichte des Feldzuges von 1815* (Berlin, 1851), pp. 108–109.
9. Petit, J., 'General Petit's account of the Waterloo Campaign' in Smith, G. (ed.), *English Historical Review* (1903).
10. Franklin, J., pers. comm.
11. He is recorded on 1 June as serving in 1st Company in 1st Battalion. SHDDT: Xab 69 Dossier *2e Chasseurs à Pied*.
12. He is recorded on 1 June as serving in 5th Company in 2nd Battalion. SHDDT: Xab 69 Dossier *2e Chasseurs à Pied*.
13. Commanding 1st Brigade comprising 1st Tirailleurs and 1st Voltigeurs.
14. Commanding 3rd Voltigeurs.
15. He is recorded on 1 June as commanding 1st Company in 1st Battalion. SHDDT: Xab 69 Dossier *2e Chasseurs à Pied*.
16. He is recorded on 1 June as commanding 4th Company in 1st Battalion. SHDDT: Xab 69 Dossier *2e Chasseurs à Pied*.
17. He is recorded on 1 June as commanding 3rd Company 1st Battalion. SHDDT: Xab 69 Dossier *2e Chasseurs à Pied*.
18. From the 2nd Battalion of the 2nd Regiment.
19. He is recorded on 1 June as commanding 1st Battalion of the 2nd Chasseurs. SHDDT: Xab 69 Dossier *2e Chasseurs à Pied*.
20. D'Avout, pp. 41–42.
21. AN: LH 628/64.
22. Captain Heuillette, *2nd Chasseurs Journal de Toulouse*, 24 October 1845, p. 2.
23. Franklin, J., pers. comm.
24. Wagner, p. 94.
25. *Ibid.*
26. Guyot, *Carnets de la Campagne du General Comte Guyot 1792–1815* (Teissèdre, 1999).

Chapter 20

1. Anon, *Tales of War* (William Mark Clarke, London, 1836), pp. 260–261.
2. Author's collection.
3. AN: 28AP *Registre* d'Erlon.
4. *La Sentinelle de l'Armée*, 4e année, No. 134, 8 March 1838.
5. Stawitzky, L., *Geschichte des Königlich Preussichen 25ten Infanterie-Regiments. Koblenz* (1857), p. 106.
6. Wagner, p. 94.
7. Chevalier Pierre Hippolyte Amillet, Captain Ordonnance Officer to Napoleon at Waterloo.

8 *Nouvelle Revue Retrospective* (Paris, January 1896), pp. 375–376.
9 SHDDT: C15 5. Dossier 23 June 1815. Kupieski to Davout.
10 Author's collection.

Chapter 21

1 SHDDT: C 15 5. Dossier 20 June 1815.
2 AN: AFIV 1939 *Registre d'Ordres du Major General*, 13–26 June 1815, pp. 54–55.
3 AN: 28AP *Registre* d'Erlon.
4 Davout, pp. 96–97.
5 AN: AFIV 1939 *Registre d'Ordres du Major General*, 13–26 June 1815, p. 96. See also SHDDT: C15 6. Dossier 23 June 1815. Soult to d'Erlon.
6 SHDDT: Xab 74 Situation report 21 June 1815.
7 AN: AFIV 1939 *Registre d'Ordres du Major General*, 13–26 June 1815, p. 79.
8 SHDDT: C15 6. Dossier 26 June 1815. Soult to Davout.
9 SHDDT: C15 6. Dossier 26 June 1815. Soult to Davout, time at 5 a.m.
10 SHDDT: C15 6. Dossier 26 June 1815. Grouchy to Davout, timed at 5.30.
11 SHDDT: C15 6. Dossier 27 June 1815. Grouchy to d'Erlon, timed at 7 a.m.
12 Weltzein, K., *Memoiren des Konglichen preussischen Genes der Infanterie Ludwig von reiche*, Vol. 2 (Leipzig, 1857), p. 249.
13 AN: AFIV 1140 Situation report, 29–30 June 1815.
14 SHDDT: MR 718 Relation Campagne 1815 par le Duc de Valmy p. 32.
15 SHDDT: C15 6. Dossier 29 June 1815. Grouchy to Davout. Copy made by Comte du Casse.
16 SHDDT: C15 6. Dossier 1 July 1815. *Ordre du Jour*.
17 Esdaile, C., *Napoleon, France and Waterloo: The Eagle Rejected* (Pen & Sword, Barnsley, 2016), p. 70.

Chapter 22

1 SHDDT: Yj11, Yj 12, Yj13. See also PRO ADM 103/513 Alphabetical List of POWs, Dartmoor, 1755–1831; ADM 103/99 Dartmoor. French prisoners of war, 1815; ADM 103/311 Plymouth. French prisoners of war, 1815; ADM 103/595 Register of French POWs Released on Parole, Okehampton and Oswestry, 1815.
2 SHDDT: C15 5. Correspondence *Armée du Nord* 1815 File 17 June 1815, *3e Corps Armée du Nord 8e Division Etat des pertes eprouver la journée du 16e Juin* 1815.
3 *Ibid*.
4 SHDDT: GR Xz 29 *22e régiment de Ligne registre des deces*.
5 SHDDT: GR Xz 33 *34e régiment de Ligne registre des deces*.
6 SHDDT: C15 35. Situations *Armée du Nord* 1815. Dossier 4e Corps.
7 SHDDT: Xz 22 *96e régiment de Ligne registre des deces*.
8 SHDDT: Xz 40 *63e régiment de Ligne registre des deces*.
9 SHDDT: Xz 23 *3e régiment de Ligne registre des deces*.
10 SHDDT: Xz 37 *51e régiment de Ligne registre des deces*.
11 SHDDT: C15 5. Dossier 17 June 1815, *Rapport du 17 Juin*.
12 SHDDT: C15 5. Dossier 17 June 1815, Daure to Soult.
13 Baudus, vol. 1, pp. 212–3.

Bibliography

Archive Sources

The bulk of this work is based primarily on archive sources held in the *Archives Nationales* and *Service Historique du Armée du Terre*, both institutions being in Paris.

Archives Nationales

AN AFIV 1940 *Garde Impériale* 1815
AN 28 AP *Registre* d'Erlon
AN 82 AP 5 *Fonds Bro de Commerce*

Service Historique Armée du Terre

C 15 4. Correspondence *Armée du Nord*, 1–10 June 1815
C15 5. Correspondence *Armée du Nord*, 11–21 June 1815
C15 6. Correspondence *Armée du Nord*, 22 June–3 July 1815
C 15 20. *Registre d'ordres du 2e regiment des Chasseurs à Pied de la Garde Impériale*, 22 April–27 August 1815
C 15 35 Situations *Armée du Nord*, 1815
C16 20 *Correspondence Militaire General* 1–7 June 1815
C16 21 *Correspondence Militaire General* 8–18 June 1815
C16 22 *Correspondence Militaire General* 19–25 June 1815
C16 23 *Correspondence Militaire General* 26 June–6 July 1815
C37 15 *Correspondence Ministre de Guerre*
GR 1M 717
GR 7 Yd 389
GR 7 Yd 603
GR 7Yd 1074
GR 8 Yd 1707
8Yd 1510
GD 2 1135
Xc 249 7e Hussard 1791–1815
Xc 250 7e Hussard 1813–1815
Xd 360 *Artillerie Armée du Nord*

Xz 22 96e Régiment de Ligne registre des deces
Xz 23 3e Régiment de Ligne registre des deces
Xz 25
Xz 29 22e Régiment de Ligne registre des deces
Xz 30 27e Régiment de Ligne
Xz 33 34e Régiment de Ligne registre des deces
Xz 37 51e Régiment de Ligne registre des deces
Xz 40 63e Régiment de Ligne registre des deces
Xz 51 *Liste de Soldats, sous-officiers et officiers tues du 5e Régiment d' Infanterie legere, tues à la bataille de Mont St Jean*
GR 20 YC 13
GR 20 YC 14
GR 20 YC 18
GR 20 YC 19
GR 20 YC 44
GR 20YC 45
GR 20 YC 46
GR 20 YC 55
GR 20 YC 56
GR 20 YC 137
GR 20 YC 154 *registre matricule Dragons Garde Impériale*
GR 20 YC 166 *Régiment de chevau-légers lanciers, créé par décret du 8 avril 1815 et formé de l'ex-corps royal des lanciers de France*, 8 April–22 December 1815 (*matricules 1 à 1,608*)
GR 21 YC 8 *1er régiment d'infanterie de ligne dit régiment du Roi*, 1 May 1814–6 December 1814 (*matricules 1 à 3,000*)
GR 21 YC 9 *1er régiment d'infanterie de ligne dit régiment du Roi*, 6 December 1814–3 July 1815 (*matricules 3,001 à 4,386*)
SHDDT: /GR 21 YC 19 *2e régiment d'infanterie de ligne dit régiment de la Reine*, 20 May 1814–21 August 1814 (*matricules 1 à 2,997*)
GR 21 YC 31 *3e régiment d'infanterie de ligne dit régiment du Dauphin*, 16 July 1814–17 December 1814 (*matricules 1 à 1,800*)
GR 21 YC 20 *2e régiment d'infanterie de ligne dit régiment de la Reine*, 9 September 1814–6 June 1815 (*matricules 3,000 à 4,723*)
SHDDT:/GR 21 YC 32 *3e régiment d'infanterie de ligne dit régiment du Dauphin*, 17 December 1814–1 July 1815 (*matricules 1,801 à 2,135*)
GR 21 YC 49 *5e régiment d'infanterie de ligne dit régiment d'Angoulême*, 6 September 1814–23 December 1814 (matricules 1 à 1,800)
GR 21 YC 50 *5e régiment d'infanterie de ligne dit régiment d'Angoulême*, 23 December 1814–25 August 1815 (*matricules 1,800 à 2,208*)
GR 21 YC 74 *8e régiment d'infanterie de Ligne dit régiment de Condé*, 30 August 1814–11 May 1815 (*matricules 1 à 1,800*)
GR 21 YC 75 *8e régiment d'infanterie de ligne dit régiment de Condé*, 14 May 1815–10 July 1815 (*matricules 1,801 à 2,379*)
GR 21 YC 92 *10e régiment d'infanterie de ligne dit régiment Colonel-Général*, 1 September 1814–6 May 1815 (*matricules 1 à 1,800*)
GR 21 YC 93 *10e régiment d'infanterie de ligne dit régiment Colonel-Général*, 6 May 1815–22 July 1815 (*matricules 1,801 à 1,943*)
GR 21 YC 100 *11e régiment d'infanterie de ligne*, 9 September 1814–4 February 1815 (*matricules 1 à 1,800*)

GR 21 YC 101 *11e régiment d'infanterie de ligne*, 4 February 1815–23 August 1815 (*matricules* 1,801 à 2,690)
GR 21 YC 158 *17e régiment d'infanterie de ligne*, October 1814–22 June 1815 (*matricules* 1 à 2,593)
GR 21 YC 178 *19e régiment d'infanterie de ligne*, 18 August 1814–26 April 1815 (*matricules* 1 à 1,800)
GR 21 YC 179 *19e régiment d'infanterie de ligne*, 26 April 1815–16 July 1815 (*matricules* 1,801 à 2,598)
GR 21 YC 197 *21e régiment d'infanterie de ligne*, 18–20 May 1815 (*matricules* 1 à 1,800)
GR 21 YC 198 *21e régiment d'infanterie de ligne*, 29 April 1815–16 June 1815 (*matricules* 1,801 à 1,817)
GR 21 YC 255 *27e régiment d'infanterie de ligne*, 1 August 1814 (*matricules* 1 à 1,800)
GR 21 YC 256 *27e régiment d'infanterie de ligne*, 1 July 1814–19 July 1815 (*matricules* 1,801 à 2,778)
GR 21 YC 264 *28e régiment d'infanterie de ligne*, 6 July 1808–23 June 1815 (*matricules* 1 à 1,762)
GR 21 YC 271 *29e régiment d'infanterie de ligne*, 21 July 1814–24 December 1814 (*matricules* 1 à 1,800)
GR 21 YC 272 *29e régiment d'infanterie de ligne*, 24 December 1814–21 July 1815 (*matricules* 1,801 à 2,226)
GR 21 YC 391 *42e régiment d'infanterie de ligne* (ex-*45e régiment d'infanterie de ligne*), 1 August 1814–4 June 1815 (*matricules* 1 à 1,800)
GR 21 YC 400 *43e régiment d'infanterie de ligne* (ex-*46e régiment d'infanterie de ligne*), 1 August 1814–31 May 1815 (*matricules* 1 à 1,800)
SHDDT:/GR 21 YC 401 *43e régiment d'infanterie de ligne* (ex-*46e régiment d'infanterie de ligne*), 31 May 1815–30 July 1815 (*matricules* 1,801 à 2,075)
GR 21 YC 456 *50e régiment d'infanterie de ligne* (ex-*54e régiment d'infanterie de ligne*), 21 July 1814–10 May 1815 (*matricules* 1 à 1,660)
GR 21 YC 463 *51e régiment d'infanterie de ligne* (ex-*55e régiment d'infanterie de ligne*), 1 August 1814–3 August 1815 (*matricules* 1 à 2,049)
GR 21 YC 516 *57e régiment d'infanterie de ligne* (ex-61e régiment d'infanterie *de ligne*), 1 August 1814–14 June 1815 (*matricules* 1 à 1,800)
GR 21 YC 599 *66e régiment d'infanterie de ligne* (ex-*72e régiment d'infanterie de ligne*), 11 August 1814–27 February 1815 (*matricules* 1 à 1,800)
SHDDT:/GR 21 YC 600 *66e régiment d'infanterie de ligne* (ex-*72e régiment d'infanterie de ligne*), 21 February 1815–4 August 1815 (*matricules* 1,801 à 2,092)
GR 21 YC 653 *72e régiment d'infanterie de ligne* (ex-*84e régiment d'infanterie de ligne*), 1 August 1814–4 Feburary 1815 (*matricules* 1 à 1,800)
GR 21 YC 655 *72e régiment d'infanterie de ligne* (ex-*84e régiment d'infanterie de ligne*), 20 January 1815–24 July 1815 (*matricules* 1,801 à 2,756)
GR 21 YC 665 *73e régiment d'infanterie de ligne* (ex-*85e régiment d'infanterie de ligne*), 16 September 1814–29 July 1815 (*matricules* 1 à 1,285)
GR 21 YC 717 *79e régiment d'infanterie de ligne* (ex-*95e régiment d'infanterie de ligne*), 26 August 1814–25 May 1815 (*matricules* 1 à 1,800)
GR 21 YC 734 *81e régiment d'infanterie de ligne* (ex-*100e régiment d'infanterie de ligne*), 24 September 1814–1 May 1815 (*matricules* 1 à 1,800)
SHDDT:/GR 21 YC 735 *100e régiment d'infanterie de ligne*, 1 May 1815–16 August 1815 (*matricules* 1,801 à 2,248)

GR 21 YC 771 *86e régiment d'infanterie de ligne* (ex-105e *régiment d'infanterie de ligne*), 13 August 1814–21 February 1815 (*matricules* 1 à 1,800)
GR 21 YC 772 *86e régiment d'infanterie de ligne* (ex-105e *régiment d'infanterie de ligne*), 24 February 1815–10 August 1815 (*matricules* 1,801 à 1,881)
GR 21 YC 781 *88e régiment d'infanterie de ligne* (ex-107e *régiment d'infanterie de ligne*), 21 July 1814–6 July 1815 (*matricules* 1 à 1,396)
GR 21 YC 790 *89e régiment d'infanterie de ligne* (ex-108e *régiment d'infanterie de ligne*), 9 September 1814–7 June 1815 (*matricules* 1 à 1,800)
GR 22 YC 19 *2er régiment d'infanterie Legere* 1814–1815
GR 22 YC 40 *4er régiment d'infanterie Legere* 1814–1815
GR 22 YC 47
GR 22 YC 48
GR 22 YC 116 *13er régiment d'infanterie Legere* 1806–1815
GR 24 YC 9
GR 24 YC 21 *Regiment de Reine* organisation 1814–29 July 1815
GR 24 YcC26 *Regiment du Dauphin* organisation 1814–June 1815
GR 24 YC 41
GR 24 YC 46 *Contrôle Nominatif Troupe 7e Cuirassiers*, 9 April 1814–6 August 1815
GR 24 YC 50
GR 24 YC 55
GR 24 YC 60 *Contrôle Nominatif Troupe 10e Cuirassiers*, 15 April–27 July 1815, organisation 1814
GR 24 YC 64
GR 24 YC 96
GR 24 YC 158
GR 24 YC 254
GR 24 YC 264
GR 24 YC 274
GR 24 YC 282
GR 24 YC 299
GR 24 YC 309
GR 25 YC 14 1er *Artillerie à Cheval*
GR 25 YC 40 3e *Artillerie à Cheval*

Printed Works

Anon, *The Relation or Journal of Three Days of the Battle of Waterloo, by an Eye Witness* (1816)
Anon, *Memoires pour servir a l'Histoire de France* (London: Richard Phillips & Co., 1820)
Anon, *Tales of War* (London: William Mark Clarke, 1836)
Aerts W., *Waterloo, opérations de l'armée prussienne du Bas-Rhin pendant la campagne de Belgique en 1815, depuis, la bataille de Ligny jusqu'a l'entrée en France des troupes prussiennes* (Spinexu: 1908)
Ali, M., *Souvenirs sur l'Empereur Napoléon. Présentés et annotés par Christophe Bourachot* (Arléa: 2000)
Aubry, T., *Memoires d'un Capitaine de Chasseurs à Cheval* (Paris: Editions Jourdan, 2011)
Avers, P., *Historique du 82e régiment d'infanterie de ligne et du 7e régiment d'infanterie légère* (Paris: Lahure, 1876)

Baudus, M. E. G., *Etudes sur Napoléon* 2 volumes (Paris: Debecourt, 1841)
de Bas, F., and de T'Serclaes de Wommersom, J., *La Compagne de 1815 aux Pays-Bas d'Après les Rapports Officiels Néerlandais* (Brussels: Libraire Albert Dewt, 1908)
Berthezene, P., Souvenirs *Militaires de la Republique et de l'Empire* (Paris: Dumaine, 1855)
Booth, J., *The Battle of Waterloo* (London: 1816)
Bro (Gen.), *Memoirs, 1796–1844* (Librerie des deux Empires: 2001)
Canler, L., Memoires *de Canler* 2 volumes (Paris: F. Roy, 1882)
Chéron, A. de, *Mémoires inédits sur la compagne de Russie—Présentés par Robert de Vaucorbeil* (Teissèdre, 2001)
Combes-Brassard, '*Notice sur la bataille de* Mont-Saint-Jean', in *Souvenirs et Correspondance sur la bataille de Waterloo* (Paris: Librerie Historique Teissèdre, 2000)
Damitz, Geschichte *des Feldzuges von 1815 in den Niederlanden und Frankreich* 2 volumes (Berlin: 1838)
Drouet, J. B., *Le Marećhal Drouet, Comte d'Erlon: Vie militaire ećrit par lui mem^e Gustave* (Paris: 1844)
Duc d'Elchingen, *Documents inédits sur la campagne de 1815* (Paris: Andelin, 1840)
Dulaure, J-A., *1814–1830: Histoire des Cent-Jours* (Paris: 1834)
Dupuy, V., *Memoires Militaire, 1794–1816* (Librerie des deux Empires, 2001)
Duthlitt, P., *Les Memoires du Capitaine Duthlitt* (Lille: 1909)
Fleischmann, T., l'*Armée Impériale racontee par la Grande Armée* (Librerie Academique Perrin, Paris)
Fleuret, F., *Description des Passages de Dominique Fleuret* (Paris: Firmin Diderot, 1929)
Fussel, P., *The Great War and Modern Memory* (Oxford: Oxford University Press, 1975)
Franklin, J. (ed.), *Waterloo Hanoverian Correspondence, Vol. 1: Letters and Reports from Manuscript Sources (Waterloo 1815)* (Ulverson, UK: 1815 Ltd, 2010)
Gourgaud, G., *Campagne de 1815,* P Mongie, Paris (1818)
Green and Troup, The *Houses of History*
de Grouchy, *Relation de la Campagne 1815*
de Grouchy, *Memoires du Marećhal Grouchy*
de Grouchy, *Relation Succinte de la Campagne de 1815 en Belgique* (Delanchy, Paris: 1845)
Guverich, A., 'The French Historical Revolution: The Annales School' in Hodder *et al., Interpreting Archaeology* (London and New York: Routledge, 1995)
Heymès, Col., *Relation de la campagne de 1815, dit de Waterloo: pour servir à l'Histoire du Maréchal Ney* Gaultier-Laguionie Paris (1829)
Houssaye, H., *1815: Waterloo* (Paris: 1903)
Janin, E. F., *Campagne de Waterloo* (1820)
Lachouque, H., *Le General Trommelin* (Tournai, no date)
Levavasseur, O., *Souvenirs militaires, 1800–1815* (A la Librerie des Deux Empires: 2001)
Lot, H., *Les deux généraux Ordener. Préf. de Félix Rocquain* (Paris: R. Roger et F. Chernoviz, 1910)
Martin, J. F., *Souvenirs d'un ex-officer 1812–1815* (Paris: 1867)
MacBride, M., *With Napoléon at Waterloo* (Philadelphia: J. B. Lippincott & Co., 1911)
de Mauduit, H., *Derniers Jours de la Grande Armée* 2 vols (Paris: 1848)

Noel, *Souvenirs Militaires d'un officer du Premier* (Empire Librerie des Deux Empires: 1999)
Nouvelle Revue Retrospective (Paris, January 1896)
Petiet, A-L., *Souvenirs militaire* (Paris: Dumaine, 1844)
von Pflug-Harttung, J., *Vorgeschichte der Schlact bei Belle-Alliance: Wellington* (Berlin: 1903)
Pontecoulant, G., *Memoires* (Paris: 1866)
Senecal, *General Le Senecal campagne de waterloo* (Philadelphia: 1818)
Shanks, M. and Hodder, I., 'Processual, post processual and interpretive archaeologies' in Hodder *et al.*, *Interpreting Archaeology* (London and New York: Routledge, 1995)
Siborne, W., *The Waterloo Campaign 1815*
Siborne, W., *The Waterloo Letters*
Steigler, *Le Maréchal Oudinot* (Paris: 1894)
Tissot, P. F., *Histoire de Napoléon, rédigée d'après les papiers d'État, les documents officiels, les mémoires et les notes secrètes de ses contemporains, suivie d'un précis sur la famille Bonaparte. L'ouvrage, orné de portraits et plans, est précédé de réflexions générales sur Napoléon* 2 vols. (Paris: Delange-Taffin, 1833)
Tondeur, J-P., Courcelle, P., Patyn, J. J., and Megnak, P., *Carnets de la Campagne No. 1 Hougoumont* (Brussels: Tondeur Diffusion, 1999)
de Vaulabelle, A., *Campagne et bataille de waterloo* (Paris: 1845)
Vaudoncourt, *Histoire des campagnes de 1814 et 1815 en France* (Paris: 1826)
Wagner, *Plane der Schlachten und Treffen* (Berlin: 1825)
Wedell, R., *Geschichte des Königlich Preussichen 18 Infanterie-Regiments von 1813 bis 1815* (Posen: 1848)